The Possibility of Pluralistic Naturalism

Understanding the Continuity Between
Philosophy and Science

Masahiko Igashira
Translated by Yu Izumi

YOUKOODOO

Table of Contents

Acknowledgement   v

Preface   vi

Chapter 1   What is Naturalism?: Quine's Characterization of Naturalism and its Development   8

    1.1 A synopsis of "Epistemology Naturalized"   8
    1.2 Interpreting "Epistemology Naturalized":
       Its Treatment of Traditional Epistemology   19
    1.3 The Early Characterization of Naturalism:
       the Nature and Basis of Naturalism   24
    1.4 A Variety of Interpretations of Naturalism and their Bases   32
    1.5 Quine's Final Characterization of Naturalism   48
    1.6 Evaluating Quine's Final Characterization of Naturalism   53
    1.7 'Treating Everything As Natural?': A Variety of Conceptions of Nature   63

Chapter 2   Ontological Options in Naturalism: Physicalist Monism and Pluralism as its Alternative   65

    2.1 The Realm of Ontological Questions   66
    2.2 The Place of Physicalism as an Ontological Option   82
    2.3 Physicalism and Indeterminacy   92
    2.4 Pluralism as an Alternative to Physicalist Monism   123

Chapter 3   Towards the Development of Pluralistic Naturalism   131

    3.1 Putnam's Pluralistic Model: Conceptual Pluralism and Conceptual Relativity   131
    3.2 The Carnapian Model of Pluralism   153

Conclusions   193

Bibliography   194

Index   201

Book design Takashi Torao

Acknowledgement

This work is based on a doctoral thesis I submitted to Tohoku University in 2008, titled "Tagenronteki Shizenshugi no Kanousei" (The Possibility of Pluralistic Naturalism). The thesis was initially published in Japanese in 2010, funded by Philosophy of Science Society Japan Ishimoto Foundation. The present book is an English translation of the Japanese book version of my thesis. The translation was done by Dr. Yu Izumi at Kyoto University. The publication of this book is supported by the Grants-in-Aid for Scientific Research from Japan Society for the Promotion of Science.

Preface

Naturalism is commonly understood as a philosophical position that views a range of human activities—in particular cognitive and linguistic activities and acts—as processes that are naturally occurring in the world. Since the publication of "Naturalized Epistemology" by the influential American philosopher W. V. O. Quine in 1969, naturalism has been a focus of contemporary debates in philosophy, and many theorists have attempted to 'naturalize' different branches of philosophy, such as epistemology, philosophy of mind, and philosophy of science. While these attempts to apply a naturalistic framework have attracted many followers in parallel with the exponential developments in biological and brain sciences, much criticism has been leveled against naturalism by 'anti-naturalistic' philosophers. Determining the scope and validity of naturalism is one of the most important tasks in contemporary philosophy, and it also has broader societal effects by contributing to a better understanding of what it means to be a human being in this golden age of natural science.

Despite a large number of publications discussing naturalism, the following fundamental questions remain unanswered: 'What is naturalism first of all?' and 'What does it mean to naturalize a branch of philosophy?' At present there is no consensus on the nature of this position called 'naturalism', and this absence of a consensus poses a serious challenge to any further development of naturalist debates.

Let me elaborate on what is encompassed by this challenge. According to the Japanese philosopher Kazuhisa Todayama, contemporary debates on naturalism can be largely classified into the following two categories (Todayama 2003):

(1) Debates between naturalists and anti-naturalists regarding the validity of the program of naturalism.
(2) Debates among naturalists regarding appropriate ways of naturalization.

Both types of debates suffer from a lack of consensus among philosophers in defining what constitutes naturalism. Debates of the first category will not be productive when there is no mutual understanding or agreement of the meaning of 'naturalism'; proponents and opponents of naturalism will talk past each other because they do not share basic assumptions. Debates of the second category face a unique obstacle to fulfilling the goals of such debates. If the nature of naturalism is underspecified, we will fail to determine possible options for realizing naturalization. For example, virtually all current naturalists develop and defend particular theses assuming physicalism, but by assuming physicalism they unreasonably restrict the possible theoretical options. As I will argue in chapter 1, given the origins and justifications for naturalism, it should not be construed as necessarily implying physicalism or scientism. Although physicalism is one of the most attractive programs within the scope of naturalism, it would be improper for us to restrict arbitrarily the scope and possibilities of naturalism by viewing physicalism as the only theoretical option available.

To overcome these problems, in this book, I primarily aim at clarifying the philosophical position called 'naturalism'. What I intend to do is to set the stage for a fertile discussion by resolving the confusions arising from current naturalist debates. The secondary aim of this book is to develop and defend a pluralistic view of naturalism that can be used as a substitute for physicalist naturalism. More specifically, I will question and revise the traditional perspective of naturalist debates that always construes 'naturalism' as necessarily implying physicalism or scientism and juxtaposes naturalism in this narrow sense with anti-naturalism, the view that is promoted as a less prejudiced position compatible with non-physicalist possibilities. Through the discussion here, I attempt to open new horizons for naturalist philosophy and provide a foundation for further productive discussion.

In what follows, I wish to present a preview of the further arguments in this book. In chapter 1, I investigate the development of naturalism and clarify its nature by examining a series of Quine's publications ranging from "Epistemology Naturalized" to "Naturalism; or Living within One's Means." I carefully unravel how naturalism was developed and defended, and characterize the kernel of naturalism as 'minimal naturalism', which is the view that assumes no justificatory means but the hypothetico-deductive method and denies any attempt of a first philosophy that precedes and grounds natural science. The basic picture to be developed is that various forms of naturalism are available to theorists; different theoretical options, such as physicalism and natural scientism, may be added to this minimal naturalism.

In chapter 2, I pursue a more appropriate naturalistic position within this basic framework of naturalism examining ontological options that can possibly be added to minimal naturalism. I analyze in particular the structure and characteristics of physicalist naturalism, a naturalistic ontology that is seen as most promising and most widely accepted. I identify the problems inherent in this ontology and propose an improved approach that maintains naturalism while avoiding the problems that physicalist considerations give rise to. The new approach to naturalism is to adopt pluralism in the place of physicalist monism.

The goal of chapter 3 is to clarify and develop the view I call 'pluralistic naturalism', which emerges from the preceding discussion. More specifically, I put forward a promising pluralistic model on the basis of the similar pluralistic views proposed by Hilary Putnam and Rudolf Carnap. The pluralistic model to be developed clearly identifies the plurality of what is asserted ('the unit of pluralization') and how pluralism is justified. Since pluralism has not been exhaustively discussed in the literature, when compared to physicalist monism, this book will help the reader map the theoretical landscape and contribute to further critical discussion of pluralism.

Chapter 1

What is Naturalism?: Quine's Characterization of Naturalism and its Development

The goal of this chapter is to specify the essence of naturalism through an examination of the development it has been subject to. First, I will briefly describe what will be discussed in each section of the chapter. Section 1 closely examines Quine's "Epistemology Naturalized," which initiated the philosophical debates on naturalism in the second half of the twentieth century. Section 2 describes how Quine's theses as presented in "Epistemology Naturalized" contributed to the popularity of naturalism from a broader perspective. The purposes of section 3 are to study the articles collected in Quine's *Theories and Things*, in which naturalism was explicitly formulated for the first time, and to provide an approximate interpretation of the naturalist view drawing on the previous sections. Section 4 reviews major attempts to clarify the obscurities that have been found in Quine's initial characterization of naturalism, discussing how they are supported and identifying their problems. Section 5 explicates how Quine dealt with the obscurities and revised the characterization of naturalism. I will point out the implications of the revised and more explicit characterization of naturalism. Section 6 shows that Quine's final characterization of naturalism is compelling given the development of naturalism, and that it provides solutions to some of the interpretive questions concerning Quine's philosophy. Section 7, finally, bridges gaps between my own formulation of naturalism and naïve conceptions of naturalism, according to which naturalistic philosophers 'view everything as natural' and 'deny non-naturalistic entities'. Finally, I will present some considerations about the relationship between naturalism and our understanding of nature.

1.1 A synopsis of "Epistemology Naturalized"

Quine's (1969) "Epistemology Naturalized" is rightly recognized as the cause of the reemergence of philosophical naturalism in the late twentieth century. Although it doesn't directly discuss naturalism itself as its main topic, the article includes important themes that indicate Quine's transition to naturalism, and so is crucially important in understanding his explicit characterization of naturalism, which was first proposed in "Five Milestones of Empiricism" and "Things and Their Place in Theories" (both in [Quine 1981]). First, I will review the discussion in "Epistemology Naturalized" (section 1), then I will turn to some of the problems it raises (section 2) and start examining Quine's characterization of naturalism around 1980 (section 3).

The structure of "Epistemology Naturalized" is the following:

(1) The tasks of epistemology are divided into a 'theory of concepts' and a 'theory of doctrine'.

(2) The history and outcomes of the conceptual side of epistemology are explicated.
(3) The history and outcomes of the doctrinal side of epistemology are explicated.
(4) It is concluded that the foundationalist project in epistemology that tries to provide a firmer foundation for natural science must be rejected.
(5) The differences and similarities between traditional epistemology and 'naturalized epistemology', which is put forward after the rejection of the foundationalist epistemology, are explicated.
(6) The relations between 'the naturalization of epistemology' and other important themes in Quine's philosophy are explicated.

Below I will summarize the main points in "Epistemology Naturalized," focusing on understanding how Quine arrived at the idea of naturalizing epistemology.

1.1.1 The history and outcomes of the conceptual side of epistemology

At the start of "Epistemology Naturalized," Quine distinguishes two different tasks of epistemology, to provide: 'a theory of concepts' and 'a theory of doctrine', evaluating how far each of these aspects of epistemology has come to attain its objective. The objective of a conceptual study is to elucidate obscure concepts using less obscure concepts to maximize clarity. For example, logicism in the foundations of mathematics has a conceptual dimension in which mathematical concepts are to be defined only in terms of clearer concepts in logic.

Quine begins the evaluation of the conceptual aspect of epistemology with Hume, who based the explanation of the concept of body in sensory terms. According to Quine, Hume proposed to identify bodies with sense impressions. This proposal, however, conflicts with our common sense views. For we intuitively distinguish bodies from our sense impressions of them and also consider bodies to endure while the impressions vary temporally.

Philosophers came to realize that identifying bodies with sense impressions was not the only way to explain the concept of body in sensory terms. To explain a term we do not need, like Hume, to specify an object to which it refers or a synonymous expression; it is only required to show how to translate whole sentences in which the term appears into others in which it does not. This insightful method of 'contextual definition', which Quine attributes to Jeremy Bentham, was not recognized at the time of Hume. Contextual definition enabled making sense of talk of bodies without equating bodies with sense impressions.

In a conceptual study, it is possible to provide an 'explicit definition', in which an obscure term is directly explained in clearer terms. The recognition of contextual definitions—in which whole sentences containing a term to be explained are translated—was a useful development for conceptual studies. Another useful development, Quine suggests, was the extension of ontological resources using set theory.

Let me illustrate, by way of example, the extension of ontological resources using set theory. It is commonsensical to acknowledge the existence of particulars, such as a red shirt and a red ball. It may be disputed, however, whether to also acknowledge the existence of properties, such as 'being red' or 'redness'. It would be less controversial to introduce a set of all red things, including red shirts and balls, and to identify it with 'redness'. This identification is compatible with our reasoning about red things and redness, since it captures an important characteristic of redness, that is, it is shared by all red particulars. As this example shows, it is not difficult to acknowledge the existence of, at least seemingly, ontologically unacceptable entities in terms of ontologically acceptable entities and sets. This is what I mean by 'the extension of ontological resources using set theory'.

Hume's austere ontology only accepted sense impressions, and he used them as the basis for clarifying the concept of physical object, equating physical objects with sense impressions. But if an epistemologist ontologically accepts set theory,[1] there would be not only sense impressions, but also sets of them, sets of sets of them, and so on, available for the sake of clarifying the concept of physical object. Quine says that the epistemologist "may hope to find in some subtle construction of sets upon sets of sense impressions a category of objects enjoying just the formula properties that he wants for bodies" (Quine 1969b, 73), suggesting that set theory may help us deal with the conceptual task of explaining 'body' in sensory terms.

Equipped with the new apparatus—contextual definition and set-theoretic construction of objects—philosophers have made significant progress in the conceptual side of epistemology. According to Quine, the efforts culminated in Russell's program to "account for the external world as a logical construct of sense data" (Quine 1969, 74) and Carnap's (1928) *Der logische Aufbau der Welt*, which was an attempt to execute the Russell program and translate all of human discourse about the world into a language of sense data, logic, and set theory ('translational reduction').[2] Such constructions would enable an understanding of our discourse about the world as clearly as we understand terms of sense data, logic, and set theory. For example, the 'problematic' concepts of ball and electron become theoretically dispensable and may be considered to be just shorthand for complicated descriptions that only contain 'unproblematic' sensory concepts. Had Carnap accomplished such a construction, it would have been a great achievement for the conceptual aspect of epistemology.

In "Epistemology Naturalized," Quine discusses three different reasons why Carnap was unsuccessful in carrying out this reductive program.

(ⅰ) Carnap's *Der logische Aufbau der Welt* does not provide translational reduction.
(ⅱ) Some scientific concepts, such as dispositional ones, resist translational reduction.

---

[1] Quine warns, however, that accepting the ontology of sets amounts to accepting "the whole abstract ontology of mathematics," and it is therefore "a drastic ontological move" (Quine 1969b, 73).
[2] It is, however, questionable whether Carnap was really engaged in a rational reconstruction. See (Iida 2007, Chapter 6).

(iii) Translational reduction is in principle impossible assuming epistemological holism.

In what follows, I will examine each of these reasons in turn, highlighting what remains implicit in "Epistemology Naturalized."

(i) First of all, let me quote Nobuharu Tanji's clear and comprehensible illustration of the first point:

> Carnap's procedure does not look like the following: if such-and-such sense experiences are given, qualities are by definition assigned to positions in physical space and time in a so-and-so way. Rather, like theory construction with limited data sets in science, it assigns qualities to space-time positions in accordance with given sense experiences in such a way that they fulfill certain desiderata *as far as possible*—such desiderata as that the assigned qualities gradually change over space and time. This procedure does not guarantee that there is a single, unique way to assign qualities to space-time positions determined by given sense experiences, and it also leaves open the possibility for the assignments to be revised in accordance with new experiences. Then if there is no determinate (unique) way to assign qualities to space-time positions for given sense experiences, the procedure cannot count as a translational reduction. As a result, Carnap's project is not successful in achieving a translational reduction. (Tanji 1997, 241-2)

In other words, Carnap merely presents guidelines for how to assign qualities to space-time positions, in which the assigned qualities are not uniquely determined and will (possibly) be revised to reflect newly acquired experiences. Thus, the Carnap plan presented in *Der logische Aufbau Der Welt*, "however illuminating, does not offer any key to *translating* the sentences of science into terms of observation, logic, and set theory" (Quine 1969b, 77, italics in original).

(ii) Now I turn to the second point, that translational reduction is impossible for dispositional statements. Dispositional statements have the form 'if x were F, then x would be G'. For example, the following statement about the solubility of salt is a dispositional statement: 'if salt were placed in water, it would dissolve'. Carnap introduced a pair of reductive sentences, (R1) and (R2) below, in his efforts to define theoretical terms including dispositional properties only by reference to observable properties (Carnap 1936, 441).

(R1) $\forall x(Q_1(x) \to (Q_2(x) \to Q_3(x)))$
(R2) $\forall x(Q_4(x) \to (Q_5(x) \to \neg Q_3(x)))$

Instances of (R1) and (R2) explain the new term $Q_3(x)$ using the familiar terms $Q_1(x)$, $Q_2(x)$, $Q_4(x)$, and $Q_5(x)$. The two instances would, however, only partially explain the sentences that contain a new term (in other words, no translational reduction would be achieved), since they explain the term "by specifying some sentences which are implied by sentences containing the term, and other sentences which imply sentences containing the term" (Quine 1969b, 77).

Let me illustrate this point with an example. For simplicity, I focus on (R1) above. Consider the following instance of (R1): 'for all x, if x is placed in water, then if x dissolves, then x is soluble in water'. This reductive sentence is designed to define the theoretical concept 'water solubility' exclusively in terms of observable properties such as 'being placed in water' and 'dissolve'.

It is, however, clearly inadequate as a definition for a dispositional concept. It basically states that whether the substance in question is 'soluble in water' is determined by the observation of whether it dissolves when placed in water. This criterion makes the entire statement true whenever the antecedent is false. That is, every substance x that is not placed in water would count as soluble in water. Since there are numerous insoluble substances that have never been placed in water, the reductive sentence fails to provide an adequate definition of 'water solubility'. Appealing to (R2) (holding 'for all x, if x is Q_4, then if x is Q_5,' then x is not soluble in water') does not save the situation.

A shortcoming of this reductive method is, Carnap acknowledges, that the terms introduced cannot be eliminated. In other words, it is impossible to translate sentences that contain the introduced terms into those that do not. Carnap was fully aware that the introduction of reductive sentences does not help execute translational reduction.

(iii) Finally, there is epistemological holism, which Quine has put forward in his previous writings, as another reason for the impossibility of the program of translational reduction.

Carnap pursued a version of Russell's project of accounting for the external world as a logical construct of sense data. The plan was to provide a translational reduction, in which all statements about the world—both singular and universal ones—are translated into statements reflecting only sense data, logic, and set theory. The significance of this plan is clearly understandable if considering a Peircean verificationist theory of meaning: "the very meaning of a statement consists in the difference its truth would make to possible experience" (Quine 1969b, 78).[3] Suppose that the meaning of a statement is its corresponding sense experience. Then to reduce a statement to sense data by translation would be to specify the very meaning of the statement. The objective of the conceptual aspect of epistemology, to replace obscure concepts with clear ones, must be understood against this verificationist background.

The impossibility of translational reduction then implies the impossibility of specifying the verificationist meaning of a statement. According to Quine, it also shows that a "typical statement about bodies has no fund of experiential implications

---

[3] Quine presents a more intelligible formulation of the verificationist theory of meaning in "Two Dogmas of Empiricism," in which Quine states, "The verification theory of meaning, which has been conspicuous in the literature from Peirce onward, is that the meaning of a statement is the method of empirically confirming or infirming it" (Quine 1953, 37).

it can call its own" (Quine 1969b, 79).[4] Quine continues to discuss his holistic view of theory revision and arrives at the same conclusion: an individual statement has no empirical meaning (that is, the impossibility of translational reduction).

> Sometimes also an experience implied by a theory fails to come off [a theoretical prediction turns out to be false]; and then, ideally, we declare the theory false. But the failure falsifies only a block of theory as a whole, a conjunction of many statements. The failure shows that one or more of those statements is false, but it does not show which. The predicted experiences, true and false, are not implied by any one of the component statements of theory rather than another. [Thus] The component statements simply do not have empirical meanings, by Peirce's standard; but a sufficiently inclusive portion of theory does. (Quine 1969b, 79)

If, as Quine states, a whole theory rather than a single statement is subjected to empirical testing, it would be impossible to specify the corresponding experience of a given statement. This would lead to the conclusion that it would be quite futile to try to reduce by translation all statements about the world into sense data (plus logic and set theory). Thus, the impossibility of translational reduction immediately follows from the acceptance of epistemological holism.

The above has detailed Quine's critical discussion of translational reduction. To sum up, Quine first explains how Carnap failed to establish a translational reduction referring to particular cases in *Der logische Aufbau Der Welt* and "Testability and Meaning," and then Quine argues for the in-principle impossibility of translational reduction on the basis of his own epistemological holism.

1.1.2 The history and outcomes of the doctrinal side of epistemology

The previous section detailed Quine's discussion of the historical development of conceptual studies. How then does Quine view the other aspect of epistemological inquiry, 'doctrinal studies'? The objective of a doctrinal study is to justify our beliefs on the basis of obvious truths to maximize certainty, or to justify "our knowledge of truths of nature in sensory terms" (Quine 1969b, 71). Quine also begins the evaluation of the doctrinal aspects of epistemology with Hume. According to Quine, Hume considered knowledge of sense impressions to have the highest degree of certainty and attempted to determine whether our more advanced beliefs about external bodies are justifiable on the basis of sense impressions. As a result of this doctrinal study, Hume concluded that the majority of our beliefs could not be justified by sense impressions. For sense experiences are information provided to agents at a certain

---

[4] This is precisely the objection to reductionism Quine presents in "Two Dogmas of Empiricism." There Quine rejects Carnap's plan for translational reduction as "radical reductionism." Quine states, "The dogma of reductionism survives in the supposition that each statement, taken in isolation from its fellows, can admit of confirmation or information at all. My countersuggetion... is that our statements about the external world face the tribunal of sense experience not individually but only as a corporate body" (Quine 1953, 41).

time and location, and they may not be used to justify—deductively or in a way that preserves the certainty of sense impressions—statements about objects enduring when there is no one to perceive them, and statements about the future as well as law-like statements that apply universally to a type of phenomenon.

The appeal to sense impressions is not the only way to provide a firm foundation for our knowledge even if, as Quine takes for granted, the underlying assumptions must conform to the tradition of empiricism. It is conceivable, for example, to conduct a doctrinal study in which scientific knowledge is grounded on observational statements, such as 'There is a brown desk at time t and position p', which replace statements concerning sense impressions, such as 'Now I see a brown square'.[5] According to Quine, however, this approach would not work either, since epistemological holism makes it impossible to identify, for a given sentence in a scientific theory, the corresponding observational statement. If it is not possible to pair a given scientific claim with an observational statement, which is presumed to be certain here, a theoretical sentence would fail to inherit the presumed certainty of an observational statement. This result is unsurprising, since doctrinal studies go hand-in-hand with conceptual studies; if a conceptual study fails in one circumstance, a doctrinal study fails under the same circumstances.[6]

These considerations led Quine to conclude that "[t]o endow the truths of nature with the full authority of immediate experience was as forlorn a hope as hoping to endow the truths of mathematics with the potential obviousness of elementary logic" (Quine 1969b, 74), declaring the defeat of the doctrinal inquiry in epistemology.

1.1.3 The abandonment of foundationalist epistemology and 'naturalizing epistemology'

As explained above, no one was able to establish a foundationalist epistemology

---

[5] Logical positivists were divided between two separate positions concerning what kind of sentences constitute the basis for scientific knowledge: on one position, 'phenomenalism', a sense-data language describing private, incorrigible direct experiences (e.g., 'Now, a red circle') constitutes such a basis; the other position, 'physicalism', defends an intersubjective, fallible physical language (e.g., 'The temperature at time t and position p is n degrees Celsius'). See (Neurath 1932; Carnap 1932a; 1932b).

[6] On the other hand, as the following passage suggests, Quine thinks that for a doctrinal study to succeed there needs to be something more than what is required for the success of a conceptual study.
> Carnap's constructions, if carried successfully to completion, would have enabled us to translate all sentences about the world into terms of sense data, or observation, plus logic and set theory. But the mere fact that a sentence is *couched* in terms of observation, logic, and set theory does not mean that it can be *proved* from observation sentences by logic and set theory. (Quine 1969b, 74, italics in original)

Quine does not explicitly state what is additionally required for the success of a doctrinal study. But a plausible candidate for the additional element is 'actual executability', given the remark that immediately follows the quoted passage: "The most modest of generalizations about observable traits will cover more cases than its utterer can have had occasion actually to observe" (74). In other words, to complete a doctrinal study, it is required not only to identify the class of observational statements corresponding to a given sentence but also to actually make observations to confirm them; the sentence would not be justified if we fail to confirm all the corresponding observational statements. Hempel (1950) discusses this point, providing a comprehensive exposition of verificationism in the philosophy of science and the problems it creates.

with our empirical knowledge and its concepts grounded in indubitable sense experiences. In response, Quine proposed to abandon a style of epistemology that attempts to put science on a more secure foundation. In what follows, I will examine how Quine arrives at this proposal.

Consider first Carnap's 'rational resconstruction', which is the culminating point in the history of conceptual studies. Carnap pursued the conceptual aspect of foundationalist epistemology in which our image of the world is to be constructed exclusively from statements about sense-data, logic, and set theory. Of course, such a construction would be different from how we actually developed 'our image of the world', which includes physics and other sciences. For it is not the case that we began with a sensory language, learned logic and set theory, and eventually learned the concepts of external bodies such as 'cup' and 'cat'. What Carnap aimed at was presenting a fictitious, rational story in which physics and other sciences are constructed from a minimum amount of reliable resources, even though this would diverge from the actual development of these sciences—this is why Carnap's project has been termed '*rational re-*construction'.

Rational reconstruction was not intended to describe faithfully the acquisition process of scientific knowledge but viewed as possessing philosophical significance: it would enable explaining epistemologically obscure concepts in terms of sense impressions (the concepts concerning sense experiences and observational terms), which have the highest degree of certainty. This was precisely the main objective of a conceptual study. If Carnap could carry out a rational reconstruction by means of translational reduction, a variety of theoretical concepts, including the concept of body, would be made as clear as observational terms or concepts in logic and set theory, and they would be shown to be nothing but a useful shorthand—in principle dispensable. For, if a translational reduction is possible, all the statements in which the concept of body or any other theoretical concepts appear can be translated into statements containing exclusively observational terms and logical and set-theoretic concepts.

Carnap's effort to develop translational reduction was a lost cause. The failure demonstrates that it is impossible to achieve the goals of rational reconstruction, that is, to "show all the rest of the concepts of science [everything but set theory, logic, and observation] to be theoretically superfluous," and to "legitimize them—to whatever degree the concepts of set theory, logic, and observation are themselves legitimate" (Quine 1969b, 76). When the significance of rational reconstruction is lost, is there any reason to construct a fictitious, rational account, which is in fact unexcutable? Wouldn't it be better to investigate the actual processes of theory formation and concept formation, figuring out how our world view is actually constructed? Reflecting on these questions, Quine states as follows:

> If all we hope for is a reconstruction that links science to experience in explicit ways short of translation, then it would seem more sensible to settle for psychology. Better to discover how science is in fact developed and learned than to fabricate a fictitious structure to a similar effect. (ibid., 78)

Quine is fully aware that replacing rational reconstruction as a part of epistemological inquiry with a branch of science, psychology, conflicts with the traditional view of epistemology. Addressing this point, Quine adds the following remarks:

> Such a surrender of the epistemological burden to psychology is a move that was disallowed in earlier times as circular reasoning. If the epistemologist's goal is validation of the grounds of empirical science, he defeats his purpose by using psychology or other empirical science in the validation. However, such scruples against circularity have little point once we have stopped dreaming of *deducing science from observations*. If we are out simply to understand the link between observation and science, we are well advised to use any available information, including that provided by the very science whose link with observation we are seeking to understand. (ibid., 75-6, italics added)

What is crucially important in this new proposal is that all available information, including science itself, may be used in the newly suggested form of epistemology, and that the foundationalist enterprise of *deducing science from observations* must be abandoned to make the new form of epistemology possible. Quine calls this shift in his perspective about the discipline of epistemology 'naturalizing epistemology'. 'Naturalized' epistemology, according to Quine, will be classified as "a chapter of psychology."

> Epistemology, or something like it, simply falls into place as a chapter of psychology and hence of natural science. It studies a natural phenomenon, viz., a physical human subject. (ibid., 82)

The main topic of naturalized epistemology is "[t]he relation between the meager input [sensory stimuli] and the torrential output [scientific theories]" (ibid., 83) that human subjects exhibit, and by shedding light on the relation, it aspires to understand "how evidence relates to theory, and in what ways one's theory of nature transcends any available evidence" (ibid., 83).

1.1.4 Differences and similarities between naturalized epistemology and traditional epistemology

(1) Topic continuity and a methodological difference

Quine's proposal of 'naturalizing epistemology' could be construed as abandoning the whole of epistemology, since epistemology was originally motivated by such questions as 'Is our belief system (including scientific knowledge) justified?' and 'If so, how is such a justified belief possible?' To answer these questions, the possibility of knowledge must be demonstrated without presupposing scientific knowledge, the legitimacy of which is called into question. If, as Quine suggests, scientific knowledge is used in an epistemological study, it seems impossible even to start addressing these questions.

The new project of naturalizing epistemology certainly abandons the goal of traditional epistemology, that is, to ground science on a more secure foundation, but according to Quine, there is a shared goal between the new and old epistemologies: to understand "how evidence relates to theory." In other words, if a more relaxed definition of epistemology is adopted—the study of the evidence-theory relation, the enterprise to understand "the relation between the meager input and the torrential output" using scientific knowledge can be legitimately called 'epistemology'.[7] These considerations prompted Quine to claim that 'naturalized epistemology' is understood as "a chapter of psychology," whereas it still qualifies as epistemology.

(2) From the containment of natural science in epistemology to the reciprocal containment between epistemology and natural science

According to the traditional understanding of the relationship between epistemology and natural science, epistemology legitimizes natural science, or the former 'contains' the latter; epistemology is understood to essentially precede natural science. Under the project of naturalized epistemology, by contrast, epistemology is contained in natural science as "a chapter of psychology," and so it becomes necessary that natural science must precede epistemology. But the containment of natural science in epistemology, as it is posited by the traditional understanding of epistemology, still obtains in a different form even after naturalizing epistemology. Quine states:

> We are studying how the human subject of our study posits bodies and projects his physics from his data, and we appreciate that our position in the world is just like his. Our very epistemological enterprise, therefore, and the psychology wherein it is a component chapter, and the whole of natural science wherein psychology is a component book-all this is our own construction or projection from stimulations ... (Quine 1969b, 83)

The gist of this quote is that natural science is assigned two different roles in the new epistemological inquiry. Epistemology in the new format explores "the relation between the meager input and the torrential output," and natural science is, on the one hand, understood as part of the object of inquiry—the "torrential output." That is, in naturalized epistemology, natural science remains as the object of investigation, and so it is still contained in epistemology. On the other hand, since the new epistemology is a component of natural science, it is also contained in natural science. Consequently, the asymmetrical containment relation between epistemology and natural science is, through the process of naturalization, transformed into a

---

[7] In later years, Quine states, "I call the pursuit naturalized epistemology, but I have no quarrel with traditionalists who protest my retention of the latter word. I agree with them that repudiation of the Cartesian dream is no minor deviation" (Quine 1992, 19). Although Quine dubbed 'naturalized epistemology' the project of understanding the evidence-theory relation with an unrestricted appeal to natural science, he is not deeply committed to the assertion that the use of the term 'epistemology' is legitimate here.

"reciprocal containment" (ibid., 83). The reciprocal containment raises the question of circularity again, but this question is moot now, since "we have stopped dreaming about deducing science from sense-data" (ibid., 84). Quine concludes that the acceptance of reciprocal containment of epistemology and natural science is what is suggested by Neurath's allegory of "the mariner who has to rebuild his boat while staying afloat in it" (ibid., 84).[8] Once the project of grounding science on an absolute foundation is discarded, the asymmetrical relation in which epistemology legitimizes natural science is replaced with the reciprocal relation in which both epistemology and science address their own agendas mutually taking advantage of the insights of both.

Let me summarize the characteristics of the new epistemology Quine presents in "Epistemology Naturalized" contrasting it with traditional epistemology.

- Naturalized epistemology shares with traditional epistemology the goal of understanding "how evidence relates to theory."
- Traditional epistemology aimed at grounding science on a more secure foundation, making it unable to use scientific knowledge, whereas naturalized epistemology can take advantage of scientific knowledge without fear of circularity, since it has abandoned this foundationalist goal of traditional epistemology.
- Traditional epistemology can be viewed as an enterprise designed to 'contain' natural science in the sense that it is aimed at legitimizing or constructing natural science relying on sense data. Under the project of naturalized epistemology, by contrast, an epistemological study is conducted using scientific knowledge, and it illuminates the actual processes of the creation of natural science. In other words, by naturalizing epistemology philosophers transform the asymmetrical containment relation between epistemology and natural science into a "reciprocal containment."

The above has explicated how Quine advocates for the transition from traditional epistemology to naturalized epistemology to take place, and the differences the new conception of epistemology creates. In the remainder of "Epistemology Naturalized," Quine continues to discuss how naturalizing epistemology relates to various concepts and theses he has developed in the past, but that discussion is not directly relevant to the present purpose, to investigate Quine's transition to naturalism. Therefore, rather than continuing to follow the discussion in "Epistemology Naturalized," I now turn to the task of situating the article "Epistemology Naturalized" in a broader context.

---

[8] "There is no way to establish fully secured, neat protocol statements as starting points of the sciences. There is no *tabula rasa*. We are like sailors who have to rebuild their ship on the open sea, without ever being able to dismantle it in dry-dock and reconstruct it from the best components" ([Neurath 1932, 206]; the quoted translation is from [Neurath 1983, 92]).

1.2 Interpreting "Epistemology Naturalized": Its Treatment of Traditional Epistemology

The previous section laid out the structure of the discussion in "Epistemology Naturalized" that arrives at the transition to naturalism. In order to assess correctly the scope and implications of the discussion, it is here necessary to understand several points that are not explicitly stated in "Epistemology Naturalized."

The article begins with the statement "Epistemology is concerned with the foundations of science" (Quine 1969b, 69), and it divides the foundations into 'conceptual' and 'doctrinal' studies, examining their historical developments separately.

<u>Quine's understanding of epistemology in "Epistemology Naturalized"</u>

Epistemology = Study concerned with the foundations of science

Conceptual study: aiming at clarifying the concepts of physical and theoretical objects in sensory terms.

Doctrinal study: aiming at justifying scientific knowledge on the basis of observational evidence.

Based on this understanding of epistemology, Quine declares traditional epistemology bankrupt and argues for naturalistic epistemology, which abandons the ambition to ground science in something foundational. There remain, however, questions about the validity of the understanding. First, it is not obvious why epistemology must include both a doctrinal study and a conceptual one. Second, while the understanding of epistemology seems to be rooted in the empiricist tradition, it must be questioned whether Quine completely ignores other traditions of epistemology. For example, it is not conceivable to use the framework of conceptual and doctrinal studies to understand Descartes's epistemology, which attempted to overcome skepticism solely on the basis of conceptual analysis and deductive reasoning; it is therefore impossible to declare the bankruptcy of traditional epistemology (understood now as including the Cartesian tradition) merely by appeal to a failure of the conceptual or the doctrinal study.

What these questions highlight is that we cannot accept without further scrutiny Quine's narrative in "Epistemology Naturalized," which goes as follows: traditional epistemology is bankrupt, and thus the transition to naturalistic epistemology is the way ahead. That is, if Quine's understanding of epistemology is inadequate in the first place, the transition to naturalistic epistemology would become less compelling. Therefore, in what follows, I will examine the origins and scope of Quine's understanding of epistemology, on which the discussion of "Epistemology Naturalized" primarily depends.

1.2.1 The origins of Quine's understanding of epistemology in "Epistemology Naturalized"

First, the dichotomy between conceptual and doctrinal studies has been clearly influenced by Carnap's epistemology. For example, consider Carnap's 1936 article "Testability and Meaning," which Quine mentions in "Epistemology Naturalized" claiming the failure of the doctrinal study. The first paragraph of the article definitely indicates that the discussion of "Epistemology Naturalized" is in the spirit of Carnap and other logical positivists.

> Two chief problems of the theory of knowledge are the question of meaning and the question of verification. The first question asks under what conditions a sentence has meaning, in the sense of cognitive, factual meaning. The second one asks how we get to know something, how we can find out whether a given sentence is true or false. The second question presupposes the first one. Obviously we must understand a sentence, i.e. we must know its meaning, before we can try to find out whether it is true or not. But, from the point of view of empiricism, there is a still closer connection between the two problems. In a certain sense, there is only one answer to the two questions. If we knew what it would be for a given sentence to be found true then we would know what its meaning is. And if for two sentences the conditions under which we would have to take them as true are the same, then they have the same meaning. Thus the meaning of a sentence is in a certain sense identical with the way we determine its truth or falsehood; and a sentence has meaning only if such a determination is possible. (Carnap 1936, 420)

Here it is clear that what Carnap refers to as 'the question of meaning' corresponds to 'conceptual studies' in "Epistemology Naturalized," and that 'the question of verification' corresponds to 'doctrinal studies'. The conceptual-doctrinal distinction in epistemological tasks strongly suggests that Quine inherited the framework of logical positivism espoused by people like Carnap. Certainly in "Epistemology Naturalized," Quine begins with the framework of Carnap, recognizes its bankruptcy, and presents naturalistic epistemology as an alternative.

However, the validity of the logical positivist understanding of epistemology may be questioned, as it makes assumptions that are necessary to ensure that 'the question of meaning' and 'the question of verification' constitute jointly important parallel problems in epistemology. One such assumption, influenced by the linguistic turn, is that the unit of epistemological inquiry is the sentence. Another important assumption is the verificationist understanding of meaning: the meaning of a sentence is identified with the empirical conditions determining the truth-value of the sentence.[9] If the meaning of a sentence is identified with the conditions for verifying

---

[9] Quine indeed discusses various issues referring to and basically accepting the Peircean empiricist understanding of meaning: "the very meaning of a statement consists in the difference its truth would make to possible experience" (Quine 1969b, 78). Also see the related discussion on pages 78-81.

the sentence, then it immediately follows that specifying the conditions under which the sentence is verified (the question of meaning) is closely tied to actually verifying the sentence (the question of verification). In other words, according to empiricism, to verify a sentence it becomes necessary to first paraphrase the content of the sentence in terms of observable phenomena and then to conduct an empirical testing—this requirement is particularly important when verifying abstract theoretical sentences. In sum, the positivist understanding of epistemology that considers the questions of meaning and verification to constitute parallel problems in epistemology is derived from an empiricist epistemology and an empiricist theory of meaning.

>   Empiricism (+ the linguistic turn)
>   ↓
>   Conceptual and doctrinal studies are viewed as parallel problems in epistemology

1.2.2 The scope of Quine's criticism of foundationalism in "Epistemology Naturalized"

The discussion so far elucidated the background to the understanding of epistemology used in "Epistemology Naturalized," which Quine shared with logical positivists. Now, the validity of this understanding must be evaluated. It is clear that logical positivists are adherents of the empiricist tradition, and Quine also takes empiricism for granted, as is shown by his claim that our knowledge about nature must be somehow based on sense experiences. Solely on the basis of the inexcutability of the logical positivist, empiricist form of foundationalist epistemology, Quine declares the entirety of foundationalist epistemology bankrupt. There exist, however, other variants of foundationalist epistemology. Why does Quine declare the bankruptcy of the entirety of foundationalist epistemology by just referring to the inexcutability of empiricist foundationalism?

Roger F. Gibson presents an illuminating discussion of this issue in *Enlightened Empiricism* (1988). Gibson (1988, 25) classifies the views in traditional epistemology into four groups using two points of difference: rationalism/empiricism and idealism/realism ("rationalistic idealism," "rationalistic realism," "empiricistic idealism," and "empiricistic realism"), outlining Quine's response to each view.[10] According to Gibson, Quine dismisses empiricistic idealism and rationalistic idealism without virtually any argument against them; Gibson states, "In short, Quine's attitude toward idealism seems to be that it deserves to be ignored rather than refuted" (ibid., 26).

As for rationalistic realism and empiricistic realism, on the contrary, Quine presents substantial arguments against them. Consider first rationalistic realism, which Gibson characterizes as the view that "reason reveals to them [rationalists] certain *a priori*, synthetic, nonscientific truths and norms (e.g., Descartes' *cogito* and its "mark" of

---

[10] Gibson categorizes, though with a question mark, Hegel as a rationalistic idealist, Descartes as a rationalistic realist, Berkeley as an empiricistic idealist, and Locke as an empiricistic realist.

clarity and distinctness) sufficient for deducing all other truths" (ibid., 26). Quine's argument against this view is based on two points: one is the rejection of the apriority of foundational truths and norms, and the other is the claim that *a priori* truths and norms, if they exist at all, would not enable the deduction of the rest of all scientific knowledge and beliefs.

According to Gibson, the former point—Quine's objection to the rationalistic realist claim that there are a priori truths—is essentially equivalent to his objection to the empiricist claim that there are analytic truths. In "Two Dogmas of Empiricism," Quine defends the idea that no statement is in principle immune from revision, on the basis of which the rationalist assumption that there are non-scientific and a priori synthetic truths is rejected. The latter point—the difficulty of deduction—is illustrated by the following remarks:

> Actually even the truths of elementary number theory are presumably not in general derivable, we noted, by self-evident steps from self-evident truths. We owe this insight to Gödel's theorem, which was not known to the old-time philosophers. (Quine and Ullian 1970, 65)

If it is impossible, even in a domain of mathematics where the deductive relations of truths seem to be most apparent, to deduce all theorems from self-evident truths (foundational truths revealed by reason) by self-evident steps (foundational norms revealed by reason), it will be all the more difficult to deduce truths in other scientific domains. Thus, even if there are *a priori*, synthetic, and non-scientific truths and norms, they alone would not enable the derivations of other truths without losing clarity and distinctness.

This sums up why Quine deems rationalistic realism bankrupt. Next, let us now consider the other view, empiricistic realism, which Gibson characterizes as contending that "sense experience reveals to them [empiricists] certain *a posteriori*, synthetic, nonscientific truths and norms from which they can deduce or rationally reconstruct all of the truths of nature" (ibid., 26). This view indeed amounts to the doctrinal and conceptual studies in epistemology, which Quine criticizes in "Epistemology Naturalized." Thus, Quine's discussion in "Epistemology Naturalized" can be viewed as refuting empiricistic realism.

The following chart summarizes the structure of Quine's narrative towards naturalistic epistemology (namely, 'traditional epistemology is bankrupt, and thus the transition to naturalistic epistemology is the way ahead').

<u>Quine's treatments of the four different variants of foundationalist epistemology</u>

Rationalistic idealism: ignored because it is idealism

Empiricistic idealism: ignored because it is idealism

Rationalistic realism: deemed inexcutable based on 'the rejection of the aprioricity of foundational truths and norms' and 'the claim that all truths are not deducible from self-evident, foundational truths and norms'

Empiricistic realism: both doctrinal and conceptual studies are deemed inexcutable or inferior to psychology based on the discussion in "Epistemology Naturalized"

Drawing on Gibson's *Enlightened Empiricism*, the discussion above examined the details of Quine's criticism of traditional epistemology from a broad perspective. Although the discussion by Gibson should not be accepted as it is stated without further scrutiny because of the obscurities it bases its arguments on (for example, the characterizations of realism and idealism), it does make sound observations that are useful to understand Quine's criticism of traditional epistemology and the importance of "Epistemology Naturalized" in the criticism. One such observation is that Quine's objection to foundationalist epistemology in "Epistemology Naturalized" is limited in scope. Since the arguments in "Epistemology Naturalized" focus on the failures of conceptual and doctrinal studies, they only undermine what Gibson calls 'empiricistic realism'; "Epistemology Naturalized" must be understood as providing a partial reason for "the bankruptcy of traditional epistemology," rather than fully substantiating a refutation—but noting this it must be borne in mind that empiricistic realism was considered the most promising form of traditional epistemology, at least, in the Anglophone philosophical tradition. Another useful observation that Gibson makes clarifies how Quine's argument for the transition to naturalistic epistemology is inadequate. While Quine makes a solid case against empiricistic realism and rationalistic realism,[11] he hardly presents an argument of any kind to reject the other variants of foundationalist epistemology. Thus, the allegation of the bankruptcy of traditional epistemology is not sufficiently supported.

This evaluation, however, does not mean that Quine's conclusion to abandon a first philosophy is groundless and therefore must be declined. For the series of discussions resulting in the transition to naturalism can be viewed as presenting an 'open conclusion', of which Quine makes use in other writings. For example, in the article "Two Dogmas of Empiricism," Quine examines a variety of promising approaches to defining 'analyticity', and by showing the inadequacy of each approach he argues that the concept of analyticity itself is unintelligible. The argument, even if sound, *does not prove the impossibility of defining analyticity; it only exposes the inadequacies of the approaches to defining analyticity that are considered promising.*[12] Thus, Quine does not exclude the possibility of a more powerful method to define analyticity being developed in the future, and in this sense, what "Two Dogmas" presents is a tentative, open conclusion that *at the present moment* there is no satisfying way to define analyticity.[13] Likewise, the abandonment of a first philosophy, entailed by Quine's

---

[11] I am here, of course, not suggesting that Quine's discussion of this is impeccable.

[12] I do not think that Quine's criticism of analyticity poses a serious threat to Carnap's project. See (Igashira 2007) and chapter 3 of this book.

[13] This interpretation of "Two Dogmas" is corroborated by the following remarks by Quine:
> My argument for the indeterminacy of translation, or for that matter my argument against analyticity in 'To dogmas', is not a proof by cases. It is not a proof at all. What went by cases was the exploration of a few avenues of definition that I or others might

criticism of foundationalist epistemology, can be understood as an open conclusion. That is, Quine regards his criticism of traditional epistemology as sufficient insofar as it reveals the deficiencies of the possible foundationalist positions that are considered promising. Whenever a feasible alternative for maintaining foundationalism is proposed, Quine is confident that it will be possible to raise a different objection to it. Until such an alternative is proposed, Quine has sufficient reason to uphold the conclusion in "Epistemology Naturalized" (that is, "the bankruptcy of traditional epistemology").

In this section, I have examined how the discussion in "Epistemology Naturalized" figures in Quine's larger picture ('traditional epistemology is bankrupt, and thus the transition to naturalistic epistemology is the way ahead'). Since the goal of this chapter is to elucidate the nature of naturalism by investigating its development, the implications and import of "Epistemology Naturalized" must be identified first, especially given that the article renewed interest in naturalism in contemporary philosophy. Sections 1.1 and 1.2 have accomplished this task. The article "Epistemology Naturalized," however, does not primarily discuss naturalism itself, since its focus is on the naturalization of epistemology, without any explicit reference to 'naturalism'. In the next section, I will turn to the task of showing the nature of naturalism examining Quine's writings in which 'naturalism' is explicitly referred to and characterized.

1.3 The Early Characterization of Naturalism: the Nature and Basis of Naturalism

The article "Epistemology Naturalized" advances a new vision of epistemology, according to which the subject matter of epistemology is human beings as natural objects, and epistemology is the study of the process of developing theories from evidence drawing on the insights of natural science. The old foundationalist epistemology, by contrast, is pronounced to be bankrupt in "Epistemology Naturalized," as Quine dismisses traditional ideas such as that the goal of epistemology is to place science on a more secure foundation, and that an epistemological inquiry can presuppose no scientific knowledge. The article augmented the naturalistic trend in late twentieth century philosophy, but it does not explicitly define naturalism; the nature of naturalism is not fully elucidated by the discussion in that article. Quine's explicit reference to 'naturalism' first appeared in the articles collected in *Theories and Things* (Quine 1981). In order to start analyzing the nature of naturalism, let me quote a couple of instructive passages from "Five Milestones of Empiricism" and "Things and Their Place in Theories":

> The fifth move, finally, brings naturalism: abandonment of the goal of a first philosophy. It sees natural science as an inquiry into reality, fallible and corrigible

---

have felt were hopeful, but that ended in dead ends. (Quine 1990, 198)
In any case, given Quine's fierce resistance to apriorism, it is plausible to suppose that Quine rejects the idea that to criticize a view in philosophy it is necessary to prove its impossibility through a philosophical discussion.

but not answerable to any supra-scientific tribunal, and not in need of any justification beyond observation and the hypothetico-deductive method. Naturalism has two sources, both negative. One of them is despair of being able to define theoretical terms generally in terms of phenomena, even by contextual definition. A holistic or system-centered attitude should suffice to induce this despair. The other negative source of naturalism is unregenerate realism, the robust state of mind of the natural scientist who has never felt any qualms beyond the negotiable uncertainties internal to science. (Quine 1981, 72)

The answer is naturalism: the recognition that it is within science itself, and not in some prior philosophy, that reality is to be identified and described. (ibid., 21)

Drawing on these passages, it is reasonable to summarize Quine's characterization of naturalism and the justification for it (at least then, at the time of writing) as follows:

Characterization: the abandonment of the goal of a first philosophy. Naturalism sees natural science as an inquiry into reality, fallible and corrigible but not answerable to any super-scientific tribunal, and not in need of any justification beyond observation and the hypothetico-deductive method. It is within science itself, and not in some prior philosophy, that reality is to be identified and described.

Justification 1: despair of being able to define theoretical terms generally in terms of phenomena.

Justification 2: unregenerate realism, the robust state of mind of the natural scientist who has never felt any qualms beyond the negotiable uncertainties internal to science.

None of these statements is easy to understand. In what follows, I will closely examine how these two justifications entail naturalism, deepening our understanding of the nature and basis of naturalism.

Consider Justification 1 first, the less enigmatic of the two. Quine presents it on the basis of a "holistic or system-centered attitude," which is basically equivalent to the 'thesis of holism': a single sentence does neither "serve as an independent vehicle of empirical meaning" nor "have observable or testable consequences," whereas a "reasonably inclusive body of scientific theory, taken as a whole, will indeed have such consequences" (ibid., 70).[14] Assuming the thesis of holism, it is easy to understand why the attempt "to define theoretical terms generally in terms of phenomena" is

---

[14] For our present purposes, it is reasonable to follow the characterization of 'holism' appearing in "Five Milestones of Empiricism," not addressing questions of interpreting whether Quine's thesis of holism subsumes semantic holism in addition to epistemological holism.

bound to fail. Here 'terms of phenomena'—in whatever way they are ultimately described—refer to the terms that appear in observational statements, and so the attempt is to define theoretical terms, such as 'electron' and 'neutrino', solely in terms of observational terms ('explicit definition') or to replace sentences containing theoretical terms with sentences that contain only observational terms ('contextual definition'). According to the thesis of holism, however, for a theoretical statement, such as 'electrons have a negative charge', there is no class of corresponding sentences based on observations. It is the "reasonably inclusive body of scientific theory" that will face "the tribunal of sense experience" (Quine 1953, 41), and it is impossible to identify a class of sentences based on observations that correspond to an individual theoretical sentence. Therefore, the attempt "to define theoretical terms generally in terms of phenomena" is shown to be unattainable by reference to the thesis of holism.

As was clearly shown in section 1.1, this effort "to define theoretical terms generally in terms of phenomena" corresponds to the project of 'translational reduction' discussed in "Epistemology Naturalized." There Quine examines three reasons for the failure of the conceptual study in epistemology, repeated below in a slightly different form.

(ⅰ) Carnap's *Der logische Aufbau der Welt* does not provide translational reduction.
(ⅱ) Dispositional statements resist translational reduction.
(ⅲ) Translational reduction is in principle impossible assuming epistemological holism.

In the article "Five Milestones of Empiricism," on the other hand, Quine just focuses on the point raised by (ⅲ), showing that it is impossible "to define theoretical terms generally in terms of phenomena" (that is, showing the impossibility of the conceptual study). Quine had different aims in writing "Epistemology Naturalized" and "Five Milestones of Empiricism." One of the main goals of the former is to review the history of conceptual studies, whereas the latter aims at concisely presenting a definitive argument against the idea of epistemology as a first philosophy. Reason (ⅲ) points out the in-principle impossibility of translational reduction, whereas (ⅰ) and (ⅱ) criticize particular attempts to carry out translational reduction. It is therefore reasonable to concentrate on (ⅲ), which sufficiently undermines translational reduction, rather than examining particular attempts and refute them one by one.

Quine's remarks on Justification 1 are straightforward, and its connection to the issues discussed in "Epistemology Naturalized" is clearly comprehensible. For Justification 2, it is difficult to understand the details and validity of the claim, however. A major cause of the difficulty lies in the absence of an explicit argument in defense of Justification 2, in contrast to the case of Justification 1, for which Quine presents the (more-or-less uncontroversial) thesis of holism. At first glance, 'unregenerate realism' appears to maintain that scientific beliefs are affirmed for what they are, requiring no assessment or justification outside of science. If there are no philosophically acceptable grounds for this affirmation, however, it would be no more than an uncritical expression of 'scientism', and naturalism would also become considered philosophically unfounded, since unregenerate realism provides a justification for naturalism—or at least such a claim would be a nonstarter from the perspective of phenomenologists, who would regard it as nothing but a 'naive naturalistic attitude'.

This shows the need why it is necessary to identify the rationale for unregenerate realism to substantiate it as a philosophically sophisticated position (and thereby defend naturalism, whose success is partially dependent on the plausibility of unregenerate realism). A promising rationale for unregenerate realism is what might be appropriately termed 'belief system immanentism', which Quine put forward in earlier work. Let us first consider the characterization of belief system immanentism.

In his article "Identity, Ostension, and Hypostasis" ([Quine 1950] in [Quine 1953]), Quine states:

> The fundamental-seeming philosophical question, How much of our science is merely contributed by language and how much is a genuine reflection of reality? is perhaps a spurious question which itself arises wholly from a certain particular type of language. Certainly we are in a predicament if we try to answer the question; for to answer the question we must talk about the world as well as about language, and to talk about the world we must already impose upon the world some conceptual scheme peculiar to our own special language. ... We can improve our conceptual scheme, our philosophy, bit by bit while continuing to depend on it for support; but we cannot detach ourselves from it and compare it objectively with an unconceptualized reality. Hence it is meaningless, I suggest, to inquire into the absolute correctness of a conceptual scheme as a mirror of reality. (Quine 1953, 78-9)

As stated above, when our belief system is compared with the 'world' or 'reality', the 'world' must be described in a particular way. This implies that the 'world', the target of comparison, is necessarily described using some belief system, and that it is impossible to evaluate our belief system by contrasting it with 'the world in itself', something that is completely independent from any belief system or conceptual system.[15] Following the above remarks, Quine continues: "Our standard for appraising basic changes of conceptual scheme must be, not a realistic standard of correspondence to reality, but a pragmatic standard" (ibid., 79). That is, our beliefs about various subjects must be revised and evaluated from the perspective 'within our belief system'. This is the view I call 'belief system immanentism' in this book.

Keeping this characterization of belief system immanentism in mind, it is now possible to make sense of what Quine means by 'unregenerate realism' (in other words, "the robust state of mind" feeling no "qualms beyond the negotiable uncertainties internal to science"). Consider as an example the scenario in which a skeptic doubts the statement 'electrons have a negative charge', which is supported

---

[15] Interestingly, John Dewey, an advocate of the naturalistic philosophy in the early twentieth century, expressed the same view in his debate with Bertrand Russell. See (Dewey 1946).

by an unlimited amount of evidence within physics. Among the possible approaches to attacking the validity of the statement, the skeptic might pose the following objection: 'no justificatory process within physics can establish a correspondence between the statement and 'the world in itself', which is completely independent of our beliefs'. The point the skeptic makes is that to prove the validity of the statement 'electrons have a negative charge' it is necessary to contrast it with 'the world in itself', to which our belief system must correspond, in addition to internally providing supporting evidence for the statement within our belief system, including physics. The demand imposed by the skeptic is, however, unfounded from the perspective of belief system immanentism.[16] If Quine is right about belief system immanentism, the conception of 'the world in itself'—something that is completely independent from our belief system—is essentially erroneous, and it cannot be used to evaluate the validity of our beliefs. According to belief system immanentism, in order to justify the claim 'electrons have a negative charge', it is not necessary to compare it with 'the world in itself' or 'reality in itself', which is independent of any belief system. What is required to ensure the truth of the claim is only a system-internal justificatory process—in this particular case the justificatory process is internal mainly to physics

---

[16] It should also be noted that belief system immanentism does not rule out all potential skeptical challenges suggesting that 'what we believe to be the case may turn out to be wrong'. Consider the definition of unregenerate realism again: "the robust state of mind of the natural scientist who has never felt any qualms beyond the negotiable uncertainties internal to science" (Quine 1981, 72). It does not follow from this definition that all of our scientific beliefs will merit the status of genuine knowledge without being left open to further challenges. The reason for this is made clearer by considering how belief system immanentism is related to skepticism.

Our beliefs, even scientific ones, have to be regarded as corrigible, since they could turn out to be wrong, as clearly shown by previously accepted beliefs in science that were eventually rejected, such as 'the earth is flat', 'combustion is caused by phlogiston', 'mass is conserved', etc. Even the belief system immanentist therefore has to acknowledge that skeptical challenges to our beliefs (including scientific ones) are meaningful. It is worth noting, however, that our beliefs have been questioned and sometimes discarded on the basis of other parts of our belief system, not on the basis of anything external to it. Quine elsewhere writes, "The crucial logical point is that the epistemologist is confronting a challenge to natural science that arises from within natural science" (Quine 1974, 2). Casting doubt on a scientific belief is acceptable for the belief system immanentist as long as doubt is raised internally within science, since what the belief system immanentist contends is that skepticism could be developed only within our belief system. (Quine discusses the following skeptical argument as an example: 'a stick in water appears to us to be bent, but it isn't actually bent; therefore our perception is not reliable'. The skeptical argument here crucially rests on the belief that the stick is not actually bent, without which the fallibility of perception would not be entailed. Thus, skeptical arguments of this kind must be understood as an argument internal to our belief system.)

Belief system immanentism, on the other hand, is incompatible with the type of skepticism that maintains that our belief system cannot be sufficiently justified without being compared with 'the world in itself', questioning the very possibility of knowledge. For belief system immanentism construes the concept of 'reality' in the terms available within a system, claiming that the idea of a 'reality that is independent from any belief system' is essentially erroneous, and so belief system immanentism conflicts with the type of skepticism that requires beliefs to be compared with 'the world in itself' for their justification. (Certainly, it is necessary to comprehensively examine different types of skepticism to be able to exhaustively discuss the relationship between naturalism and skepticism, and so my discussion here is not really exhaustive enough for that purpose. The present purpose is, however, more specific: to understand how belief system immanentism rejects a typical assumption that skeptics make in their skeptical arguments. For this purpose, the discussion here is sufficient, pointing out the type of skepticism that is incompatible with belief system immanentism.)

and chemistry. Given these considerations, it is now simple to recognize belief system immanentism in the definition of unregenerate realism. In other words, Quine's characterization of unregenerate realism, "the robust state of mind of the natural scientist who has never felt any qualms beyond the negotiable uncertainties internal to science" (Quine 1981, 72), is an expression of (at least a kind of) belief system immanentism.

Construed in this way, unregenerate realism can be viewed not as an uncritical expression of scientism but as a philosophically plausible thesis that is based on a philosophical argument—the idea of 'the world in itself' is essentially erroneous.[17] Furthermore, on this construal of unregenerate realism, it is now possible to understand clearly how Justifications 1 and 2 entail naturalism, according to which "it is within science itself, and not in some prior philosophy, that reality is to be identified and described" (ibid., 21). In what follows, I will examine the details of how Justifications 1 and 2 entail naturalism, corroborating the interpretation of unregenerate realism I have just presented.

Let me first repeat Quine's early characterization of naturalism and the justification for naturalism.

> Characterization: abandonment of the goal of a first philosophy. Naturalism sees natural science as an inquiry into reality, fallible and corrigible but not answerable to any supra-scientific tribunal, and not in need of any justification beyond observation and the hypothetico-deductive method. It is within science itself, and not in some prior philosophy, that reality is to be identified and described.
>
> Justification 1: despair of being able to define theoretical terms generally in terms of phenomena.
>
> Justification 2: unregenerate realism, the robust state of mind of the natural scientist who has never felt any qualms beyond the negotiable uncertainties

---

[17] According to Roger Gibson, Quine's unregenerate realism "is ... logically grounded on the recognition that the skeptical challenge to science presupposes science" (Gibson 1988, 42). This line of interpretation is, however, slightly off the mark. It is certainly undeniable that the example Quine brings up represents the type of skepticism that is internal to a belief system ('a stick in water appears to us to be bent, but it isn't actually bent; therefore our perception is not reliable'). But this particular example does not generalize to all skeptical challenges; the general claim that every kind of skepticism is internal to a belief system is not entailed by the claim that a particular kind of skepticism is internal to a belief system. The possibility of another type of skepticism—our beliefs are not sufficiently justified until they are compared with 'the world in itself'—has not yet been ruled out. To make a generalization about skeptical challenges it must be pointed out that the concept of 'the world in itself' is essentially erroneous. Given this point or belief system immanentism that it entails, it becomes possible to claim that a skeptical argument could be presented only internally within a belief system. This shows that, in order to contend that a skeptical challenge to science presupposes science, it is necessary to rule out the type of skepticism that requires beliefs to be compared with 'the world in itself' for their justification. Thus, Gibson's interpretation puts the cart before the horse by considering unregenerate realism grounded in "the recognition that the skeptical challenge to science presupposes science." Although the observation that "the skeptical challenge to science presupposes science" is closely related to unregenerate realism or belief system immanentism, it is the latter that grounds the former, not the other way around.

internal to science.

As already discussed, Justification 1 points to the failure of an empiricist foundationalist project, such as the one examined in "Epistemology Naturalized," and it is based on the thesis of holism that Quine advanced earlier. According to the interpretation of unregenerate realism presented above, Justification 2 is an expression of belief system immanentism, which abandons any idea of 'reality in itself that is independent of our belief system', and understands the concept of reality in the terms available within our belief system. This interpretation of the two justifications makes the derivation of naturalism intelligible. First, since belief system immanentism renders the concept of reality internal to our belief system, there is no need to justify our scientific beliefs from a perspective outside of our belief system ("it is within science itself, and not in some prior philosophy, that reality is to be identified and described").[18] Second, from the perspective within our belief system, given the thesis of holism, it is impossible to conceptually clarify or justify all of our scientific beliefs by means of deriving them from observational terms (namely, from sense-data and observation statements). Putting it differently, having discarded the expectation of defining 'theoretical terms generally in terms of phenomena', the holistic perspective within our belief system also does away with empiricist foundationalism, which demands the translational reduction of scientific beliefs into observational terms. Thus, the enterprise of legitimizing science by placing it on a more secure footing is abandoned, and so is the conception of first philosophy that views philosophy as being prior to and more solidly secure than science, in favor of naturalism, according to which natural science is "an inquiry into reality, fallible and corrigible but not answerable to any supra-scientific tribunal, and not in need of any justification beyond observation and the hypothetico-deductive method" (ibid., 72).[19]

This section has attempted to clarify the basis and nature of naturalism as well as its derivation, relying on Quine's remarks in "Five Milestones of Empiricism" and

---

[18] As this description of naturalism clearly indicates, naturalism must be conceived as subsuming belief system immanentism. And one of the two justifications for naturalism Quine presents—"despair of being able to define theoretical terms generally in terms of phenomena as well as epistemological holism"—does not entail belief system immanentism. It is therefore inescapable to have to conclude that the other justification—unregenerate realism—entails belief system immanentism. Together with the discussion so far, the fact that naturalism subsumes belief system immanentism supports my interpretation of unregenerate realism as an expression of belief system immanentism.

[19] At the risk of oversimplification, unregenerate realism, understood as an expression of belief system immanentism, ensures that natural science is "not answerable to any supra-scientific tribunal," and the impossibility of translational reduction derived from holism ensures that science is "not in need of any justification beyond observation and the hypothetico-deductive method." Belief system immanentism shows that, since having the following criterion of justification is completely useless for evaluating our beliefs: there must be correspondence between beliefs and the world in itself that is completely independent of our belief system, it is impossible to appeal to a tribunal external to our (scientific) belief system. Furthermore, the thesis of holism shows that the possibility of translational reduction into observational terms cannot serve as the criterion of justification either. What is left in the criterion of justification is the fitness to the collected data or a successful application of the hypothetico-deductive method, which falls short of translational reduction, requiring only the implications of a theory to fit observations.

"Things and Their Place in Theories." What follows is a summary of the discussion presented in this section. First, the two justifications for naturalism that Quine presents—namely, "despair of being able to define theoretical terms generally in terms of phenomena" and unregenerate realism—were examined, and their interpretations and rationales explicated. The former was interpreted as the abandonment of foundationalist epistemology, which demands translational reduction, and its rationale is found in Quine's thesis of holism. The latter, unregenerate realism, was interpreted as an assertion of belief system immanentism based on the claim that the idea of 'the world in itself—something that is completely independent of any belief system—is essentially erroneous. These two justifications lead to the abandonment of any project in the tradition of first philosophy, namely to place science on a secure philosophical foundation, and they thereby derive naturalism, the view that science itself is an inquiry into reality requiring no justification from philosophy. The structure of the derivation of naturalism can be schematically represented as below:

Belief system immanentism (← the impossibility of justification from outside belief systems)
+
The impossibility of empiricist foundationalism (← holism)
↓
Naturalism: first philosophy has been abandoned; science itself is an inquiry into reality

Though the discussion so far clarifies Quine's early characterization of naturalism and its derivation, it does not identify the exact nature of naturalism. For one thing, in the Quine articles discussed above, there were two different expressions, 'science' and 'natural science', whose interpretations are not immediately apparent; there seems to be no clear criterion for distinguishing the two. As a result, it is unclear what is intended by 'science itself', when Quine concludes, "it is within science itself, and not in some prior philosophy, that reality is to be identified and described," as quoted above. It must also be elucidated what other inquiries than natural science are probable when Quine says that naturalism "sees natural science as *an inquiry* into reality" (my emphasis). If there is no other probable inquiry into reality than natural science, then what are the criteria to delineate 'natural science' from everything else? These interpretive questions indicate that the early characterization of naturalism Quine presented in *Theories and Things* contains obscurities that will hamper efforts to determine the nature of naturalism or to state precisely what is and is not implied by naturalism, the prominent position Quine resurrected in contemporary philosophy.

Despite the obscurities in the characterization of naturalism, Quine put forward a variety of philosophically important theses on the basis of naturalism. As naturalism has received increasing attention from contemporary philosophers, many have attempted to determine the nature of naturalism drawing on Quine's remarks. Some have developed arguments against naturalism relying on their own interpretations of naturalism, and others have developed their own naturalistic philosophical theses assuming their own interpretations of naturalism.[20] The next section examines some of the common interpretations of naturalism, evaluating their bases and identifying their problems.

1.4 A Variety of Interpretations of Naturalism and their Bases

This section takes up three different interpretations of naturalism, examining their textual bases and identifying the problems they present. In extant research on naturalism, the following three answers are given to the question "What is and is not implied by naturalism?":

> Naturalism implies that epistemology is to be replaced with descriptive empirical psychology. (1.4.1)

> Naturalism implies natural scientism. (1.4.2)

> Naturalism implies physicalism. (1.4.3)

Let me first briefly explicate the goal of the current section. Since the early characterization of naturalism was presented in a confusing manner, and as some obscurities exist in Quine's remarks, theorists have proposed different interpretations of naturalism. Multiple interpretive possibilities have been an obstacle to forming a basis for further debates among theorists (proponents and opponents of naturalism alike), hampering constructive criticism and fruitful discussion of naturalism. One of the main aims of this chapter is to provide a clear characterization of naturalism to set the stage for moving the discussion ahead, resolving the confusions arising from current naturalist debates. Accordingly, the goal of this section is to examine the interpretations of naturalism previously proposed and to understand their bases and the problems they create. With this, I will propose the characterization of naturalism to be adopted in this book (section 5), and try to bridge gaps between the proposed characterization and the previous interpretations of naturalism (section 6).

1.4.1 The 'replacement thesis' interpretation

Now, I will examine the idea that naturalism implies the 'replacement thesis'—the view that epistemological questions can be replaced with psychological questions, and I will elucidate why this interpretation of naturalism has been put forward. By considering a typical objection to the replacement thesis-the 'normativity charge', I will also explore the significance of the enterprise of epistemology understood as

---

[20] As I will discuss later, this dialectical development has contributed to the unfortunate circumstance that theorists debating naturalism often talk past each other. That is, in order to eliminate the obscurities contained in the early characterization of naturalism, many theorists developed their own interpretations of naturalism, on the basis of which they advanced their own views, and as a result, no mutual understanding or agreement about the characteristics of the very topic, naturalism, has emerged to date.

descriptive, empirical psychology, and identify the problems of naturalism under this interpretation. To forestall confusion, the goal of this subsection is not to defend or criticize the idea of epistemology as descriptive, empirical psychology. The goal is narrower: it is to understand the implications and problems of the enterprise of descriptive epistemology, and to clarify the bases for this interpretation of naturalism.

(1) The descriptive-normative distinction and descriptive epistemology

Before delving into the significance and problems of the idea of epistemology as descriptive, empirical psychology, it is necessary to have a basic understanding of the descriptive-normative distinction, which is commonly appealed to when classifying statements in ethics and other areas of philosophy. The descriptive-normative distinction is usually understood as deriving from the contrast between what *is* the case and what *ought* to be the case. For example, the statement 'Billy fired a gun' is a descriptive statement, whereas 'Billy ought not to have fired a gun' is normative. Importantly for the current discussion, the distinction is crucially relevant to the oft-asserted thesis that normative statements cannot be reduced to descriptive ones. It is impossible to derive a normative claim, such as 'Billy ought not to have fired a gun', exclusively from descriptive statements, such as 'there were many people around Billy' and 'it is possible that people around are shot dead', no matter how many descriptive statements are enumerated; a normative statement could only be derived together with other normative statements, such as 'it is wrong to kill people' or 'you ought not to kill people'. Another point worth keeping in mind with respect to the descriptive-normative distinction is that it is generally believed that natural science is a descriptive study including no normative component. That is, theses in natural science are meant to be descriptive statements ('the atomic weight of hydrogen is smaller than that of carbon', 'the sun mostly consists of hydrogen and helium', etc.), and putting forward normative statements falls outside the scope of natural scientific inquiry.

Keeping this descriptive-normative distinction in mind, let us consider the development of the interpretation of naturalism according to which naturalism implies the enterprise of descriptive epistemology: the task of epistemology is limited to producing a specific type of descriptive statements. The textual evidence for this interpretation may be found in "Epistemology Naturalized" and "Five Milestones of Empiricism." There Quine makes the following remarks with respect to the task remaining for naturalistic epistemology after the abandonment of the traditional ideal of foundationalist epistemology:

> Epistemology, or something like it, simply falls into place as a chapter of psychology and hence of natural science. It studies a natural phenomenon, viz., a physical human subject. This human subject is accorded a certain experimentally controlled input—certain patterns of irradiation in assorted frequencies, for instance—and in the fullness of time the subject delivers as output a description of the three-dimensional external world and its history. The relation between the meager input and the torrential output is a relation that we are prompted to study for somewhat the same reasons that always prompted epistemology:

namely, in order to see how evidence relates to theory, and in what ways one's theory of nature transcends any available evidence. (Quine 1969b, 82-3)

Naturalism does not repudiate epistemology, but assimilates it to empirical psychology. Science itself tells us that our information about the world is limited to irritations of our surfaces, and then the epistemological question is in turn a question within science: the question how we human animals can have managed to arrive at science from such limited information. Our scientific epistemologist pursues this inquiry and comes out with an account that has a good deal to do with the learning of language and with the neurology of perception. He talks of how men posit bodies and hypothetical particles, but he does not mean to suggest that the things thus posited do not exist. Evolution and natural selection will doubtless figure in this account, and he will feel free to apply physics if he sees a way. (Quine 1981, 72)

These remarks show that Quine views the task of the new epistemology as a study of a "natural phenomenon," the "relation between the meager input and the torrential output." More specifically, the new epistemology investigates how human beings, physical objects, "have managed to arrive at science from such limited information" (namely, "irritations of our surfaces"). Thus, Quine considered (at least then, at the time of writing) the task of epistemology as a descriptive inquiry into how human beings form theories about nature, not as a normative study that explains how human beings *ought* to form theories about nature, since epistemology is a part of empirical psychology, a study of natural phenomena concerning humans as physical objects, which is nothing but a descriptive, natural scientific inquiry.

Hilary Kornblith calls the view that traditional questions in epistemology can be replaced with questions in empirical psychology the 'replacement thesis', explicating its motivation as follows:

Once we see the sterility of the foundationalist program, we see that the only genuine questions there are to ask about the relation between theory and evidence and about the acquisition of belief are psychological questions. (Kornblith 1994, 4)

The interpretation Kornblith suggests is that Quine puts forward the replacement thesis as a result of the historical analysis of epistemology in "Epistemology Naturalized," which has concluded that no one succeeded in justifying or conceptually clarifying scientific theories on the basis of epistemologically unproblematic evidence. The replacement thesis here is understood as the view that the objectives of traditional epistemology, such as 'to provide a foundation for science', are all replaced by descriptive problems concerning the evidence-theory relation in empirical psychology. The two quotes above indeed seem to support this interpretation.

I have so far elaborated why the idea of epistemology as a descriptive project has been attributed to Quine. It is important to understand the textual basis of this interpretation, since several philosophers indeed discuss naturalism while interpreting naturalism as implying the idea of epistemology as a descriptive project. Now, the remaining task is to identify the problems with the interpretation. Before turning to this task, let us consider a typical objection to descriptive epistemology, the 'normativity charge', and Quine's response to it, so that the problems with the 'replacement thesis' interpretation of naturalism can more clearly be put in perspective.

(2) The replacement thesis and the charge of normativity

As a matter of course, the replacement thesis and the conception of epistemology it suggests were regarded as a threat to the long-standing field of epistemology itself, and the new conception, epistemology as a descriptive enterprise, has been subjected to much criticism. Here I will discuss the most powerful and most widely shared criticism, the 'normativity charge', according to which epistemology is essentially a normative study, and because of this replacing epistemological questions with questions in empirical psychology is to change the subject. The following details this challenge to the idea of descriptive epistemology and explains the implications and problems it gives rise to.

At the beginning of the article "What is 'Naturalized Epistemology'?" Jaegwon Kim (1988) describes traditional epistemology as consisting of the following two parts, using Descartes's *Meditations* as an example:

- Epistemology aims at identifying the criteria of justification: the criteria on which beliefs are accepted or rejected.

- Epistemology determines what we know according to the criteria of justification.

Since Descartes, it has been a commonplace among empiricists and rationalists alike to hold that the concept of 'justification' is central to the theory of knowledge. According to Kim, the concept of 'justification' is "what makes knowledge itself a normative concept" (Kim 1988, 35)[21], and traditional epistemology becomes an essentially normative study by placing justification at the center of the inquiry. Kim presents a plausible defense of this view as follows:

> If a belief is justified for us, then it is *permissible* and *reasonable*, from the epistemic point of view, for us to hold it, and it would be *epistemically irresponsible* to hold beliefs that contradict it. If we consider believing or accepting a proposition to be an "action" in an appropriate sense, belief justification would then be a special case of justification of action, which in its

---

[21] In this part of the article, where Kim claims that the normativity of the knowledge concept derives from the concept of justification, he refers to the classical definition of knowledge ('justified true belief'), and states that neither the concept of belief nor the concept of truth is (at least superficially) normative or evaluative—the former is a psychological concept and the latter is a semantical-metaphysical concept (Kim 1988, 35). Later on (ibid., 43-6), however, Kim argues that the concept of belief itself is normative and hence naturalized epistemology "cannot even be thought of as being about beliefs" (ibid., 43).

broadest terms is the central concern of normative ethics. Just as it is the business of normative ethics to delineate the conditions under which acts and decisions are justified from the moral point of view, so it is the business of epistemology to identify and analyze the conditions under which beliefs, and perhaps other propositional attitudes, are justified from the epistemological point of view. It probably is only an historical accident that we standardly speak of "normative ethics" but not of "normative epistemology." Epistemology is a normative discipline as much as, and in the same sense as, normative ethics. (Kim 1988, 35, italics in original)

If Kim is right about the status of epistemology here—it has to be an essentially normative study—and then there is a serious challenge to the new conception of epistemology suggested by the replacement thesis (and also a challenge to naturalism itself if interpreted as implying the idea of descriptive epistemology). For, if naturalized epistemology is concerned with empirical psychological questions about 'natural phenomena', the processes of producing 'the torrential output' from 'the meager input', as Quine occasionally states it to be, then the task of naturalized epistemology would be purely descriptive, and it would thereby be impossible to replace the 'essentially normative' epistemology with a descriptive naturalized epistemology.[22] Kim argues against Quine's position as follows:

Thus, it is normativity that Quine is asking us to repudiate. Although Quine does not explicitly characterize traditional epistemology as "normative" or "prescriptive," his meaning is unmistakable. Epistemology is to be "a chapter of psychology," a law-based predictive-explanatory theory, like any other theory within empirical science; its principal job is to see how human cognizers develop theories (their "picture of the world") from observation ("the stimulation of their sensory receptors"). Epistemology is to go out of the business of justification. We

---

[22] It will be helpful here to quote at length Kim's discussion of the new conception of epistemology Quine proposed. Kim illuminates the differences between the new conception of epistemology and other views previously proposed in the theory of knowledge.
The Cartesian project of validating science starting from the indubitable foundation of first-person psychological reports (perhaps with the help of certain indubitable first principles) is not the whole of classical epistemology—or so it would seem at first blush. In our characterization of classical epistemology, the Cartesian program was seen as one possible response to the problem of epistemic justification, the two-part project of identifying the criteria of epistemic justification and determining what beliefs are in fact justified according to those criteria. In urging "naturalized epistemology" on us, Quine is not suggesting that we give up the Cartesian foundationalist solution and explore others within the same framework —perhaps, to adopt some sort of "coherentist" strategy, or to require of our basic beliefs only some degree of "initial credibility" rather than Cartesian certainty, or to permit some sort of probabilistic derivation in addition to deductive derivation of nonbasic knowledge, or to consider the use of special rules of evidence, like Chisholm's "principles of evidence," or to give up the search for a derivational process that transmits undiminished certainty in favor of one that can transmit diminished but still useful degrees of justification. Quine's proposal is more radical than that. He is asking us to set aside the entire framework of justification-centered epistemology. That is what is new in Quine's proposals. Quine is asking us to put in its place a purely descriptive, causal-nomological science of human cognition. (Kim 1988, 39-40)

earlier characterized traditional epistemology as essentially normative; we see why Quine wants us to reject it. Quine is urging us to replace a normative theory of cognition with a descriptive science. (ibid., 40)

It is none of the naturalized epistemologist's business to assess whether, and to what degree, the input "justifies" the output, how a given irradiation of the subject's retinas makes it "reasonable" or "rational" for the subject to emit certain representational output. His interest is strictly causal and nomological: he wants us to look for patterns of lawlike dependencies characterizing the input-output relations for this particular organism and others of a like physical structure. (ibid., 41)

But it is difficult to see how an "epistemology" that has been purged of normativity, one that lacks an appropriate normative concept of justification or evidence, can have anything to do with the concerns of traditional epistemology. And unless naturalized epistemology and classical epistemology share some of their central concerns, it's difficult to see how one could *replace* the other, or be a way (a better way) of doing the other. To be sure, they both investigate "how evidence relates to theory." But putting the matter this way can be misleading, and has perhaps misled Quine: the two disciplines do not investigate the same relation. As lately noted,[23] normative epistemology is concerned with the evidential relation properly so-called—that is, the relation of justification—and Quine's naturalized epistemology is meant to study the causal-nomological relation. For epistemology to go out of the business of justification is for it to go out of business. (ibid., 43)

To summarize the main point of Kim's normativity charge expressed in these remarks, a naturalized epistemology (which is nothing but a descriptive inquiry in empirical psychology) cannot supersede traditional epistemology (an essentially normative study); if epistemology is an essentially normative study, then it is impossible to conceive a 'naturalized epistemology' as epistemology.

Kim's discussion presented here is sufficiently convincing, and it seems difficult to sustain the replacement thesis against the challenge it poses—the thesis that epistemology is replaced by empirical psychology. Thus, if naturalism implies the replacement thesis (or the idea of descriptive epistemology), then Kim's normativity charge would extend to naturalism itself, creating a potentially insoluble problem for

---

[23] Just prior to this, Kim states, "The causal relation between sensory input and cognitive output is a relation between "evidence" and "theory"; however, it is not an *evidential relation*" (Kim 1988, 42, italics added), and then continues as follows:

> In any event, the concept of evidence is inseparable from that of justification. When we talk of "evidence" in an epistemological sense we are talking about justification: one thing is "evidence" for another just in case the first tends to enhance the reasonableness or justification of the second. And such evidential relations hold in part because of the "contents" of the items involved, not merely because of the causal or nomological connections between them. A strictly nonnormative concept of evidence is not our concept of evidence; it is something that we do not understand. (ibid.)

naturalism.

In his "Reply to Morton White," however, Quine (1986) suggests the possibility of treating normativity within naturalistic epistemology. If Quine's suggestion is valid, then the normativity charge would not pose any insoluble problem to naturalism (note that Quine's suggestion appeared before the publication of the Kim article considered here). In what follows, I will examine Quine's suggestion as a response to the normativity charge.

(3) Quine's response to the normativity charge

Before closely examining Quine's response to the normativity charge by Kim, let us briefly review its line of reasoning.

(a) Traditional epistemology is an essentially normative study to which the normative concept of justification is central.
(b) At the same time, naturalized epistemology is fully elucidated by the study of the purely descriptive input-output relation.
(c) Thus, although both investigate the evidence-theory relation, the former treats it as a normative relation, an 'evidential' or 'justificatory' relation, whereas the latter treats it as a descriptive, causal-nomological relation.
(d) Therefore, the two studies share neither subject matter nor goal of inquiry, and it would hence be unjustifiable to replace traditional epistemology with naturalized epistemology.

Quine certainly appears to support (b) above given the remarks in "Naturalized Epistemology" and "Five Milestones of Empiricism," and the normativity charge seems to apply well to such a conception of epistemology. Then, how does Quine respond to the normativity charge? The following two remarks clearly indicate the direction that this response takes:

> Naturalization of epistemology does not jettison the normative and settle for the indiscriminate description of ongoing procedures. For me normative epistemology is a branch of engineering. It is the technology of truth-seeking, or, in a more cautiously epistemological term, prediction. ...There is no question here of ultimate value, as in morals; it is a matter of efficacy for an ulterior end, truth or prediction. (Quine 1986a, 664-5)

> But they [the critics] are wrong in protesting that the normative element [of naturalized epistemology], so characteristic of epistemology, goes by the board. Insofar as theoretical epistemology gets naturalized into a chapter of theoretical science, so normative epistemology gets naturalized into a chapter of engineering: the technology of anticipating sensory stimulation. (Quine 1992, 19)

Quine here maintains that epistemological normativity can be accounted for in naturalized epistemology. That is to say, in the context of naturalized epistemology, a question concerning epistemological normativity can be understood as a question concerning the "efficacy for an ulterior end," and it may be answered, more specifically, by a hypothetical imperative: 'if you aim at x, then you ought to do y'. Provided that questions concerning epistemological normativity can be dealt with in this manner within the orbit of naturalized epistemology, there would be little force in the objection that naturalized epistemology is improper as an epistemology because it cannot account for the normativity concept, an essential component of epistemology. This is a distillation of how Quine responds to the so-called normativity charge.

It is at this point important to understand the relation between naturalism and the idea of 'normative epistemology based on instrumental normativity'. As argued in section 3, naturalism is derived from the thesis of holism and belief system immanentism, and it demands the abandonment of traditional epistemology, which attempts to justify science on the basis of a more secure foundation than science itself. Many theorists have interpreted Quine as denying the possibility of any attempt to justify scientific beliefs. The following remark also reinforces this interpretation: "Naturalism does not repudiate epistemology, but assimilates it to empirical psychology" (Quine 1981, 72). But the idea of a normative epistemology based on the concept of instrumental normativity would seem to admit of the possibility of justifying scientific beliefs. Now the question to be asked here is: Is abandoning the ideal of traditional epistemology while embracing naturalism really compatible with accepting the idea of normative epistemology based on the concept of instrumental normativity?

To answer this question it is necessary to understand which part of traditional epistemology is rejected by naturalism, and on what grounds an epistemological project of this kind can be rejected by naturalism. First, notice that the traditional epistemological project rejected by naturalism is understood as a first-philosophical, foundationalist epistemology attempting to justify science *based on a more secure foundation*. That is, what naturalism rejects is the conviction that we can and ought to justify science on the basis of something more secure than science itself; naturalism by no means rejects the possibility of justifying scientific beliefs. Second, on what grounds does naturalism reject this first-philosophical, foundationalist epistemology? As discussed in section 2, naturalism does so on the basis of belief system immanentism and holism. If it is impossible to compare our belief system (our conceptual scheme or theory) with unconceptualized reality, as Quine states in "Identity, Ostension, and Hypostasis," then beliefs need to be justified only internally within our belief system. It is, however, impossible to ground our theoretically sophisticated beliefs in statements about sense data or observations by means of deduction or translational reduction alone, as implied by the discussion in "Epistemology Naturalized" and the thesis of holism.

Even though 'correspondence to reality' and 'justification through translational reduction' cannot be used as the criteria for justifying our belief system (including science), that does not amount to the abandonment of the whole project of normative epistemology. Certainly, naturalism rejects an epistemological project that takes 'correspondence to reality external to a belief system' or 'the possibility of deduction from an empirical basis' to be the criteria for justifying beliefs, but the reason for the rejection is that such a project is incompatible with belief system immanentism and the thesis of holism. Conversely, if an epistemological project becomes compatible with both belief system immanentism and the thesis of holism, then the project would be acceptable for naturalists.

The epistemological project Quine proposes using the concept of instrumental normativity is indeed compatible with belief system immanentism and holism. To observe that this is the case, consider how Quine arrived at the view that normative questions are questions concerning the "efficacy for an ulterior end" answerable by hypothetical imperatives. This view was expressed in response to the suggestion by Norton White that Quine endorses normative epistemology in the following remark: "Concepts are language, and the purpose of concepts and of language is efficacy in communication and in prediction. Such is the ultimate duty of language, science, and philosophy, and it is in relation to the duty that a conceptual scheme has finally to be appraised" (Quine 1953, 79).[24] Agreeing with White's suggestion, Quine claims that it is the instrumental normativity that figures in normative epistemology. The passage White quoted together with the part immediately preceding it makes it clear that Quine's treatment of epistemological normativity nicely fits with the basic principles of naturalism.

> We can improve our conceptual scheme, our philosophy, bit by bit while continuing to depend on it for support; but we cannot detach ourselves from it and compare it objectively with an unconceptualized reality. Hence it is meaningless, I suggest, to inquire into the absolute correctness of a conceptual scheme as a mirror of reality. Our standard for appraising basic changes of conceptual scheme must be not a realistic standard of correspondence to reality, but a pragmatic standard. Concepts are language, and the purpose of concepts and of language is efficacy in communication and in prediction. Such is the ultimate duty of language, science, and philosophy, and it is in relation to the duty that a conceptual scheme has finally to be appraised (Quine 1953, 78-9).

As explicitly stated in this quoted passage, the idea of instrumental normativity emerges only after conceding the impossibility of applying "a realistic standard of correspondence to reality" and abandoning such a standard. Based on this, it must be accepted as conclusively shown that Quine here does not adopt the criterion of justification unacceptable for naturalists, namely 'correspondence to reality'. Furthermore, as is clear from the contrast between the criterion of effectiveness to fulfill the purpose ("efficacy in communication and in prediction") and the criterion of justification depending on translational reducibility to something observational, the idea of instrumental normativity does not require a foundationalist justificatory structure, such as the one rejected in "Epistemology Naturalized."[25] The discussion so

---

[24] Directly quoting from Quine's comments on White, Quine states, "When in a passage quoted by White I referred to "the ultimate duty of language, science, and philosophy" I was using the word somewhat as when we speak of a heavy-duty cable or tractor. It was what language, science, and philosophy are for, as eyes are for seeing" (Quine 1986a, 665).

[25] In "Two Dogmas of Empiricism," Quine proposes this strategy of employing a pragmatic criterion for revising or justifying beliefs, dismissing the foundationalist criterion depending on the possibility of translational reduction. There Quine first argues for holism, rejecting 'radical reductionism', the

far reveals that the treatment of epistemological normativity as instrumental normativity does not use criteria of justification depending on ideas such as 'correspondence to reality' or 'justification through translational reduction'. It must be concluded that the treatment of epistemological normativity as instrumental normativity is compatible with the basic principles of naturalism.

Note here that the conclusion above does not presuppose the correctness of Quine's view that "efficacy in communication and in prediction" is "the ultimate duty of language, science, and philosophy" (quoted in full above). Such a view is problematic for several reasons. (The most significant problem is that Quine seems to have no argument for it, and it is also not obvious if such an argument can be given at all.) The correctness of the view is, however, irrelevant to the conclusion that epistemological normativity construed as an instrumental kind is compatible with the basic principles of naturalism. Epistemological normativity is understood in instrumental terms (effectiveness to fulfill whatever 'purpose' language and science may have), and this instrumentalist approach to normativity clearly does not require a criterion of justification depending on ideas such as 'correspondence to reality' or 'justification through translational reduction'. Thus, whatever 'purpose' language and science has, it is irrefutable that the idea of instrumental normativity is compatible with the basic principles of naturalism.

I have so far explicated the replacement thesis interpretation of naturalism and the basis for the interpretation, as well as the main challenge to naturalism so interpreted, discussing how the challenge has been resolved.[26] Now, it is possible to identify two problems in the interpretation according to which naturalism implies the replacement thesis:

- Naturalism faces a serious problem (it is impossible to develop epistemology within naturalism, since epistemology is an 'essentially normative' study).

- Some of the later remarks by Quine reject this interpretation.

For the moment, let me just point out these problems, and a fully developed assessment of this interpretation of naturalism will have to wait till section 6. The next subsection examines an interpretation of naturalism according to which

---

view that "[e]very meaningful statement is held to be translatable into a statement (true or false) about immediate experience"
(Quine 1953, 38). He then states, "The myth of physical objects is epistemologically superior to most in that it has proved more efficacious than other myths as a device for working a manageable structure into the flux of experience" (ibid., 44).

[26] As is pointed out above, the later Quine states, "Naturalization of epistemology does not jettison the normative and settle for the indiscriminate description of ongoing procedures" (Quine 1986a, 664). But he also seems to limit the scope of epistemology to a descriptive inquiry into the causal relation between the input and output of human beings as physical objects, saying that "[n]aturalism does not repudiate epistemology, but assimilates it to empirical psychology" (Quine 1981, 72). It is important to determine whether these statements by Quine are compatible with one another: the earlier statement should not be lightly dismissed in the light of later writings. I will return to this point in section 6, where I try to bridge gaps between the previous interpretations of naturalism and the interpretation of naturalism to be proposed in this book.

naturalism implies natural scientism.

1.4.2 The 'natural scientism' interpretation

In what follows, I will discuss the rationale for the interpretation that naturalism implies natural scientism, together with the problems of the interpretation. Before defining the central notion, natural scientism, let us first look at the following remarks by Quine:

> It [naturalism] sees *natural science* as an inquiry into reality, fallible and corrigible but not answerable to any supra-scientific tribunal, and not in need of any justification beyond observation and the hypothetico-deductive method. (Quine 1981, 72, italics added)

> The other negative source of naturalism is unregenerate realism, the robust state of mind of the *natural scientist* who has never felt any qualms beyond the negotiable uncertainties internal to science. (ibid., italics added)

> Epistemology, or something like it, simply falls into place as a chapter of psychology and hence of *natural science*. It studies a natural phenomenon, viz., a physical human subject. (Quine 1969b, 82, italics added)

As the highlighted parts of the passages here suggest, it is important to keep in mind that Quine seems to particularly focus on 'natural science' rather than on any special discipline. As discussed in section 3, naturalism is in part based on the idea of belief system immanentism, according to which beliefs must be revised or evaluated internally within a belief system. Recall, however, that, Quine leaves unspecified the extension of the belief system within which beliefs are revised or evaluated, or the meaning of 'science itself'. In any case, in the above quotes, Quine refers to 'the robust state of the mind of the natural scientist' as one of the sources of naturalism and considers naturalism to view 'natural science as an inquiry into reality', while taking epistemology to be 'a chapter of natural science'. It is then reasonable that many commentators have assumed that naturalism confers a special status on natural science.[27] In this essay, let 'natural scientism' be the name of the view that natural science is the single genuine inquiry into reality and truth.[28] (Natural scientism can be understood either as an epistemological or an ontological thesis: the former is that only the methods and procedures of natural science allow an inquiry into reality and

---

[27] For example, in the introduction to their anthology on naturalism, Steven Wagner and Richard Warner consider "naturalism to be the view that only natural science deserves full and unqualified credence" (Wagner and Warner, 1993, 1).

[28] Such a view is usually called 'scientism', but I will stick to the name 'natural scientism' in this book, since 'science' in 'scientism' is potentially misleading. Many of the objections to naturalism from the perspective of scientism address the methodology of natural science or monistic ontology of natural science. Thus, it is probably more appropriate to understand the objections to naturalism from the perspective of scientism as objections to 'natural scientism'.

truth, whereas the latter is that entities posited in natural science are the only genuine entities. Unless noted otherwise, I will use the term 'natural scientism' to include both theses.) The interpretation of naturalism to be examined here is that naturalism implies natural scientism.

Quine's remarks quoted above appear to suggest this 'natural scientism' interpretation of naturalism, and it is not surprising that many objections have been raised against naturalism interpreted in this way. Paul Moser and David Yandell, for example, criticize naturalism on this construal, claiming that naturalism is self-defeating because the theses of naturalism themselves are not defensible from a viewpoint of empirical science,[29] and that naturalism arbitrarily determines what counts as a genuine inquiry (Moser and Yandell, 2000).[30] Of course, Moser and Yandell's criticism of naturalism does not prove natural scientism to be unsustainable, but if naturalism implies natural scientism, then naturalists would have to at least address such questions as, 'How can naturalism be motivated from the perspective of empirical science?' and 'What is the basis for singling out and conferring a special status on natural science rather than any of our wide-ranging intellectual activities?'[31]

This kind of criticism of naturalism clearly shows the problems of the natural scientism interpretation of naturalism. As pointed out by Haruki Ito,[32] Quine's thesis of holism and other theses presented in "Epistemology Naturalized" are not themselves theses in natural science, nor do they appear to have been proposed following the method of natural science. Therefore, naturalism construed as implying

---

[29] There is a close relation between criticisms of natural scientism and the normativity charge, since natural science is usually regarded as purely descriptive. For example, according to epistemological natural scientism, the methodology of natural science is the only reliable method of inquiry, and an epistemological inquiry then has to occur in accordance with the methodology of natural science; therefore, epistemology inevitably becomes a descriptive study. Thus, it appears that natural scientism would imply the replacement thesis if natural science is understood as purely descriptive, and the normativity charge, an objection to the replacement thesis, would also be an objection to natural scientism on this understanding of natural science. Nevertheless, there is no complete overlap between the contexts in which these two types of criticism are made, as well as there is none between the targets of the criticism. (For example, the normativity charge only focuses on the context of epistemology, criticizing naturalism for failing to account for normativity, whereas criticisms of natural scientism not only address this epistemological problem but also contend that the distinction between genuine and non-genuine belief systems is unfounded.) I will therefore distinguish criticisms of natural scientism from the normativity charge, at least for now, in this chapter.

[30] See (Moser and Yandell 2000). There the criticism of naturalism goes roughly as follows:
1. Quine's scientism can be summarized in two theses.
   - There is no such thing as 'epistemologically legitimate philosophy' being prior to or independent from empirical science.
   - Hence, no philosophical claim transcending empirical science should be made.
2. There is a dilemma in Quine's scientism. The two theses above are apparently not claims in empirical science, and so they are either self-defeating or lose force by arbitrarily selecting what claims fall within empirical science. Therefore, scientism is not sustainable.

[31] Following the discussion in the previous section, naturalism implies belief system immanentism, according to which the notions of reality and truth are accounted for from a perspective within our belief system. Our belief system, however, encompasses a variety of intellectual activities besides natural science, and there is no argument for selecting or prizing natural science alone, at least, in Quine's derivation of naturalism. Section 6 will address this point.

[32] See Ito's exegesis of "Epistemology Naturalized," p.63.

natural scientism can be suspected of being internally incoherent. Furthermore, the fact that there is no positive argument for singling out and conferring a special status on natural science (at least in Quine's derivation of naturalism) suggests that this interpretation is open to question. (Recall that the two justifications for naturalism— 'despair of being able to define theoretical terms generally in terms of phenomena' and 'unregenerate realism'—are characterized as 'negative sources'.)

The above has provided a thorough elaboration of the interpretation of naturalism according to which naturalism implies natural scientism and of possible objections to the interpretation. On the one hand, since Quine's discussion of the method of naturalized philosophy sometimes shows great respect for natural science, the natural scientism interpretation of naturalism is to some extent convincing. This interpretation, on the other hand, has been pointed out to have several problems:

- It is hard to conceive of the theses of naturalism based on the bankruptcy of foundationalist epistemology and belief system immanentism as theses in natural science, so it must be doubted that naturalism construed as implying natural scientism is internally coherent.

- Although there is some support for belief system immanentism, there is no explicit support for the further claim that natural science is to be distinguished from the rest of our belief system, meriting a special status.

The final verdict on this interpretation will have to wait for section 6 (like verdict on the replacement thesis interpretation in section 1.4.1). Let us now turn to an interpretation asserting that naturalism implies physicalism.

1.4.3 The physicalist interpretation of naturalism

This subsection gives an overview of the interpretation of naturalism according to which naturalism implies physicalism. For the central notion of physicalism, let us for now adopt Quine's characterization: "there is no difference in matters of fact without a difference in the fulfillment of the physical-state predicates by space-time regions" (Quine 1979, 166). (A stricter definition of physicalism will be proposed in chapter 2, where I will primarily discuss physicalism.)[33]

A motivation for the physicalist interpretation of naturalism comes from Quine's discussion of the indeterminacy of translation,[34] immediately below in a brief

---

[33] The currently dominant approach to the definition of physicalism is to appeal to some sort of supervenience relation. As is clear from the wording, Quine's characterization is also along the lines of the supervenience approach (even when it is not as strict as recent characterizations). See (Kim 2002) for different versions of the relation between physicalism and supervenience. There are many questions to be considered to provide an adequate definition of physicalism—for one thing, 'Do physical predicates exclusively describing facts depend on current physics or a completed future physics?' See (Craine and Mellor 1990; Papineau 1993; Todayama 2003). Such questions are not directly relevant to the discussion in this subsection, however.

[34] Another motivation for the interpretation is to understand naturalism as the thesis that 'everything

summary. (Section 2.3.1 details the relation between the indeterminacy of translation and physicalism.) In the widely influential work *Word and Object*, Quine advances the thesis of the indeterminacy of translation, according to which there are multiple manuals for translating one language into another (Quine 1960, 27). The thesis asserts that it is impossible to determine uniquely a synonymy relation between sentences in different languages, or to determine, for a given sentence of one language, a sentence of another language that is synonymous with it. From this Quine reaches a further conclusion: "What the indeterminacy of translation shows is that the notion of propositions as sentence meanings is untenable" (Quine 1992, 102).[35] Here a 'proposition' is understood as the meaning of a sentence, and two synonymous sentences are assumed to have the same propositional content despite their notational differences. (For example, if the Japanese sentence 'yuki wa shiroi' and the English counterpart 'snow is white' are synonymous, then they are said to have the same propositional content, though they are apparently different sentences.)[36] In whatever way the concept of proposition is characterized, if propositions are conceived of as the meanings of sentences, it must at least be held that there is a unique proposition assigned to each sentence. However, if the indeterminacy of translation is correct—if it is impossible to determine a unique synonymy relation—then the very concept of propositions would become untenable. Thus, on the basis of the indeterminacy of translation, Quine rejects the concept of propositions as well as the idea that every sentence has a corresponding meaning.[37]

At this point, one might raise the following objection: even if it is impossible to

---

is in nature' ('nothing is supernatural') and to combine it with the physicalist conception of nature (physicalist worldview), according to which nature is ultimately explained by physics. This will lead to the physicalist interpretation of naturalism. As will be discussed in section 6, Quine did not presuppose the physicalist conception of nature in reviving naturalism in contemporary philosophy. I will therefore not pursue this line of reasoning because the main goal of this chapter is to determine the nature of naturalism by examining how Quine derived it.

[35] Understanding the basis of this conclusion would require more detail than I will present in this section. Here I will focus on the rationale for the physicalist interpretation of naturalism; Section 2.3.1 contains a fuller discussion of the logic of Quine's denial of meaning.

[36] For this concept of propositions, see (Carnap 1956, in particular sections 6 and 33). The thesis of the indeterminacy of translation was originally proposed as a criticism of Carnap's concept of propositions. See (Nakamura 2001) for this point.

[37] Let me discuss this line of reasoning in a little more detail. For Carnap, a proposition is the intension of a sentence, and there are two conditions to be met by propositions: first, for a given sentence, the proposition to be assigned is uniquely determined, and second, two sentences are assigned the same proposition if and only if they share the same truth value, and they share the same truth value only by virtue of their semantic rules. Carnap proposed a definition of propositions intended to satisfy these conditions: the proposition expressed by a sentence is the class of all sentences that are synonymous with it. This definition seems reasonable because it preserves our important intuition that the meaning of a sentence is shared by all synonymous sentences, and it also makes propositions (meanings of sentences) learnable by defining them using publicly accessible sentences (rather than using publicly inaccessible entities such as mental ideas). Propositions defined in this way, however, clearly fail to satisfy the first condition ('for a given sentence, the proposition to be assigned is uniquely determined') if the thesis of the indeterminacy of translation is correct. When one manual of translation pairs sentence A with sentence a, whereas another pairs A with β, which is not usually taken to be synonymous with A, it is impossible to determine whether the proposition expressed by A is {A, a, ...} or {A, β, ...}. Thus, the indeterminacy of translation refutes the view that a sentence expresses a uniquely determined proposition (the set of all sentences it is synonymous

Chapter 1 What is Naturalism?: Quine's Characterization of Naturalism and its Development

determine a unique synonymy relation, that would only imply that we are unable to do so, and the impossibility would still admit of the existence of a genuinely synonymous sentence or a genuinely correct manual of translation. This objection appears to presuppose that, even if an answer to a question cannot be given within our belief system, there could be a 'genuine answer' to the question outside the belief system.[38] Quine's response to this objection rests on naturalism. Consider the following remarks:

> I have argued that two conflicting manuals of translation can both do justice to all dispositions to behavior, and that, in such a case, there is no fact of the matter of which manual is right. The intended notion of matter of fact is not transcendental or yet epistemological, not even a question of evidence; it is ontological, a question of reality, and to be taken *naturalistically within our scientific theory of the world.* (Quine 1981, 23, italics added)

Restating what Quine describes here, the question as to which one of two conflicting manuals of translation is correct has to be solved "naturalistically within our scientific theory of the world," and there can be no 'genuinely correct' translation manual if an answer to the question cannot be uniquely determined, no matter what method is used.[39] That is, it is naturalism that provides the basis for refuting the

---

with) as well as the commonsensical view that sentences have a corresponding meaning.

[38] One might argue that, in figuring out what a sentence really means, there is no need to seek an answer outside our belief system. The thesis of the indeterminacy of translation presupposes a third-person perspective from which the meaning of a sentence must be determined depending on publicly available evidence such as the speaker's behavior and contextual circumstances. If such a perspective is replaced by a first-person perspective, and the meaning of a sentence is apparent from a first-person perspective, then the question asking what a sentence really means would perhaps disappear. Indeed, Searle (1987) presented a similar argument against the indeterminacy of translation. However, proponents of this line of argument would face serious problems in explaining successful linguistic communication and language learning (Quine 1992, 37-8). Therefore, although first-person authority is an important topic in the understanding of utterance content, it alone fails to pose a serious challenge to the indeterminacy of translation. (Evolving Quine's philosophy of language in an original way, the work of Donald Davidson develops a unified approach to explaining the public and private aspects of language, successful linguistic communication as well as language learning and first-person authority concerning the understanding of utterance content. See, for example, [Davidson 2001].)

[39] Nobuharu Tanji characterizes Quine's position until 1980s as 'metaphysical realism', discussing the relation between the indeterminacy of translation and the underdetermination of theory.

> Hilary Putnam criticizes what he calls 'metaphysical realism', the view that a theory resulted from an ideal inquiry is still fallible, and that the world as it really is can be different from what the theory describes. Quine held the view of this 'metaphysical realism' for some time. (Tanji 1997, 184)

Nonetheless, as the quoted passage above clearly indicates, Quine naturalistically construes the notion of matter of fact, and so the notion is understood in a belief system immanentist way. Thus, Quine here does not support metaphysical realism. (Note that the passage is quoted from the 1981 collection of essays.)

It has sometimes been pointed out that the early Quine was inclined to pluralism, whereas the later Quine shifted toward physicalist monism (see [Noe 1993, 225-6]). In my view, Quine was committed to metaphysical realism at no point in this transition period. (Quine sometimes characterized his own position as realism, but it seems that the position would be more appropriately called 'belief system immanentist realism'.) My interpretation here seems to be supported by the texts from both early and later stages of the transition period ([Quine 1953, 78-9] and [Quine 1981, 23]), in which Quine explicitly rejects ideas similar to metaphysical realism.

objection above ('it is certainly impossible to determine a unique translation relation, but that is our failure and by no means undermines the idea that there exists a meaning that a sentence really has'). Recall Quine's characterization of naturalism in section 3, which states, "It is within science itself, and not in some prior philosophy, that reality is to be identified and described" (Quine 1981, 21).

However, what does Quine specifically mean by 'our scientific theory' in the above quote? From what does Quine deduce the conclusion that there is no definite way to select one translation manual as the right one? (Towards the end of section 3, I pointed out that Quine's early characterization of naturalism leaves it unclear what 'science' and 'natural science' refer to. That point is directly relevant to the questions here.) The following remarks seem to suggest how Quine would answer these questions:

> In respect of being under-determined by all possible data, translational synonymy and theoretical physics are indeed alike. [...] Where then does the parallel fail? Essentially in this: theory in physics is an ultimate parameter. There is no legitimate first philosophy, higher or firmer than physics, to which to appeal over physicist heads. (Quine 1969c, 302-3)

> ...when I say there is no fact of the matter, as regards, say, the two rival manuals of translation, what I mean is that both manuals are compatible with all the same distributions of states and relations over elementary particles. In a word, they are physically equivalent. (Quine 1981, 23)

It is recognizable in these remarks that Quine viewed theory in physics to be the ultimate judge of facts and thought there to be no question of factuality ("no fact of the matter") that cannot be answered within theory in physics. That is, in claiming that an answer to the question about choosing the right translation manual has to be provided "naturalistically within our scientific theory," Quine contends that the matter of factuality has to be described within theory in physics.[40]

The view, expressed in the remarks, that theory in physics is the ultimate

---

[40] Physicalism, in which physics is the ultimate determinant of facts, has drawn much criticism, while also attracting many supporters. (Proponents of the physicalist interpretation of naturalism, of course, consider criticism of physicalism to be criticism of naturalism.) A major criticism of physicalism calls into question the basis for the special status that physics enjoys. (Going one step further than questioning the basis for this, I have argued that physicalism cannot be justified within the framework of naturalized epistemology [Igashira 2005]. For a defense of physicalism see [Papineau 2001], in which Papineau considers physicalism to be an empirical hypothesis and defends the background for and plausibility of physicalism.) For example, Quine proposed the thesis of the underdetermination of theory, according to which it is impossible to determine uniquely a theory based on available evidence. There seems to be a parallelism between the underdetermination thesis and the thesis of the indeterminacy of translation, but Quine sees no problem in theory in physics while judging there to be no fact of the matter about translation manuals. We may ask what the reason for distinguishing physical theory from linguistic theory concerning semantic questions is. Why does physics merit special treatment, monopolizing the study of matters of fact? Much debate on the indeterminacy of translation has revolved around the problem concerning the basis of physicalism, and a number of critics have accused physicalism of lacking justification. (The most important criticism along these lines can be found in [Chomsky 1969; 1975; 1980; Rorty 1972].)

determinant of facts is nothing but physicalism. (The relation between the indeterminacy of translation and physicalism will be closely examined in the next chapter.) In discussing the thesis of the indeterminacy of translation, Quine seems to express naturalism through claims such as that the matter of fact must be described in theory in physics and that there is no fact concerning questions unanswerable within the bounds of theory in physics. Thus, Quine's discussion of the indeterminacy of translation supports the interpretation of naturalism according to which naturalism implies physicalism.

I have explicated how the physicalist interpretation of naturalism has been motivated, regardless of its plausibility. Certainly, the above quote unquestionably suggests that Quine's belief system immanentism is a physicalist position. The problem of the interpretation, however, is that no reason has been presented for restricting in a physicalist way our belief system, through which reality is to be identified and described. Quine did not present any argument for physicalism, at least, in the discussion supporting the naturalistic turn. In other words, even though Quine is obviously a physicalist, no argument has been given for the claim that *naturalists in general* have to be physicalists. If it is claimed that naturalism implies physicalism, it must be shown not only that the naturalist Quine is a physicalist, but also that there is some reason for naturalists to be physicalists (for example, it could be shown that physicalism is a premise for the justification of naturalism). This is a task remaining for proponents of the physicalist interpretation of naturalism.

The above has examined the textual basis for and the problems of the physicalist interpretation of naturalism. Just as the two interpretations previously discussed, Quine's own remarks support this interpretation, adding considerable plausibility (it is at least unquestionable that Quine is a physicalist). At the same time, the discussion so far revealed that the interpretation is inadequate, since it fails to explain the implications of physicalism from the standpoint of naturalism, providing no reason for naturalists to endorse physicalism. Together with the other interpretations, section 6 will give the final verdict on this interpretation.

As I stated at the end of section 3, since "Epistemology Naturalized," Quine not only advocated for the naturalistic turn but also presented on various occasions methodological considerations concerning naturalistically conceived philosophical inquiry. Extant interpretations of naturalism reflect those considerations, trying to provide an adequate definition of naturalism by removing the obscurities in Quine's early characterization of naturalism. The current subsection has focused on some of the extant interpretations and discussed their backgrounds and the problems they pose. The next subsection turns to Quine's own discussion of the obscurities in the early characterization of naturalism, leading to Quine's final characterization of naturalism.

1.5 Quine's Final Characterization of Naturalism

The previous section examined three different interpretations of naturalism, according to which naturalism implies, respectively, the replacement thesis, natural scientism, and physicalism; this was done while discussing the basis and problems of each interpretation. As I have mentioned earlier, these interpretations of naturalism were inferred and reconstructed from Quine's writings on naturalistic inquiry, not explicitly stated in the texts. The obscurities in Quine's early characterization of naturalism left theorists with no choice but to speculate on possible interpretations. For example, Quine characterized naturalism as 'viewing science as an inquiry into reality' but here Quine leaves the referent of 'science' underspecified. As a result, in order to clearly delineate the notion of naturalism, theorists discussing naturalism found it necessary to appeal to Quine's remarks on other topics. In the efforts to remove the obscurities, some theorists identifed 'science' here with natural science,[41] and others identified it with physics (or the system of studies in which physics is the pinnacle of its ontological hierarchy). (Thus, in contemporary debates on naturalism, there is no shortage of interpretations of naturalism, making it difficult to pursue a meaningful discussion based on any common ground; the obscurities in Quine's early characterization are partially responsible for this situation.)

In later years Quine himself became aware of this and attempted to resolve the obscurities in the early characterization of naturalism. (What was proposed was not compatible with the extant interpretations of naturalism.) In what follows, I will explore Quine's ultimate conception of naturalism referring to the 1995 article "Naturalism; or Living within One's Means."

1.5.1 Quine's elaboration of the early characterization of naturalism

Quine begins the article "Naturalism" with the definition of naturalism presented in *Theories and Things*:

- Naturalism is "the recognition that it is within science itself, and not in some prior philosophy, that reality is to be identified and described" (Quine 1981, 21)

- Naturalism is an "abandonment of the goal of a first philosophy prior to natural science (ibid., 67)

As has been repeatedly pointed out, the characterization here is inadequate; the scope of 'science itself' is not clearly delineated, nor is 'a first philosophy prior to natural science' clearly understandable. In elucidating the characterization of naturalism, Quine elaborates on what counts as 'scientific'.

- 'Science itself' includes "the farthest flights of physics and cosmology," experimental psychology, history, social sciences, and mathematics, "insofar at least as it [mathematics] is applied." (Quine 1995, 275)

- If I saw indirect explanatory benefit in positing sensibilia, possibilia, spirits, a

---

[41] The scope of 'natural science' too deserves more explication, but for the moment, it can be understood to be 'what is commonly termed natural science'.

Creator, I would joyfully accord them scientific status too, on a par with such avowedly scientific posits as quarks and black holes. (ibid., 275)

According to Quine, the possible scope of 'science itself' not only encompasses the natural sciences but also extends to the social sciences and theories positing spirits and a Creator. Below is a further elaboration of the early characterization.

> My point in the characterizations of naturalism that I quoted is just that the *most* we can reasonably seek in support of an inventory and description of reality is testability of its observable consequences in the time-honored hypothetico-deductive way-whereof more anon. Naturalism need not cast aspersions on irresponsible metaphysics, however deserved, much less on soft sciences or on the speculative reaches of the hard ones, expect insofar as a firmer basis is claimed for them than the experimental method itself. (ibid., 276, italics in original)

The above quote indicates that Quine's characterization of naturalism derives from the distinction between science itself and some prior philosophy, and that the distinction depends on the methodological consideration as to whether a basis firmer than the experimental method is claimed or demanded, rather than on the topic of an inquiry or the types of entities posited in the inquiry.[42] Thus, naturalism is "boiling down to the claim that in our pursuit of truth about the world we cannot do better than our traditional scientific procedure, the hypothetico-deductive method" (ibid., 281). Following these statements, even Descartes's dualism—typically considered to be a metaphysical thesis—"could as well be reckoned as science, however false" (ibid., 275). Now, based on these remarks, Quine's final characterization of naturalism can be summarized as follows:

> Naturalism: rejecting any other justificatory procedure than the hypothetico-deductive method, the view turns its back on the first-philosophical project in which philosophy precedes science and provides its foundation.

1.5.2 Quine's final characterization of naturalism and what it excludes

---

[42] In recent years the distinction between 'epistemological naturalism' and 'ontological naturalism' is often presupposed in debates on naturalism (see [Todayama 2003] and [Borchert 2006]). Following that distinction, it is tempting to suppose that Quine's characterization only aims at the epistemological aspects of naturalism, a subcategory of naturalism. As will be discussed in chapter 2, however, naturalism in Quine's conception has ontological implications, and construing it only as a variant of epistemological naturalism would seem imprecise and misleading. In my view, the epistemological-ontological naturalism distinction is useful for classifying questions concerning the legitimacy of naturalism, but it also possibly thwarts a unified understanding of naturalism by disconnecting epistemological and ontological themes, essential components of naturalist debates; therefore, the distinction would not be useful to understand the whole project of naturalism.

The previous subsection has explicated Quine's final characterization of naturalism, but there are still some issues to be addressed with respect to the characterization. First, an empirical test in the hypothetico-deductive method is "a negative test" (Quine 1995, 280). The hypothetico-deductive method is a way to measure the validity of a theoretical hypothesis, a procedure in which an observable consequence is deduced from the hypothesis under consideration and tested in comparison with actual observations. Simply put, the validity of a hypothesis is evaluated by testing the predictions deduced from the hypothesis. As for prediction, Quine states, "I said that prediction is not the main purpose of science, but only the test. It is a negative test at that, a test by refutation" (Ibid., 280).

The use of negative tests here must be understood to be in contrast to verificationism (confirmationism), as is clear from the paraphrase of 'a negative test' —'a test by refutation'. (According to verificationism or confirmationism, amassed observations fitting a hypothesis establish the correctness of the hypothesis or increase its plausibility. By contrast, according to falsificationism, a hypothesis is no more likely to be correct irrespective of how many observations fitting the hypothesis are amassed, and the role of the observations is limited to refuting conflicting hypotheses.) Quine maintains that a test in the hypothetico-deductive method is a procedure of falsification, in which a hypothesis incompatible with observations is refuted. It follows that for a group of hypotheses to pass a test in the hypothetico-deductive method—the only justificatory procedure for Quine—there is no need to increase the plausibility of the hypotheses by continuously producing successful predictions. A test by means of prediction, testing in the hypothetico-deductive method, is a negative test, and that alone does not disprove hypotheses as long as they produce correct predictions.

The second issue to be addressed is the intended meaning of the claim that there is no justificatory procedure other than the hypothetico-deductive method. As I have already stated, the hypothetico-deductive method is a procedure evaluating the validity of a hypothesis by testing observable consequences deduced from the hypothesis. In stating that the method is the only justificatory procedure, Quine does not intend to assert that there has to be a testable and observational consequence for every single naturalistically acceptable claim, hypothesis, or theory. Consider the following passage:

> As a further disavowal let me add, contrary to positivism, that a sentence does not even need to be testable in order to qualify as a respectable sentence of science. A sentence is testable, in my liberal or holistic sense, if adding it to previously accepted sentences clinches an observation categorical that was not implied by those previous sentences alone; but much good science is untestable even in this liberal sense. We believe many things because they fit in smoothly by analogy, or they symmetrize and simplify the overall design. Surely much history and social science is of this sort, and some hard science. Moreover, such acceptations are not idle fancy; their proliferation generates, every here and there, a hypothesis that can indeed be tested. Surely this is the major source of testable hypotheses and the growth of science. (ibid., 280)

As is explicitly stated here, according to the descriptions in "Naturalism; or Living within One's Means," naturalism can accept sentences with no observable consequences as a 'respectable sentence of science'. It then follows that, in claiming there to be no other justificatory procedure than the hypothetico-deductive method, Quine does not in effect exclude sentences that are not directly testable through the hypothetico-deductive method. Although empirical testing in the hypothetico-deductive method is construed as falsification, it is not required for a sentence to be falsifiable to qualify as a scientific sentence. Rather, the claim is intended to reject a demand and deny an allegation for a foundation that is more secure than the experimental method—whether the alleged foundation is correspondence to reality or translational reducibility to observation statements; Quine intends to point out that any claim can be certain only to the extent that it is able to pass the hypothetico-deductive testing, or that it is not falsified.[43]

It is important to understand this point in connection with the problem of the obscurities in the early characterization of naturalism discussed at the end of section 3, that is, the indeterminate scope of 'our belief system', from within which reality and truth are to be described. The threshold for a sentence to belong to our belief system or to 'respectable' science is set fairly low: a sentence is required neither to be a sentence in natural science nor even to have observable consequences. (Quine earlier refers to "explanatory benefit" [Quine, 1995, 275] in discussing the scope of science, but it is unclear if this is a part of the conditions for something to be scientific.) After all, all that Quine explicitly excludes as being incompatible with naturalism is a basis that is firmer than the experimental method. Now, it is possible to identify Quine's ultimate answer to the question raised at the end of section 3, What is included in 'science itself' when he says, "It is within science itself, and not in some prior philosophy, that reality is to be identified and described" (Quine 1981, 21) ? The answer would be that science possibly includes everything as long as it does not require a more secure foundation than the experimental method. (Therefore, Quine's final characterization of naturalism seems incompatible with the three interpretations of naturalism examined in section 4. More of this will be discussed in the next section.)

---

[43] One might ask how the hypothetico-deductive method itself can be justified. Perhaps, a plausible answer to that question would be that there is no positive argument for the validity of the hypothetico-deductive method.

This answer may be easy to grasp if it is considered together with justificatory procedures appealing to correspondence to reality or translational reduction. These procedures used to be thought of as being able to provide a more secure or solid basis for our beliefs than the hypothetico-deductive method (experimental method), but Quine concluded neither to be executable; as a result, the naturalist position—the abandonment of a first philosophy and rejection of any other justificatory procedure than the hypothetico-deductive method (experimental method)—has been proposed. The justificatory processes appealing to correspondence to reality or translational reduction are importantly different from the hypothetico-deductive method in that they have been pointed out to be inexecutable. Thus, the hypothetico-deductive method is accepted only to the extent that it has not been proven to be inadequate. In approving no other form of justification than the hypothetico-deductive method, Quine is mainly suggesting that there is no executable justificatory procedure stronger than the hypothetico-deductive method, not that there is some specific virtue in the method.

1.6 Evaluating Quine's Final Characterization of Naturalism

Section 4 has discussed three interpretations of naturalism proposed in the effort to resolve the obscurities in Quine's early characterization of naturalism. Each interpretation is motivated by some of Quine's own remarks on the philosophical methodology after the naturalistic turn. Given the remarks that are cited, it is indeed undeniable that naturalism is closely related to the replacement thesis, natural scientism, and physicalism. A straightforward reading of the texts motivating the interpretations makes it even appear that Quine was committed to the idea that naturalism implies all of the replacement thesis, natural scientism, and physicalism. (In fact, many contemporary thinkers consider natural scientism or physicalism as an essential part of the definition of naturalism. For example, it is usually assumed that naturalizing the mind amounts to explaining mental phenomena retaining a physicalist ontology or the natural scientific worldview.)[44] At the same time, the characterization of naturalism presented in "Naturalism; or Living within One's Means" seems incompatible with those interpretations. For, as discussed in the previous section, the final characterization of naturalism excludes only any stress on or demand for a more secure foundation than the experimental method, and neither natural scientism nor physicalism constrains the scope of our belief system.

In this way, there appears to be a tension between Quine's remarks on the philosophical methodology after the naturalistic turn and the final characterization of naturalism. However, the three interpretations of naturalism—taking naturalism to imply the replacement thesis, natural scientism, or physicalism, respectively—should not be lightly dismissed, since they are supported by persuasive textual evidence. Did Quine change his views of naturalism in the 1980s through the late 1990s? Or is there a plausible explanation making all the remarks coherent? In any case, an explanation must be provided for the (at least superficial) tension between Quine's variously interpretable wide-ranging remarks.

This section is devoted to the task of explaining away the (seemingly troubling) tension between Quine's remarks, which will contribute to our understanding of the nature of naturalism. First, in section 1.6.1, I will examine how Quine's final conception of naturalism relates to other important theses such as the replacement thesis, natural scientism, and physicalism. (A new notion, 'minimal naturalism', will be introduced for the naturalist position defined by Quine's final characterization of naturalism.) Next, in section 1.6.2, I will argue that naturalism should be understood in accordance with Quine's final characterization of it. The argument partially depends on the way in which naturalism has been justified, in particular, how the premises in the justifications relate to the conclusions deduced by Quine. Finally, in section 1.6.3, distinguishing naturalism itself from the position endorsed by the naturalist Quine, I will bridge gaps between Quine's final characterization of naturalism and the three interpretations of naturalism discussed in section 4 (as well as Quine's remarks

---

[44] Yukihiro Nobuhara (2004), for example, often uses the word 'naturalization' with such an assumption.

1.6.1 Naturalism without the replacement thesis, natural scientism, or physicalism

According to the three interpretations of naturalism examined in section 4, naturalism implies, respectively, the replacement thesis, natural scientism, or physicalism, whereas Quine's final characterization of naturalism, outlined in section 5, seems to include none of such philosophical theses. This subsection clarifies the relations between the final characterization of naturalism and these three theses. To state the conclusion at the outset, I will argue for the following two points:

(1) Although physicalism and natural scientism are compatible with naturalism, they are not necessary parts of naturalism.
(2) Naturalism has justificatory priorities over physicalism and natural scientism; it is naturalism that makes these two positions philosophically plausible, and not the other way around.

Consider first how naturalism relates to physicalism. As I have mentioned earlier, Quine's definition of physicalism suffices for present purposes: "there is no difference in matters of fact without a difference in the fulfillment of the physical-state predicates by space-time regions" (Quine 1979, 166). (A more detailed definition of physicalism will be introduced in chapter 2.) The following paragraph describes Quine's final assessment of physicalism in connection with naturalism.

> Naturalism is naturally associated with physicalism, or materialism. I do not equate them, as witness my earlier remark on Cartesian dualism. I do embrace physicalism as a scientific position, but I could be dissuaded of it on future scientific grounds without being dissuaded of naturalism. (Quine 1995, 281)

What is suggested here is that physicalism is neither equivalent to nor necessary for naturalism; the status of physicalism is rather analogous to that of scientific positions or hypotheses that can be developed within the naturalistic framework.[45] First, it naturally follows from the final characterization of naturalism that physicalism is a scientific hypothesis, since otherwise physicalism would be unfalsifiable by empirical evidence, having a firmer basis than the hypothetico-deductive method and clearly conflicting with the basic principles of naturalism.[46] Second, Quine's final

---

[45] Similar remarks can be found also in (Quine, 2000, 411). It should be noted that, according to Quine's understanding of physicalism, physicalism as a scientific hypothesis in itself is not testable, but it allows deductions of other testable hypotheses (Quine 1995, 285). Recall that naturalism can accept sentences with no observable consequences as a 'respectable sentence of science' under Quine's final characterization of naturalism, examined in Section 5. The physicalist hypothesis is precisely an instance of such scientific sentences.
[46] David Papineau is an example of a theorist who also explicitly acknowledges physicalism to be a scientific hypothesis. See (Papineau 2001).

characterization makes it sufficiently plausible that it is possible to abandon physicalism while retaining naturalism. On the final characterization, all that naturalism explicitly excludes is a foundation allegedly more secure than the experimental method, and there is nothing incoherent in removing physicalism from the picture. Since physicalism is a scientific hypothesis, naturalists are of course free to adopt physicalism. Physicalism, however, is not an essential component of naturalism.[47]

Next, consider the relation between naturalism and natural scientism. As is stated in section 1.4.2, natural scientism is defined in this book as the view that natural science is the only genuine inquiry into reality and truth. How it relates to naturalism is not difficult to grasp. The discussion of physicalism in the previous paragraph extends to natural scientism. Natural scientism must be understood as a scientific hypothesis because otherwise it would be incompatible with the basic principles of naturalism. Furthermore, naturalism can accept a discipline outside natural science as long as it does not make claims for a foundation that is more secure than the experimental method. Therefore, it is theoretically possible to adopt naturalism while rejecting natural scientism.

At last, let us consider the replacement thesis. First, notice that not all normative statements are excluded by naturalism under Quine's final characterization. Since all that is excluded by naturalism characterized in this way is a claim for a foundation more secure than the experimental method, normative statements satisfying this condition are acceptable within naturalism, and some hypothetical normative statements, such as those suggested by Quine, clearly satisfy the condition: for example, 'if the goal is to build a bridge that can hold one thousand people without collapsing, then it must be built in such-and-such way'; 'if the goal is to accurately detect the conditions of an individual from two kilometers away, then some other means than direct visual information must be employed'. (The former may be refuted and revised as empirical sciences such as architecture and mechanics develop, and the latter as medicine and physiology develop.)[48] Thus, it is not necessary for naturalism to accept the replacement thesis. Second, it is obvious that the naturalist framework is compatible with the development of descriptive epistemology indicated by the replacement thesis—an empirical psychological investigation of the input-output relation of human beings understood as physical objects. In sum, it is possible to descriptively study the evidence-theory relation as part of empirical psychology, but it is also possible to normatively study the same relation.

The above discussion has elucidated the relations that the naturalism in Quine's final conception has to the replacement thesis, natural scientism, and physicalism, but it has not emphasized one important aspect of these relations: that naturalism has justificatory priorities over physicalism and natural scientism; that it is an adoption of naturalism that renders views such as natural scientism and physicalism

---

[47] Noe has already pointed out the theoretical possibility of abandoning first philosophy while rejecting physicalism and natural scientism. See (Noe 1993, 209, 215).
[48] What is excluded here would be categorical normative statements that are presented as being immune to revision (for example, because they are credited by holy texts).

philosophically plausible.

It has been traditionally assumed in epistemology that there must be some philosophical foundation for scientific knowledge to qualify and vouch for it as genuine knowledge, regardless of the practical implications, when the legitimacy of scientific knowledge is evaluated from a philosophical perspective. (Translational reduction to observation statements, a main topic of Quine's "Epistemology Naturalized," is one of such foundational projects in epistemology.) Considered from this assumption, it follows that natural scientism and physicalism, which view natural science and physics to be a genuine inquiry into reality and truth, have no plausibility (at least as philosophical theses) until they are somehow philosophically grounded.

Different from this, naturalism implies belief system immanentism and rejects the need for providing a foundation for science, which it sees "as an inquiry into reality, fallible and corrigible but not answerable to any supra-scientific tribunal, and not in need of any justification beyond observation and the hypothetico-deductive method" (Quine 1981, 72). That is, naturalism jettisons the need for a first-philosophical basis in which philosophy precedes science and provides its foundation. As a result, a naturalist becomes able to examine the legitimacy of scientific knowledge from a perspective within science, irrespective of whether there is a philosophical foundation for the scientific knowledge. Given the failures of the various forms of foundationalist epistemology (section 1.2), it will remain extremely difficult to present natural scientism or physicalism as a philosophically plausible thesis while holding onto the epistemological tradition in which scientific knowledge needs a philosophical foundation to qualify as genuine knowledge. Therefore, the naturalistic turn is a prerequisite for developing natural scientism and physicalism as philosophically plausible theses.

Here is a summary of the discussion so far. First, according to Quine's final characterization of naturalism, theses such as natural scientism and physicalism are not essential components of naturalism, but theoretical options available to naturalists. Second, it is the adoption of naturalism that renders these theses philosophically justifiable. Therefore, the three interpretations of naturalism examined in section 4 outline different extensions of naturalism (positions that become plausible only after adopting naturalism), rather than define naturalism itself.

Now, it becomes justifiable to offer the following expositions to understand the relations among the three interpretations of naturalism presented in section 4.[49] Naturalist positions essentially containing physicalism or natural scientism share in common the rejection of the first-philosophical project in which philosophy precedes and provides a foundation for science, and the denial of the existence of any other useful justificatory procedure than the hypothetico-deductive method. The common thread proposed here is nothing but Quine's final characterization of naturalism. In this book, let us call this shared view 'minimal naturalism'. Accordingly, 'physicalist

---

[49] Of course, I have not examined all the interpretations of naturalism proposed in today's literature; and I do not generalize my conclusion here to all forms of naturalism. However, given that most interpretations of naturalism are dependent on Quine's discussion of naturalism, it is not unreasonable to suppose that all contemporary characterizations of naturalism share in common the abandonment of a first philosophy—nothing is more to be trusted than the hypothetico-deductive method after all.

naturalism' for example, which implies physicalism, is to be understood as minimal naturalism with the physicalist hypothesis added onto it. Likewise, 'natural scientism naturalism' can be understood in the same manner. Naturalists can take a variety of naturalist positions by adding different theses to minimal naturalism. Moreover, this way of understanding naturalism would seem applicable to the various definitions of naturalism offered in the contemporary literature. For example, Roseberg (1996) defines naturalism as 'the abandonment of a first philosophy + scientism + Darwinism + scientific progressivism', a position that without any distortion can be paraphrased as minimal naturalism with multiple theses added onto it. In this manner naturalists will be able to make multiple additions to minimal naturalism when specifying their particular forms of naturalism.

This subsection has discussed the relations between Quine's final characterization of naturalism ('minimal naturalism') and the three interpretations of naturalism examined in section 4, showing that these three fail to capture the final characterization. Rather than prematurely jumping to the conclusion that, since the final characterization is the last version of Quine's description of naturalism, we should limit its application to understanding naturalism, I wish to reconsider the justifications for naturalism Quine presented and how they support naturalism in order to throw light on the problems with the three interpretations and show that minimal naturalism is the optimum interpretation of contemporary naturalism.

1.6.2 The strength of Quine's final characterization of naturalism

As has been exhaustively discussed in section 1.5, according to Quine's final characterization of naturalism, naturalism denies the existence of any other justificatory procedure than the hypothetico-deductive method and rejects the first-philosophical project in which philosophy precedes science and provides its foundation. There is an important strength in this characterization of naturalism, as opposed to other interpretations of naturalism such as those discussed in section 4 (containing physicalism or natural scientism as necessary components). The strength lies in that the justifications for naturalism Quine presented indeed warrant the minimal interpretation of naturalism, whereas the other interpretations go beyond what is warranted by the Quine justifications. To clearly understand this strength, let me quote again the passage in which Quine expresses the bases of naturalism.

> Naturalism has two sources, both negative. One of them is despair of being able to define theoretical terms generally in terms of phenomena, even by contextual definition. A holistic or system-centered attitude should suffice to induce this despair. The other negative source of naturalism is unregenerate realism, the robust state of mind of the natural scientist who has never felt any qualms beyond the negotiable uncertainties internal to science. (Quine 1981, 72)

Quine cites as the bases of naturalism 'despair of being able to define theoretical terms generally in terms of phenomena' and 'unregenerate realism'. Recall that section 1.3 has shown that the bases are supported by the thesis of holism and the impossibility of justifying beliefs from outside belief systems. At the end of section 1.3, I schematically represented the logical structure of the derivation of naturalism as follows:

> Belief system immanentism (← the impossibility of justification from outside belief systems)
> +
> The impossibility of empiricist foundationalism (← holism)
> ↓
> Naturalism: first philosophy has been abandoned; science itself is an inquiry into reality

The question to be addressed here is whether it is justifiable to read natural scientism or physicalism into the outcome of this line of reasoning (namely, naturalism). What is relevant to answering this question is probably only one of the two justifications, belief system immanentism. More specifically, what needs to be made clear is whether the belief system immanentism stated in the justification is (i) a simple expression of the idea that reality and truth are to be described within our belief system, (ii) a natural scientism variant of belief system immanentism, or (iii) a physicalist variant of belief system immanentism. I will point out two reasons for taking (i) to be the right answer.

The first reason is that Quine's rationale for belief system immanentism allows directly deriving neither a natural scientism nor a physicalist variant of belief system immanentism. Quine supports belief system immanentism by arguing against the concept of 'the world in itself' (the world is completely independent from our belief system), saying that the concept is essentially erroneous in the context of justifying beliefs. This claim, however, only entails the simple form of belief system immanentism, according to which reality and truth are to be described within our belief system. A further qualification is needed in order to derive a more constrained variant of belief system immanentism that is able to confer a special status on natural science or physics, identifying the notions of reality and truth within these disciplines.

The second reason is that Quine included no reference to the success of natural sciences or to the completeness of physics, which probably would have been needed for the transition from the simple form of belief system immanentism to a natural scientism or physicalist variant of belief system immanentism. Quine only cites belief system immanentism and the impossibility of foundationalist epistemological projects in support of the naturalistic turn. The articles "Epistemology Naturalized" and "Five Milestones of Empiricism," which detail the derivation of naturalism, contain no discussion that could be seen to favor a different version of belief system immanentism; Quine could have distinguished natural science from other studies by referring to the success of the natural sciences, or have acknowledged a special status for physics bringing up the completeness of physics. The absence of such a discussion also supports the simple interpretation of belief system immanentism.

To present a plausible and well-founded thesis, in general, it is necessary to provide a justification with a content that is sufficiently complex to support the presented thesis. As already observed, the justifications for naturalism are 'despair of being able to define theoretical terms generally in terms of phenomena' and 'unregenerate realism', which in turn are justified by the thesis of holism and the impossibility of justifying beliefs from outside belief systems. This also holds for naturalism: for naturalism to be plausible and well-founded it has to be defined in such a way that it can be derived from the justifications presented for it. Now, one of the justifications for naturalism, belief system immanentism, is understood as having the simple form (i) above, so it cannot be seen to imply physicalism or natural scientism on its own. If naturalism were construed as containing physicalism or natural scientism, that would leave no grounds for warranting Quine's argument for naturalism.

Let me summarize the discussion here. Quine acknowledges the existence of obscurities in his own characterization of naturalism in *Theories and Things*. In the effort to resolve these obscurities, Quine formulates a naturalist view that objects to the existence of any justificatory procedure other than the hypothetico-deductive method and that also rejects the first-philosophical project in which philosophy precedes and provides a foundation for science. (This view as formulated is termed 'minimal naturalism' in this book.) The minimal characterization of naturalism has been shown to be not only a matured conception that Quine finally arrived at, but also an appropriate understanding of naturalism that is well grounded by the presented justifications for naturalism. What is crucial in this conception is that in deriving naturalism Quine included no reference to the success of natural sciences or the completeness of physics. In this conception neither natural scientism (the natural scientism conception of nature) nor physicalism (the physicalist conception of nature) can serve as a premise for naturalism. Rather, naturalism assumes justificatory priorities over natural scientism and physicalism, and it is the adoption of naturalism that renders these two philosophically plausible.

Based on these considerations, let us adopt the minimal characterization of naturalism in what follows in this book. Henceforth 'naturalism' will always be understood as minimal naturalism (except where it is otherwise noted). Furthermore, 'minimal naturalism' or just 'naturalism' will be prefaced by a qualifier to distinguish different versions of naturalism deriving from auxiliary theoretical additions ('physicalist naturalism', 'natural scientism naturalism', 'pluralistic naturalism', 'descriptive naturalism', etc). I have now explicated an outline of the theory of naturalism to be detailed in the rest of the book.

1.6.3 The distinction between naturalism and the commitments held by the naturalist Quine

Sections 1.6.1 and 1.6.2 have shown that theses such as natural scientism and physicalism are not an essential part of naturalism but are possible theoretical additions available to naturalists. Thus, the three interpretations of naturalism examined in section 4 are laying out different ways to extend naturalism rather than defining naturalism itself. The remaining task is to bridge whatever gaps there may be between the proposed minimal characterization of naturalism and Quine's remarks on the philosophical methodology after the naturalistic turn, on which the three interpretations are based.

As discussed in section 1.6.1, Quine's final characterization of naturalism implies neither physicalism nor natural scientism, but the particular remarks on the philosophical methodology after the naturalistic turn occasionally indicate that Quine is in fact committed to the idea that embracing naturalism amounts to endorsing such theses as the replacement thesis, natural scientism, and physicalism. (These remarks are what gave rise to and motivated the previous interpretations of naturalism.) The key to explaining away this superficial tension contained in Quine's remarks is in distinguishing between naturalism and the commitments held by the naturalist Quine.

To drive home this distinction, consider again how Quine views the relation between physicalism and naturalism. Quine states, "I do embrace physicalism as a scientific position, but I could be dissuaded of it on future scientific grounds without being dissuaded of naturalism" (Quine 1995, 281). This statement clearly shows that there is no complete overlap between naturalism itself and the particular theoretical commitments Quine holds as a naturalist. This mismatch between naturalism and the naturalist Quine is very well accounted for by the theory of naturalism presented in the previous section—a variety of forms of naturalism may be developed by adding different theses to minimal naturalism. More specifically, there is nothing puzzling in Quine's statement above, since 'naturalism' there is understood as using the minimal characterization of naturalism, and Quine is additionally committed to physicalism, embracing 'physicalist naturalism'.

In this way, naturalism itself is distinguished from the commitments held by the naturalist Quine, and there is a mismatch between the two.[50] The distinction allows

---

[50] The importance of the distinction is further illustrated by the following passage from Takashi Iida's writing:

> Quine's view illustrated above is most commonly characterized as 'naturalism'. Naturalism is originally the view that all that exists is nature, denying the existence of supernatural things such as God and spirits, and that everything occurring in nature is explained within nature. Given the overwhelming success of natural sciences, especially physics, in describing and explaining nature, it is reasonable to elaborate the notion of naturalism by further adding that what natural sciences deem to exist constitutes the whole nature, and that nothing but natural sciences can account for processes taking place in nature. Naturalism held by Quine is indeed this elaborated kind of naturalism. (Iida 2007, 631)

Here Iida identifies the naturalism held by Quine with 'natural scientism naturalism'. It is, however, arguable whether the 'naturalism held by Quine' is equivalent to Quine's general characterization of naturalism or to the commitments that Quine holds as a naturalist. Using the terminology developed in this book, the former corresponds to the question: 'What is Quine's characterization of naturalism?' and the latter to 'What theoretical options does Quine add to minimal naturalism?' Unless what Iida intended by the statement 'naturalism held by Quine' is determined, it will be hard to evaluate the Iida claim in the quoted passage. The two questions are clearly distinct and their answers are also likely to be distinct.

Let us consider both interpretive possibilities. First, suppose that Iida tries to answer the question 'What is Quine's characterization of naturalism?' claiming that the naturalism held by Quine is natural scientism. Then, the answer would have to be judged incorrect on the basis of the discussion so far. For, as observed in Section 1.6.1, the view of naturalism held by Quine depends on a distinction between science itself and some prior philosophy, which in turn depends on whether the existence of a firmer foundation than the experimental method is claimed. As long as the existence

explaining the superficial tension between Quine's remarks. For example, consider the following passage:

> I have argued that two conflicting manuals of translation can both do justice to all dispositions to behavior, and that, in such a case, there is no fact of the matter of which manual is right. The intended notion of matter of fact is not transcendental or yet epistemological, not even a question of evidence; it is ontological, a question of reality, and to be taken naturalistically within our scientific theory of the world.
> …Then when I say there is no fact of the matter, as regards, say, the two rival manuals of translation, what I mean is that both manuals are compatible with all the same distributions of states and relations over elementary particles. In a word, they are physically equivalent. (Quine 1981, 23)

In the first quoted paragraph, Quine describes the notion of matter of fact to be "taken naturalistically within our scientific theory of the world," while providing a physicalist treatment of it in the second paragraph, stating that the fact of the matter is to be determined by physical states. If these two quotes are hastily connected with one another, then there would appear to be a tension between these quotes and Quine's minimal characterization of naturalism, since Quine here suggests treating naturalism as implying physicalism. The apparent tension is, however, dissolved by considering the distinction between naturalism itself and the commitments held by

---

of such a foundation is not claimed, naturalism could accept whatever theses there may be, including Cartesian dualism or a theory positing a Creator. (They are most likely to be dismissed given their poor efficacy, however.) Moreover, Quine included in 'science itself' experimental psychology, history, and social sciences, which are usually not classified as natural sciences. This inclusion would be a counterexample to Iida's identification of the naturalism held by Quine with natural scientism. (There is no useful discussion in Quine's writings that delineates the scope of natural science, however.) So, if Iida is trying to answer the question 'What is Quine's characterization of naturalism?', then the claim that the naturalism held by Quine is natural scientism would have to be rejected.

Second, suppose that Iida identifies the naturalism held by Quine with natural scientism to answer the other question, 'What theoretical options does Quine add to minimal naturalism?' Then, the identification would be defensible. At least, at many points in the writings, Quine shows a strong sympathy for and support of natural sciences. This interpretation is, however, not perfect; it leaves a twofold task: the notion of natural scientism must be clarified, and textual evidence is needed for assuming Quine to actually adopt natural scientism. As for the former part, it is perhaps justifiable to characterize natural scientism as the view that what natural sciences deem to exist constitutes the whole of nature, and that nothing but natural sciences can account for the processes taking place in nature. But even if it is so, then unless what falls under the category of natural sciences is unambiguously determined, it would be unclear what Iida effectively attributes to Quine with the identification, and so Iida's claim could not be properly evaluated. The latter part of the remaining task would also pose a serious problem. Quine explicitly commits himself to physicalism, not natural scientism, and hence there would have to be some reason for attributing natural scientism to Quine, in whatever way natural scientism is characterized. A possible solution to both parts of the task is, of course, to define natural science as 'the study that is compatible with physicalism'. That definition is, however, underspecified to a large extent, and current physicalists are making great efforts to establish that physicalism is compatible with folk psychology, which is usually not included in the category of natural sciences. Therefore, there are obviously many problems left in the second way to interpret Iida's identification of the naturalism held by Quine with natural scientism.

Quine as a naturalist. The first quoted paragraph can be viewed as commenting on naturalism in general, while the second paragraph can be understood as describing particular naturalistic commitments held by Quine. Thus, it is not necessary to conclude that Quine's characterization of naturalism changed from the 1980s to the 1990s.[51] As I have already argued, it is very probable that some naturalists adopt physicalist naturalism, but naturalism in general by no means requires inclusion of physicalism. Since Quine himself regards physicalist naturalism as the most plausible form of naturalism, a physicalist treatment of the fact of the matter appears with no qualification in the above quote. This superficial appearance, however, does not show that Quine has changed the characterization of naturalism, even if it shows that his discussion at this point failed to articulate adequately the nature of naturalism.

Section 1.4 discussed some of Quine's remarks on the philosophical methodology after the naturalistic turn. The methodological vision expressed in those remarks assumes various theses such as the replacement thesis, natural scientism, and physicalism, and thereby inspired the interpretations of naturalism as implying such a thesis. However, assuming the discussion so far as correct, the remarks only suggest that Quine makes commitments to particular proposals he considers plausible within the naturalistic framework, and there is no reason to imagine that Quine intends to constrain naturalism using such commitments. According to the theory of naturalism proposed in this book, naturalism is a broad program that can take various shapes depending on different theses added to the basic minimal naturalism, and so a general characterization of naturalism itself can diverge from the commitments held by a particular naturalist (Quine in this case).

It is undeniable that Quine's remarks on the philosophical methodology after the naturalistic turn have encouraged interpretations according to which embracing naturalism amounts to also adopting other theses such as the replacement thesis, natural scientism, and physicalism. In my view, however, the remarks can best be understood as expressing the commitments to particular proposals Quine considers plausible within the naturalistic framework, or as indicating that Quine did not fully realize the precise nature of naturalism and the difficulties in characterizing it.[52] The

---

[51] I wish to thank Takashi Naruse for helping me crystallize my thinking on this point.

[52] There are two turning points in the development of naturalism in the second half of the twentieth century, initiated by the article "Epistemology Naturalized." One is the introduction of normativity in "Reply to Morton White" (1986) and the other is the recognition of the separability of naturalism from natural scientism and physicalism.

Quine, "Epistemology Naturalized" (1969)
The article declares the bankruptcy of traditional foundationalist epistemology, proposing the enterprise of descriptive epistemology: to assimilate epistemology to empirical psychology, which causally describes our belief formation processes.
↓

Quine, "Reply to Morton White" (1986)
The article presents the view that naturalized epistemology will not be exhausted by a sweeping description of ongoing processes with everything normative discarded; naturalized epistemology pursues to account for epistemological normativity in terms of instrumental normativity. This idea is also a response to the normativity charge, according to which

three interpretations of naturalism examined in section 4 are to blame for failing to articulate adequately their target, but they should not merely be dismissed as incorrect. (This assessment may only be apparent in hindsight, after Quine has provided his final characterization of naturalism, even though it is well supported by the considerations of how Quine justifies naturalism and the cited sources.) Of course, naturalists may adopt natural scientism or physicalism, and they may as well address philosophical problems concerning mind, morality, and knowledge from a perspective of 'natural scientism naturalism' or 'physicalist naturalism'. Inquiries from such a perspective can be authentically called 'naturalistic philosophical inquiries', but it would be wrong to suppose that such inquiries are naturalistic by virtue of presupposing natural scientism or physicalism. As the discussion so far has revealed, the essence of naturalism, the position revived by Quine in contemporary philosophy, resides in the abandonment of a first philosophy or foundationalist epistemology, not in the inclusion of physicalism or natural scientism.

1.7 'Treating Everything As Natural?': A Variety of Conceptions of Nature

Naturalism has often been defined as the denial of supernatural entities or as an attitude that treats everything as natural. This definition alone, however, is of little use to determine the nature of naturalism, since it will be unclear what treating as natural amounts to and also what falls under the category of supernatural entities, as long as the borderline between being 'natural' and 'supernatural' remains implicit.[53] This has led many current thinkers to appeal to natural scientism or physicalism when specifying the notion of naturalism, claiming, for example, that what natural sciences deem to exist constitute the whole of nature, or that the aggregate of physical facts is nature. Different from this, according to the theory of naturalism outlined in this chapter, physicalism and naturalism are merely two among the theoretical options available to naturalists and are not essential components of

---

       epistemology is an essentially normative study, and so descriptive psychology cannot be epistemology.
       ↓

       Quine, "Naturalism; or Living within one's Means" (1995)
       Encouraged by Quine's writings concerning the philosophical methodology after the naturalistic turn, many theorists have considered naturalism to imply natural scientism or physicalism. Nonetheless, the article characterizes naturalism only as the abandonment of a first philosophy that claims or demands for justification beyond empirical testing.

In this book, the outlined development of the understanding of naturalism is not construed as the changes of Quine's basic treatment of naturalism. Rather, Quine has continuously improved the characterization of naturalism, a position that remains the same over time. A reason for this construal is that naturalism can be understood as a consistent view with a definite contour, rather than as a nebulous notion. Another reason is that Quine's wide-ranging remarks can be most coherently interpreted on this construal (for example, the final characterization of naturalism in [Quine, 1995] is said to be a specification of the characterization presented in [Quine, 1981]).

[53] Other theorists have made the same point. See (Todayama 2003) and (De Caro and Macarthur 2004), among others.

naturalism. Therefore, any effort to specify the notion of naturalism by appealing to physicalism or naturalism is bound to be inadequate, certainly as an attempt to determine the nature of naturalism. Then it will be in order to ask how the theory of naturalism outlined here describes the conception of nature?

First of all, it is impossible to provide a definite answer to this question before presenting a specific extension of naturalism, since naturalism is not a philosophical position that is developed presupposing a fixed picture of the world or nature. I have argued that naturalism is the abandonment of a first-philosophical project, derived from belief system immanentism and the impossibility of foundationalist epistemology, and that it affirms, without requiring philosophical justification, the outcomes of scientific inquiries as descriptions of fact and reality or of nature (assuming their corrigibility, of course). On this understanding of naturalism, even if it includes the attitude of treating everything as natural, nature only gradually takes shape as a belief system evolves, and so the shape of nature is not somehow fixed in advance.

Considering the current state of debates concerning naturalism, I should also point out that the strategy of defining naturalism beginning with 'the attitude of treating everything as natural' in itself is wrongheaded. For, there is widespread disagreement among naturalists about how to define 'nature', even though that is precisely the first question to be addressed under this strategy. Resolving the disagreement is equivalent to providing a unified answer to the question about what naturalism is. When "there is little consensus on its [the term 'naturalism'] meaning," (Papineau 1993, 1), it will remain extremely difficult to start understanding naturalism with the question about what nature is. In my view, naturalism should be investigated focusing on how it has been developed and justified. This strategy is precisely what I have employed for the current chapter.

The theory of naturalism proposed in this chapter is that various forms of naturalism can be produced by adding different theses to minimal naturalism. Even if naturalism is construed as the attitude that treats everything as natural, its details will vary from naturalist to naturalist depending on the conception of nature that she adopts. Theorists endorsing physicalist naturalism understand nature in physicalist terms and dismiss everything outside the physicalist framework as 'supernatural'. Theorists endorsing 'natural scientism naturalism' define nature as the domain of natural scientific inquiry and dismiss everything outside of it. Here, it is important to keep in mind that there is no unified picture of nature, even though both types of theorists treat everything as natural. There is no determinate conception of nature that theorists share prior to arguing for naturalism on its basis; rather, a variety of conceptions of nature will emerge depending on the particular theoretical commitments that naturalists make. Now, recall that the rationale for naturalism includes belief system immanentism as well as the impossibility of a foundationalist epistemology, but not the completeness of physics or the success of natural sciences. Then, the range of conceptions of nature available to naturalists can be extended beyond those that are possible within physicalism or natural scientism.

Chapter 2

Ontological Options in Naturalism: Physicalist Monism and Pluralism as its Alternative

In chapter 1, I have discussed how to understand the nature of naturalism, one of the focal points in contemporary philosophy. The outcome of the discussion is that naturalism should be characterized as 'minimal naturalism', the view that denies the existence of any other justificatory procedure than the hypothetico-deductive method, and rejects the first-philosophical project in which philosophy precedes science and provides a foundation for it. Furthermore, the last chapter has also presented the basic framework for the theory of naturalism to be advanced in this book, according to which there are a number of theoretical options available to naturalists, and a variety of naturalist positions can be formed by adding different theses such as physicalism and natural scientism to minimal naturalism. Here, in chapter 2, on the basis of this minimal characterization of naturalism and the basic picture of the theory of naturalism, I will explore an ideal form of naturalism. More specifically, the goal of this chapter is to sketch a solution to the question of what theoretical option should be adopted to add to minimal naturalism to obtain a more convincing formulation of the naturalist view.

It must be recognized, however, that there are a number of theoretical options available to naturalists, and that those options compete variously with one another in different contexts. For example, in the context of epistemology, one can conceive of various positions other than a moderate one that rejects a first-philosophical epistemological project, an attempt to provide a foundation for science completely independently from scientific beliefs (in a broad sense).

The conceivable positions include 'epistemological natural scientism'—the view that the single most effective way of acquiring knowledge on any subject is a natural scientific methodology (which clearly deserves more explanation)—and 'epistemological descriptivism'—the view that the objective of epistemology is restricted to causally describing how sensory stimuli become theoretical outputs (a view that Quine once suggested). Likewise, various theoretical options are also conceivable in the field of ontology: physicalist monism, according to which all truth or facts is physical (or something that supervenes on the physical), phenomenological monism, according to which only sense impressions constitute genuine facts, Cartesian dualism, pluralism, etc. Although only two domains of inquiry, epistemology and ontology, are touched on here, there may well be more theoretical options in other domains, too, such as in ethics and aesthetics. In the present chapter, I will address the question of what theoretical options should be adopted in addition to minimal naturalism, focusing on debates in ontology, in particular, those concerning physicalism.

Here is an outline of the current chapter. Section 2.1 extracts a (more or less comprehensive) framework for discussing contemporary debates in ontology, examining the article "On What There Is," through which Quine brought ontology to the forefront of contemporary analytic philosophy. Section 2.2 studies physicalism, a representative ontological position within naturalism as often assumed, and identifies the questions to be asked to evaluate physicalism as an addition to minimal naturalism, locating it within the framework presented in section 2.1. Section 2.3 discusses criticism of physicalism based on the thesis of the indeterminacy of translation and interpretation, identifying the difficulties it poses for physicalism. Section 2.4 proposes, as a solution to the difficulties to be exposed in this chapter, a pluralist approach to the ontology of naturalism that replaces physicalist monism with pluralism.

2.1 The Realm of Ontological Questions

According to Hilary Putnam, ontology "became a respectable subject for an analytic philosopher to pursue" (Putnam 2004, 78) due to Quine's 1948 article "On What There Is."[1] The arguments Quine presented there have indeed provided a basis for current debates on ontology in the Anglo-Saxon tradition. (Of course, this by no means suggests that Quine's conclusions are widely accepted today.) Accordingly, first, the current section briefly reviews the discussion in "On What There Is," outlining a method Quine presents to cope with ontological questions. Second, I will extract a general framework for understanding debates concerning ontological questions, abstracting away from peculiar commitments held by Quine. The framework will provide a foundation for pursuing the main goal of this chapter, namely, to explore ontological options in naturalism focusing on physicalism.

2.1.1 The framework for ontological debates in "On What There Is"

The first question Quine asks in the article "On What There Is" is about how to express disagreement over ontological issues. Quine describes the gist of the problem as follows:

> Suppose now that two philosophers, McX and I, differ over ontology. Suppose McX maintains there is something which I maintain there is not. McX can, quite consistently with his own point of view, describe our difference of opinion by saying that I refuse to recognize certain entities. ...
> When *I* try to formulate our difference of opinion, on the other hand, I seem to be in a predicament. I cannot admit that there are some things which McX countenances and I do not, for in admitting that there are such things I should be contradicting my own rejection of them.
> It would appear, if this reasoning were sound, that in any ontological dispute the proponent of the negative side suffers the disadvantage of not being able to admit that his opponent disagrees with him. (Quine 1953, 1, italics in original)

---

[1] Putnam, however, is skeptical about the significance of this thriving field of analytic philosophy.

If Pegasus *were* not, McX argues, we should not be talking about anything when we use the word; therefore it would be nonsense to say even that Pegasus is not. Thinking to show thus that the denial of Pegasus cannot be coherently maintained, he concludes that Pegasus is. (ibid., 2, italics in original)

Let us illustrate the problem with an example. Suppose that A answers positively to the question about whether Pegasus *is*, while B answers in the negative. Then, B would not be able to claim that there is something called 'Pegasus' such that A acknowledges it whereas B does not. For by doing so, as B denies the existence of Pegasus, B would in a way acknowledge the existence of something called 'Pegasus' that A acknowledges whereas B does not. (In this case, what would be asserted is not that Pegasus, an object of flesh and blood, exists in a spatio-temporal location, but that Pegasus exists as an idea in the mind.)

The example has illustrated the problem that launches the inquiry in "On What There Is," that is, in describing ontologically different opinions, that those who deny the existence of something, those representing negating views, are disadvantaged. Now, a conceivable approach to overcoming this problem is to classify the uses of expressions for existence in a finer-grained fashion. Quine introduces an imagined philosopher, Wyman, who adopts this fine-grained approach distinguishing a word 'exist' that is only applicable to actualized objects, and a word 'be' that is applicable also to unactualized possibilia. According to Wyman, Pegasus *is*, as an unactualized possibilium, and our claim that Pegasus *isn't* must be paraphrased, strictly speaking, as 'Pegasus definitely *is*, but it does not *exist* in the sense that it has no attribute of actuality'.

Certainly at first sight, the Wyman approach seems to enable those denying existence to describe ontologically different opinions. For example, it can make sense of the debates over the existence of Homer: all parties acknowledge that Homer *is* as a possibilium, and disagree about whether Homer has the attribute of actuality. Quine, however, points out several difficulties in this Wyman approach. One is that Wyman's ontology, the domain of objects whose beings are acknowledged by Wyman, would be enormous and lack elegance. (Indeed, on the Wyman approach, everything conceivable becomes included as being.) The biggest difficulty in the approach, Quine observes, is the obscured identity conditions of things that presumably are. The following paragraph thoroughly describes this difficulty:

Take, for instance, the possible fat man in that doorway; and, again, the possible bald man in that doorway. Are they the same possible man, or two possible men? How do we decide? How many possible men are there in that doorway? Are there more possible thin ones than fat ones? How many of them are alike? Or would their being alike make them one? Are no *two* possible things alike? Is this the same as saying that it is impossible for two things to be alike? Or, finally, is the concept of identity simply inapplicable to unactualized possibles? But what sense can be found in talking of entities which cannot meaningfully be said to be identical with themselves and distinct from one another? (ibid., 4, italics in original)

To summarize, according to Quine, the Wyman approach, which boldly acknowledges unactualized possibilia, is incompatible with the basic ontological requirement that no entity is without identity.

After all, the problem with which Quine begins "On What There Is" remains unsolved: in describing ontologically different opinions, theorists who deny existence, those on the negative side, are disadvantaged. To get around this problem Quine chooses to undermine one of the basic presuppositions in McX's and Wyman's reasoning. Assuming that to make a claim about something it is necessary to acknowledge its existence in some way, McX claims Pegasus to have a being, since otherwise "we should not be talking about anything when we use the word; therefore it would be nonsense to say even that Pegasus is not" (ibid., 2). On the basis of the same assumption, Wyman introduces the notion of 'unactualized possibilia' as a conceptual device necessary for making sense of talk of Pegasus and thereby overcoming the ontological problem for theorists who deny the existence of something. If it is, however, justifiable to dismiss the assumption that to make a claim about something it is necessary to acknowledge its existence in some way — that is, if the meaningfulness of talk of something does not require its existence — then the ontological problem that McX points out does not arise in the first place. This opens the way to a resolution; a method of talking about something without acknowledging its existence is the key to solving the problem that, in describing ontological disagreement, those on the negative side are disadvantaged. Quine indeed attempts to provide such a method relying on Bertrand Russell's theory of descriptions — an analysis of definite descriptions.

Consider the sentence 'the present king of France doesn't exist' as an example. The sentence contains a definite description, 'the present king of France', which stands for a unique object by describing a uniquely identifying property of that object. According to the assumption above, which both McX and Wyman take for granted, then, for the sentence to be meaningful there must be an object that is 'the present King of France'. Since France today is not a monarchy, however, there is no king of France acknowledged as such in the ordinary sense of the phrase. McX, hence, would acknowledge the existence of the present king of France as an idea in the mind, and Wyman would acknowledge it as an unactualized possibilium.

For McX and Wyman, a definite description, such as 'the present king of France', is a referring term, whose presence requires the existence of an object that it refers to for the whole sentence to be meaningful. According to Russell, however, a definite description is not a referring term, since a sentence containing it can be paraphrased into a sentence containing no referring terms. Such a paraphrase will secure the meaningfulness of the sentence 'the present king of France doesn't exist' without introducing dubious objects such as unactualized possibilia. Consider the following paraphrase:

The present king of France doesn't exist = $\neg\ (\exists x(Fx \& \forall y(Fy \rightarrow (x=y))))$
(where F is the predicate 'being a present king of France')

The paraphrase contains no referring term. (Note that F above is a predicate, not a referring term; it can be restated as 'sitting currently on the throne of France', if that is less confusing.) The paraphrase asserts that there is nothing having the property of 'being a present king of France' and that of 'being whoever is a present king of France'. What is crucial here is that for these assertions to be meaningful there does not have to be an object that is 'the present king of France'. Therefore, the paraphrase shows that the existence of an object referred to by 'the present king of France' is not required for a meaningful understanding of the sentence 'the present king of France doesn't exist'.

Given these considerations, it is justifiable to reject the assumption that to make a claim about something it is necessary to acknowledge its existence in some way. Now, let us turn to 'Pegasus', which is the focus of the imaginary dialogues with McX and Wyman. The expression 'Pegasus' is not a definite description, which stands for a unique object by describing its uniquely identifying property, but a proper name used to name a winged horse in Greek mythology; Russell's analysis of definite descriptions does not directly apply to 'Pegasus', but it is applicable to 'Pegasus', as Quine suggests, if the proper name can be replaced by a definite description. (One of such descriptions Quine suggests is 'the winged horse that was captured by Bellerophon'.) Alternatively, Quine further proposes that if the notion of Pegasus is too obscure or too basic to identify a corresponding description, then the new predicate 'pegasizes' could be created to paraphrase the sentence 'Pegasus doesn't exist' into a sentence containing no referring term. Either way, a Russellian analysis would be applicable to sentences in which proper names occur if proper names can be replaced by definite descriptions.

In this way, since it is possible to paraphrase sentences that contain proper names, rather than descriptions, into sentences that contain no referring term, it is possible to circumvent the idea that to make a claim about something it is necessary to acknowledge its existence in some way. Therefore, the ontological problem—in describing ontologically different opinions, theorists who deny the existence of something, those on the negative side of a debate, are disadvantaged—does not arise in the first place.

The discussion so far has elucidated how to overcome the ontological problem at the beginning of "On What There Is"—that theorists denying the existence of the disputed object are disadvantaged. After overcoming this problem, the next issue is, what approach does Quine adopt to investigate the realm of ontological problems? The reason for scrutinizing "On What There Is" to answer this second question is to identify the framework for discussing ontology Quine presented in "On What There Is." What follows will focus on achieving this.

Quine as well as the imagined philosophers, Wyman and McX, share the idea that ontological views are made explicit through sentences asserted to be true. The difference arises from the way in which ontological views are derived from asserted sentences. The imagined philosophers believe that to make a claim about something the existence of that 'something' must be acknowledged in some way, and that ontological views are made explicit on the basis of singular terms that refer to objects. More specifically, to assert that the present king of France doesn't exist it is necessary to commit oneself to accepting the existence of the king of France, since otherwise the whole sentence containing the singular term 'the present king of France' would be meaningless. Here, Quine states, "A singular term need not name to be significant" (ibid., 9), since Russellian paraphrases dispel "the delusion that the meaningfulness of a statement containing a singular term presupposes an entity named by the term" (ibid., 8-9). Thus, accepting a claim containing a singular term alone does not amount to accepting the existence of an object that is seemingly referred to by the singular term. Then, according to Quine, under what circumstances is it necessary to commit oneself to accepting the existence of an object?

Here enters the influential thesis that to be is to be the value of a variable. Consider, for example, the sentence 'the author of *Waverly* is a poet'. It is now possible to eliminate the singular term in the sentence, 'the author of *Waverly*', by paraphrasing the whole sentence as follows:

$(\exists x(Fx \& \forall y(Fy \rightarrow (x=y))) \& Gx)$
(where F and G are predicates, 'authored *Waverly*' and 'being a poet', respectively)

(This precisely illustrates the method of paraphrasing enabling Quine to maintain that singular terms do not have to name an object to be meaningful.) If this method of paraphrasing is legitimate, there is an object the existence of which must be acknowledged in accepting the paraphrase as true: an object that fulfills the three predicates at the same time ('authored *Waverly*', 'being identical to whoever authored *Waverly*', and 'being a poet'); if nothing does so, the paraphrase would simply be false.[2]

These considerations have led Quine to the following characterizations of 'ontological commitment':

> ...we are convicted of a particular ontological presupposition if, and only if, the alleged presuppositum has to be reckoned among the entities over which our variables range in order to render one of our affirmations true. (ibid., 13)
> ...a theory is committed to those and only those entities to which the bound variables of the theory must be capable of referring in order that the affirmations made in the theory be true. (ibid., 13-14)

---

[2] As for this particular example, irrespective of whether Russell's theory of descriptions is adopted, the original sentence would be meaningful because 'the author of *Waverly*' exists; it may be unclear what difference the paraphrase makes, as opposed to the approach the imagined philosophers assume. The crucial difference is that the paraphrase introduces an ontological claim in terms of what predicates must be fulfilled for the sentence to be true, whereas the imagined philosophers would derive an ontological claim on the basis of singular terms that seemingly refer to objects. To appreciate that these two approaches can yield different ontological views, it is enough to consider the negative existential 'the present king of France doesn't exist', observing its ontological implications. On the approach the imagined philosophers assume, to assert meaningfully that 'the present king of France doesn't exist' one needs to commit to the existence of an object that is 'the present king of France'. (Consequently, the approach creates the ontological problem that, in describing ontologically different views, those who deny the existence of the disputed object are disadvantaged.)

There are two important ideas in the criterion for ontological commitment suggested here: one is that an ontological commitment is determined by replacing all singular terms in a sentence with descriptions and obtaining a quantified statement.[3] The other is that entities to which an individual or a theory affirming a sentence has to be ontologically committed are regarded as entities that are indispensable for the sentence to be true. (The latter motivates what are usually known as 'indispensability arguments'.)

This subsection has explicated the framework for discussing ontology Quine proposed in "On What There Is." As I mentioned earlier, although Quine's framework has greatly influenced contemporary debates on ontology, his own ontological position is not widely shared among contemporary theorists working on ontology. For this reason, in what follows, I will attempt to distill a general framework for ontology analyzing and relativizing Quine's particular proposal.

2.1.2 The generalized ontological framework[4]

Below I will reconstruct Quine's argument for the ontological commitment to abstract objects such as numbers and classes, examining an alternative possibility for each step of the argument. This will elucidate alternative views to Quine's ontological position. The line of reasoning showing the ontological commitment to abstract objects to be inevitable goes as follows:[5]

---

[3] Iida doubts that singular terms are eliminable across the board. See the discussion in (Iida 1987, 208f).

[4] It is commonplace in ontological debates to distinguish 'ontology' and 'metaontology'. The term 'ontology' stands for an 'inventory of entities', so to speak. The ontology of a theory, for example, is equivalent to an inventory of objects to which the theory is committed, or an inventory of objects that anyone who accepts the theory as true must acknowledge. To illustrate, consider the contrast between realism and nominalism: the former acknowledges abstract entities, whereas the latter acknowledges only concrete particulars; the disagreement between them boils down to their 'ontological' disagreement. The word 'metaontology' stands for a framework introducing a specific 'ontology' in the sense discussed above. For example, it is asked at the level of 'metaontology' whether the appropriate criterion of ontological commitment is based on referring terms or the 'indispensability arguments', in which sentences are transformed into quantified sentences. (See the entry 'Metaontology' in [Burkhardt and Smith 1991], among others.)

Given the ontology-metaontology distinction, the framework to be developed in section 2.1.2 may be more appropriately called a 'metaontological framework' rather than an 'ontological' one. To avoid further complicating the terminology, I will use 'ontology' broadly, rather than employing the ontology-metaontology distinction; instead 'the level of objects or entities' will be distinguished from 'the level of the criterion of ontological commitment' as well as 'the level of a set of statements entailing an ontological commitment'.

[5] See (Quine 1953, 1-19, 102-29) and (Putnam 1979). Quine became outspoken about his commitment to physicalism after the 1960s, and so another line could be added to the argument below deriving an ontological commitment. (To be specific, the class of statements from which an ontological commitment is derived could be identified with the class of physicalistically acceptable statements, rather than with the class of statements we accept as true.) Nevertheless, section 2.2 discusses the role of physicalism in deriving an ontological commitment, and physicalism is not a necessary premise in Quine's argument for abstract mathematical objects; so I will discuss the argument in the form presented prior to the explicit adoption of physicalism.

1. By accepting a statement as true, one assumes some kind of ontological commitment.
2. We accept the whole of our science, including physics and chemistry, as true.
3. A part of physics and chemistry includes mathematics as an essential component.
4. Quine derives an ontological commitment from an accepted statement assuming the correctness of indispensability arguments. (Whether an object is indispensable is determined after the accepted statement is transformed into a quantified statement in which no singular terms appear.)
5. For mathematical statements to be true, there must be abstract mathematical objects.
C. Therefore, we must assume the ontological commitment to abstract objects.

Now, what are possible responses to this argument for abstract objects? To begin with, as an objection to step 5, one could argue that it is not necessary to be committed to mathematical objects, such as numbers and classes, to accept mathematical statements as true. According to Putnam, for example, "[e]very statement about the "existence" of any mathematical entities is equivalent (equivalent mathematically, and equivalent from the point of view of application as well) with a statement that doesn't assert the actual existence of any mathematical objects at all, but only asserts the *mathematical possibility* of certain structures" (Putnam 2004b, 67, italics in original). That is, there is no need to accept the existence of mathematical objects, such as numbers and classes, to hold mathematical statements to be true.[6]

Step 4 can also be challenged by an alternative approach, neo-Fregeanism, represented by philosophers like Bob Hale and Crispin Wright—it is often described as one of the two major approaches to contemporary ontology together with the Quinean approach, which depends on indispensability arguments. According to the neo-Fregean approach, a specific ontology is deduced depending on a grammatical notion, that of a singular term, rather than on an indispensability argument involving the translation into quantified statements. Consider, for example, a scenario in which 'Pegasus has wings' is accepted as true. Quine would paraphrase the sentence as 'there is exactly one thing that 'pegasizes' and has wings', and so require an entity to exist to make the paraphrase true, namely a unique thing that 'pegasizes' and has wings. By contrast, the neo-Fregean approach would introduce an entity, Pegasus, into an inventory of entities in virtue of the singular term 'Pegasus' in the sentence.[7]

---

[6] This view was presented earlier in (Putnam 1967), to which Quine responded in (Quine 1992, 30-1).
[7] See (Eklund 2006b) for an overview of neo-Fregeanism in ontology. Let me briefly discuss how neo-Fregeanism is different from McX's approach, rejected by Quine. Although McX characterizes the word 'Pegasus' as a singular term, giving no particular reason (probably based on the surface grammar), the neo-Fregean approach provides various criteria to identify a singular term. (The basic strategy of providing such criteria is to determine the pattern of inference in which statements are valid only when a specific constituent of them is a singular term. See [Wright 1983, 57f].) For neo-Fregeans, Pegasus would exist only when the word 'Pegasus' is among those that fulfill the criteria for singular terms. Thus, if 'Pegasus' is not a singular term, then neo-Fregeans would be able to assert meaningfully that 'Pegasus doesn't exist', and therefore, they would not necessarily face the ontological problem that those denying the existence of something are disadvantaged in an

This shows that there is an alternative criterion of ontological commitment to the indispensability arguments, in which singular terms are eliminated through quantificational paraphrases.

For step 3, Hartry Field has proposed an alternative nominalist theory maintaining that for physics, mathematics is no more than a dispensable tool.[8] First, Field suggests that it is possible to build a nominalistically acceptable alternative to our current scientific theories. (In support of this suggestion, Field brings up a version of the Newtonian theory of gravity constructed in such a way that it has no need for the ontological commitment to mathematical objects.) Next, Field argues that, even if a mathematical theory is added to such a nominalist theory, a statement would not be a theorem of the new theory unless it is a theorem of the original theory. (Field points this out stating that mathematical theories are 'conservative' in relation to nominalist theories [Field 1980, x].) This leads Field to claim that mathematics can be severed from physics, and that the severing would not change the substance of physics. The significance of Field's theory to present purposes is that it opens up the possibility of avoiding the ontological commitment to abstract mathematical objects, claiming that mathematical theories are not necessary for everything we accept as science, even though they are committed to abstract mathematical objects.

There are also a number of reactions to step 2. One is that it is only a part of science, not all of science, that has an ontological commitment. Penelope Maddy criticizes Quine's argument for abstract mathematical objects, which involves indispensability arguments, pointing out that actual scientists do not consider all of our best theories to be true — "indispensability for scientific theorizing does not always imply truth" (Maddy 1992, 289).[9] What Maddy's criticism implies is that

---

ontological dispute.

An important characteristic of the neo-Fregean approach to ontology is that the syntactic categories have priority over ontological ones. The neo-Fregean conception of object inherits Frege's idea that an object is what is referred to by a singular term (See [Wright 1983, 53]), and so neo-Fregeans are unable to identify the syntactic category of singular terms using the standard of whether expressions refer to objects. Thus, the biggest challenge of the neo-Fregean approach is how to determine singular terms without using the concepts of entity and reference. For the thesis of the priority of the syntactic categories over ontological ones and its problems, see (Dummett 1981, Ch.12; Wright 1983, 53-64; Iida 1987, 69-73; Kaneko 2006, Ch.1), among others.

[8] See (Field 1980). The ensuing exposition is partly dependent on (Todayama 1998).

[9] This is only a part of Maddy's criticism of the indispensability arguments; the overall criticism goes as follows:

(i) "An argument based on scientific and mathematical practice can only succeed from a sufficiently naturalistic perspective" (Maddy 1992, 275).

(ii) "From the perspective of this scientific naturalism, a philosopher can criticize scientific practice, but only on scientific grounds. ...[it follows that] a conflict between scientific practice and philosophy must be resolved by revising the philosophy" (ibid., 276).

(iii) The indispensability arguments that Quine used to argue for abstract objects "will be judged by their ability to account for actual mathematics as practiced" (ibid., 276); if they turn out to be incompatible with mathematical practice, they will be discarded.

(iv) "[A] simple indispensability argument for the existence of mathematical entities goes like this: we have good reason to believe our best scientific theories, and mathematical entities are indispensable to those theories, so we have good reason to believe in mathematical entities" (ibid., 278). This argument, however, is incompatible with mathematical practice. In pure mathematics, there are a number of justificatory steps that do not appeal to indispensability in science. Even

74   Chapter 2 Ontological Options in Naturalism: Physicalist Monism and Pluralism as its Alternative

endorsing a scientific theory does not amount to taking all the statements in the theory to be true, and so, even if mathematics turns out to be necessary for a scientific theory, it is not justifiable to conclude that those accepting the theory are committed to the existence of abstract mathematical objects.

The above discussion has examined Quine's argument for the ontological commitment to abstract mathematical objects and recent responses to the argument. Almost all steps in the argument are challenged by an alternative proposal; my remarks at the end of section 2.1.1 can now be readily understood: Quine's framework has greatly influenced contemporary debates on ontology, but his own ontological position is not widely shared among contemporary theorists working in ontology. (Nevertheless, none of the criticism is insurmountable. Quine's position remains as a possible and viable option.) Of course, the current section is not intended to provide a comprehensive survey of ontological frameworks in contemporary metaphysics; instead it focuses on indispensability arguments—how they are used to derive the ontological commitment to abstract objects and the alternatives that have been proposed.[10] It must be clear by now, however, that we face a complicated dialectical

---

   with respect to the part of mathematics that is applied in science, mathematicians accept the theorems of number theory and analysis not because "they are useful in applications but ... [because] they are provable from the appropriate axioms" (ibid., 279). (The 'appropriateness' of axioms is determined on the basis of mathematical intuition and elegance in systematization; scientific applications are very rarely cited for it.)
(v) A modified indispensability argument is proposed to overcome the difficulty of the simple indispensability argument. In the simple argument the applicability in science is the criterion of justifying mathematical statements, whereas in the modified version the indispensability in scientific theorizing confirms the existence of some mathematical objects, letting actual practitioners determine what exactly they are and what properties they have.
(vi) The modified indispensability argument is criticized for being incompatible with scientific practice. According to epistemological holism, on which the modified approach is based, every statement in a theory that fits experience is equally true. But in scientific practice there is a distinction between parts of a theory that are considered true and the parts that are considered merely useful. Maddy states, "the merely useful parts might in fact be indispensable, in the sense that no equally good theory of the same phenomena does without them. ... [therefore] the indispensability of mathematics in well-confirmed scientific theories no longer serves to establish its truth" (ibid., 281).
(vii) The modified indispensability argument is criticized also for being incompatible with mathematical practice. On the modified approach, for the existence of mathematical objects to be endorsed, mathematical theories referring to the objects are required to be indispensable to scientific theorizing. Actual mathematicians, however, evaluate the legitimacy of mathematical statements and endorse mathematical objects independently of developments of foundational physics and what mathematical devices are necessary for it. Therefore, the way in which the modified indispensability argument endorses the existence of mathematical objects conflicts with mathematical practice.
(viii) As a result indispensability arguments fail to provide an adequate account for the epistemology and ontology of mathematics.
   Based on the discussion in chapter 1, (ii) expresses a radical naturalist position acceptable within naturalism, rather than characterizing naturalism itself. This inexact description of naturalism, however, does not reduce the significance of Maddy's point (vi): the indispensability of mathematics in scientific theories does not necessarily imply their truth.
[10] This is why I by no means suggest that the issues raised here cover the whole ground of ontology. In fact, Daisuke Kachi has pointed out a new trend in ontology that does not rely on the basic

situation concerning contemporary ontology, given the various perspectives discussed above.

Now, two caveats with respect to the ontological debates outlined above deserve further attention. First, although theorists engage in disputes over ontology, the point of contention is not what objects exist—the disputes are not at the level of objects or entities. More specifically, the opponents of Quine discussed above do not reject Quine's ontological position through an outright denial of the existence of abstract mathematical objects, but they raise objections to some part of Quine's argument for the ontological commitment to abstract mathematical objects.[11] The second caveat is that, although theorists including Field and Maddy present a different ontological framework than that of Quine, there is a common basic idea, namely, step 1 above: a specific ontology is derived from statements accepted as true.

Having these caveats in mind, let us revisit the ontological debates presented above. Now, the points of contention can be clearly stated as follows: 'From which set of statements should an ontological commitment be derived?' and 'What is the method of deriving an ontological commitment from the determined set of statements?' To summarize the dialectical situation presented so far on the basis of these two questions, both Field and Maddy are trying to answer the former question—Field attempts to eliminate mathematics from physics, while Maddy claims only some, but not all, statements comprising our best science have to be considered in deriving an ontological commitment. On the other hand, Putnam and neo-Fregeans are trying to answer the latter question—Putnam suggests the possibility of paraphrasing mathematical statements into modal statements that have no ontological commitment to mathematical entities while accepting the truth of mathematical statements, whereas neo-Fregeans attempt to define the criterion of ontological commitment in terms of the category of singular terms, rather than appealing to indispensability arguments.[12] These considerations give rise to the following perspective illuminating

---

ontological perspective adopted in this book (ontological questions are answered by identifying true statements and determining the criteria of ontological commitment). According to Kaji, in addition to the language-oriented approach, represented by Dummett's work, as well as the epistemology-oriented approach in the naturalist literature, the ontology-oriented approach started to attract much attention in recent years. (Kachi labels the approach 'neo-Aristotelian analytic metaphysics', an important feature of which is that "metaphysics is not studied as inquiry into language or conceptual scheme, something on *our* side, but as inquiry into the fundamental structure of the world existing independently from us" [Kachi 2004, 168-9].) Of course, the ontology-oriented approach seems to conflict with the main topic of this book, naturalism (in particular, with belief system immanentism). It must be noted in any case that the current chapter covers only a fraction of a large number of recent debates surrounding ontology.

This lack of completeness, however, will not impede achieving the objective of this chapter. For the current chapter is not intended to provide an overview of the main themes in ontology; it rather intends to expose my own view of how to approach physicalism, an ontological option within naturalism. Moreover, as will be discussed in the next section, no further distinction is required to understand the significance of physicalism, as an ontological thesis, to the debates in ontology.

[11] Of course, the opponents may raise an objection being motivated by a belief at the level of objects (for example, nominalist intuitions), but what is crucial is a publicly presented claim, not an implicit motivation.

[12] In fact, Putnam (2004b) also proposes a thesis concerning the former question, which will be examined in chapter 3.

the process of deriving a particular ontological position, from which a number of ontological debates will be clearly understood:

The basic perspective for ontological debates

The set of statements from which an ontological commitment is derived is determined (in other words, what is true is determined).
+
The method of deriving an ontological commitment from a statement set is determined (the criterion of ontological commitment is determined)
↓
A list of entities is created.

Now, I need to explicate how the discussion developed so far relates to the main objective of this chapter, to explore convincing ontological options in naturalism. As I have stated in chapter 1, naturalism is defined in this book as minimal naturalism with some or other theses added to it. Naturalists can formulate a variety of naturalist views by adding different theses to minimal naturalism. The above perspective for ontological debates helps evaluating ontological theses that naturalists may add to minimal naturalism. In particular, the current chapter focuses on physicalist monism, a commonly held ontological thesis in contemporary naturalism, and pluralism as an alternative; the perspective will illuminate at what level physicalist monism and pluralism compete with one another.

From the next section and in the following, I will focus on achieving the objective of this chapter, to explore and elucidate convincing ontological options in naturalism. Before doing so, to conclude the current section, I wish to go over the constraints on ontology arising from naturalism.

2.1.3 Constraints on naturalist ontology

(1) The constraint from belief system immanentism

The first constraint to be discussed comes from belief system immanentism, one of the justifications for naturalism, and it is concerned with the first question above, 'From which set of statements should an ontological commitment be derived?' To get the discussion off the ground, let 'the set of statements from which an ontological commitment is derived' be 'a set of true statements'. Now, what is encompassed by true statements? More precisely, under what conditions are statements evaluated as true? Quine's belief system immanentism suggests that truth cannot be defined completely independently from our belief system. The following passages clearly indicate this core idea of belief system immanentism (some of these were also quoted earlier in chapter 1).

> The fundamental-seeming philosophical question, How much of our science is merely contributed by language and how much is a genuine reflection of reality? is perhaps a spurious question which itself arises wholly from a certain particular

type of language. Certainly we are in a predicament if we try to answer the question; for to answer the question we must talk about the world as well as about language, and to talk about the world we must already impose upon the world some conceptual scheme peculiar to our own special language. ... We can improve our conceptual scheme, our philosophy, bit by bit while continuing to depend on it for support; but we cannot detach ourselves from it and compare it objectively with an unconceptualized reality. Hence it is meaningless, I suggest, to inquire into the absolute correctness of a conceptual scheme as a mirror of reality. (Quine 1953, 78-9)

It is rather when we turn back into the midst of an actually present theory, at least hypothetically accepted, that we can and do speak sensibly of this and that sentence as true. (Quine 1960, 24)
Have we now so far lowered our sights as to settle for a relativistic doctrine of truth—rating the statements of each theory as true for that theory, and brooking no higher criticism? Not so. The saving consideration is that we continue to take seriously our own particular aggregate science, our own particular world-theory or loose total fabric of quasi-theories, whatever it may be. [...] Within our own total evolving doctrine, we can judge truth as earnestly and absolutely as can be; subject to correction, but that goes without saying. (ibid., 25-5)

Given that naturalism presupposes belief system immanentism, it is justifiable to suppose that naturalists cannot characterize truth as correspondence to reality-in-itself. A set of true statements from which an ontological commitment is derived—whether it is a set of ordinarily accepted statements or the totality of science (or a part of it)—has to be located within our belief system. To illustrate, consider the statement 'electrons have a negative charge'. One might argue that the statement can be judged true, and that for it to be true, there must exist electrons, and so electrons exist. Naturalism conceptually excludes the following kind of objection to this argument: the truth of the statement 'electrons have a negative charge' is not confirmed by correspondence to reality-in-itself, which is independent from our belief system; therefore, whether electrons *really* exist is not known.

However, characterizing truth internally within our belief system does not amount to uncritically considering all statements we have currently accepted as true. Such a consequence would create a serious problem by conflicting with the commonly accepted meaning of the term 'truth'. For example, consider the currently believed statement 'Napoleon died on the island of St. Helena'. If it were necessary to accept this statement as true just because it is currently believed, then it would be difficult to make sense of the property of being true attributed to this belief if future research discovers contrary evidence, rejecting the belief (it is unlikely, but possible, to happen). Therefore, it seems justifiable to conclude that naturalists must endorse belief system immanentism with respect to the notion of truth, while distinguishing truth from currently accepted beliefs—these must not be equated.

These two ideas—endorsing belief system immanentism and distinguishing truth from what is believed—appear to be incompatible. In what follows, two attempts to resolve the apparent conflict will be examined: one is Putnam's conception of 'idealized rational acceptability' and the other is Quine's view of truth being internal and 'transcendental' at the same time. Of course, there may be other plausible naturalistic ways to resolve the conflict, but the present purpose is to understand how the constraint on a naturalistic theory of truth is compatible with the ordinary usage of the term 'truth', and not to select the best naturalistic theory of truth examining all the candidates; so considering these two concrete proposals will be sufficient for the purpose here.

Putnam endorses belief system immanentism, rejecting metaphysical realism,[13] which views truth as correspondence to belief-independent reality. To get around the difficulty of the verificationist idea that identifies truth with verification—recall the Napoleon statement mentioned above—Putnam presented an approach that views truth as 'idealized rational acceptability'.

> To reject the idea that there is a coherent 'external' perspective, a theory which is simply true 'in itself', apart from all possible observers, is not to *identify* truth with rational acceptability. Truth cannot simply *be* rational acceptability for one fundamental reason; truth is supposed to be a property of a statement that cannot be lost, whereas justification can be lost. The statement 'The earth is flat' was, very likely, rationally acceptable 3,000 years ago; but it is not rationally acceptable today. Yet it would be wrong to say that 'the earth is flat' was *true* 3,000 years ago; for that would mean that the earth has changed its shape. [...]
> What this shows, in my opinion, is not that the externalist view is right after all, but that truth is an *idealization* of rational acceptability. We speak as if there were such things as epistemically ideal conditions, and we call a statement 'true' if it would be justified under such conditions. 'Epistemically ideal conditions', of course, are like 'frictionless planes': we cannot really attain epistemically ideal conditions, or even be absolutely certain that we have come sufficiently close to them. But frictionless planes cannot really be attained either, and yet talk of frictionless planes has 'cash value' because we can approximate them to a very high degree of approximation. (Putnam 1981, 55, italics in original)

As is clear from these remarks, Putnam attempts to reconcile the two apparently conflicting ideas: truth defined in terms of belief system immanentism and truth distinguished from what is currently believed. The former is established by dismissing metaphysical realism and an 'external' perspective, while the latter by viewing truth, not as present rational acceptability, but as idealized rational acceptability.

Quine also attempts to reconcile truth defined in terms of belief system immanentism and truth distinguished from what is currently believed. Consider the

---

[13] There Putnam (1981) characterizes metaphysical realism referring to the following three theses:
- [T]he world consists of some fixed totality of mind-independent objects.
- There is exactly one true and complete description of 'the way the world is'.
- Truth involves some sort of correspondence relation between words or thought-signs and external things and sets of things. (Putnam 1981, 49)

following:

> We naturalists say that science is the highest path to truth, but still we do not say that everything on which scientists agree is true. Nor do we say that something that was true became false when scientists changed their minds. What we say is that they and we *thought* it was true, but it wasn't. We have scientists pursuing truth, not decreeing it. Truth thus stands forth as an idea of pure reason, in Kant's apt phrase, and transcendent indeed. ...
> C.S. Peirce tried to naturalize truth by identifying it with the limit that scientific progress approaches. This depends on optimistic assumptions, but if we reconstrue it as mere metaphor it does epitomize the scientists' persistent give and take of conjecture and refutation. Truth as goal remains the established usage of the term, and I acquiesce in it as just a vivid metaphor for our continued adjustment of our world picture to our neural intake. Metaphor is perhaps a handy category in which to accommodate transcendental concepts from a naturalist point of view. (Quine 1995, 285-6, italics in original)

According to Quine, Peirce's definition of truth as "the limit that scientific progress approaches" is an attempt to "naturalize truth," since it reflects the basic naturalist idea that reality is to be identified and described within science. Quine points out both positive and negative aspects of the definition. The negative aspect of this conception of truth is that it depends on an "optimistic assumption," and it is suggested to be reinterpreted as a "mere metaphor." The grounds for this negative assessment can be found in the following remarks in *Word and Object*:

> ... we have no reason to suppose that man's surface irritations even unto eternity admit of any one systematization that is scientifically better or simpler than all possible others. (Quine 1960, 23)

That is, Peirce is too optimistic in assuming that a best theory is uniquely determined by all experiences at the ideal limit of scientific inquiry. This assumption is unacceptable for Quine because of the thesis of the underdetermination of theory, according to which the theory to be adopted will never be uniquely determined even given all possible observations (See section 2.3.1 for the thesis).

At the same time, Quine appreciates the positive aspect of Peirce's definition of truth, stating, "Metaphor is perhaps a handy category in which to accommodate transcendental concepts from a naturalist point of view" (Quine 1995, 286). One of the 'transcendental concepts' here is the 'truth' in "We have scientists pursuing truth, not decreeing it" (ibid.), something that our inquiry aims at and that we do not merely decree. The reference to 'metaphor' relates to 'the ideal theory' Peirce imagined. Peirce's definition of truth serves as a metaphor for "the scientists' persistent give and take of conjecture and refutation" and "our continued adjustment of our world picture to our neural intake" (ibid.). To summarize, Quine's mixed assessment of Peirce's truth definition can be reformulated as follows:

'The ideal theory' has to be a mere metaphor in the sense that it does not actually exist, but it aptly expresses our condition that our inquiry will never cease and there is no definite end point at some future time. For this reason, this metaphor helps naturalistically incorporating the transcendental aspect of truth —truth is the goal of our inquiry, not something decreed.

Then, how does the metaphor of 'the ideal theory' help incorporating truth 'from a naturalist point of view'? Identifying truth with Peirce's 'ideal theory', it would be possible to dissociate what is *currently* believed from truth, and at the same time, truth would be understood as something internal to our science (even though it cannot be reached). To put more simply, Quine wished to retain both the naturalist (internalist) spirit and transcendental aspect of truth—claiming everything to be within our reach and denying that truth can be decreed. 'The ideal theory' Peirce suggested should not be literally accepted for its problems, but it serves as a useful metaphor for accomplishing what Quine wished to accomplish.[14]

Here is a summary of the discussion concerning the constraint from belief system immanentism. The naturalist answers to the first question specified in the perspective for ontological debates—from which set of statements should an ontological commitment be derived?—are subject to the constraint that a set of statements (namely, truth) must be provided internally within our belief system. At the same time, as exemplified by Putnam's internal realism and Quine's view of truth as being internal as well as transcendental, defining truth internally within our belief system does not imply identifying truth with what is currently justified to believe. Defining truth as being in-principle unreachable is contradictory to the general principles of naturalism, and identifying truth with our belief system is fundamentally misguided. Naturalists rather locate truth at the end point of our inquiry, avoiding the dilemma of naturalizing truth. ('The end point of our inquiry' exists only as an idealization, as the quotes from Putnam and Quine above indicate.)

---

[14] It is plausible enough that, for Quine, 'the ideal theory' should not be accepted literally, given the thesis of the underdetermination of theory. Then, how does Quine himself reconcile the transcendental aspects of truth and naturalism? What does Quine offer in the place of 'the ideal theory' to understand the notion of truth from a naturalist viewpoint?

A possible answer to this is the idea of an 'empirically adequate theory', which fits all experiences. It is important to realize that the condition of empirical adequacy is also an idealization, like the notion of 'the ideal theory'. (For, whether a theory is empirically adequate cannot be definitely determined at any point of the inquiry.) The main reason for Quine's denial of the existence of an ideal theory is that a theory will never be uniquely determined even given all of experience, and Quine does not deny the importance of scientific inquiry, whose main objective is to fit experience to theory. It follows that assuming empirical adequacy as the goal of our inquiry causes no trouble, even though there may be more than one empirically adequate theory. Given Quine's (somewhat) positive assessment of Peirce's definition of truth—as an effort to 'naturalize truth'—it is reasonable to suppose further that the idea of 'empirical adequacy' is a promising interpretation of Quine's position.

What is, after all, the goal of our inquiry according to Quine? (Of course, the uniquely determined 'ideal theory' cannot be an answer, as Quine refutes that.) The answer proposed above is 'idealized empirical adequacy' or 'only ideally existing empirical adequacy'. If this proposal is correct, then 'idealized empirical adequacy' substitutes for Peirce's 'ideal theory' to understand naturalistically the notion of truth, accounting for the transcendental aspect of truth—it is the goal of our inquiry but not something decreed.

(2) The constraint from the abandonment of foundationalism

As stated in section 1.5, the boundary between what is naturalistically acceptable and what is not is based on whether a foundation more secure than the experimental method—more secure than science—is claimed. From this it follows that any naturalist claim must be presented in an empirical and fallible way, and this consequence yields a constraint on ontology within a naturalistic framework. To illustrate the constraint, consider the following exposition of seventeenth-century physicalism by Tim Crane and David Mellor:

> But physicalism differs significantly from its materialist ancestors. In its seventeenth-century form of mechanism, for instance, materialism was a metaphysical doctrine: it attempted to limit physics a priori by requiring matter to be solid, inert, impenetrable and conserved, and to interact deterministically and only on contact. But as it has subsequently developed, physics has shown this conception of matter to be wrong in almost every respect: the 'matter' of modern physics is not all solid, or inert, or impenetrable, or conserved; and it interacts indeterministically and arguably sometimes at a distance. Faced with these discoveries, materialism's modern descendants have—understandably—lost their metaphysical nerve. No longer trying to limit the matter of physics a priori, they now take a more subservient attitude: the empirical world, they claim, contains just what a true complete physical science would say it contains. (Crane and Mellor 1990, 186)

If the old conception of matter, the ontological view that matter is "solid, inert, impenetrable and conserved, and to interact deterministically and only on contact," were treated as an *a priori* principle immune to revision, then no naturalist would be able to accept it, since one of the general principles of naturalism is that there is no other justificatory procedure than the hypothetico-deductive method, and a physicalism that is construed as a principle immune to revision obviously violates this. The thesis that nothing contradicts the old materialist view is not problematic in itself; the problem is its epistemological status. If the thesis is advanced as an incorrigible truth deduced from an *a priori* conceptual analysis of the term 'exist', it would be, of course, naturalistically unacceptable. What is acceptable from a naturalist viewpoint is, at most, the following materialist view, a working hypothesis open to revision:

> The idea that every existing object has the properties of being solid, inert, impenetrable, etc. nicely captures our intuitions. To determine whether the intuitions are sustainable, let us for the moment adopt this idea as a materialist hypothesis, observing how far it will be able to explain our scientific practice.

The materialist hypothesis formulated in this way is justified to the extent of our intuitions, but it is not conferred a special epistemic status of being incorrigible (because intuitions are fallible). Therefore, materialism understood in this way is compatible with the general principles of naturalism, since it can be discarded by empirical facts (for example, it can be shown to be incompatible with scientific practice).

It has become clear by now that any ontological claim from a naturalist perspective always has to have the epistemological status of being open to revision or of being fallible. No naturalist can accept an ontological claim, such as mechanistic materialism, that determines the domain of existing objects in an *a priori* way, exempting itself from objections. On the contrary, if an ontological claim is formulated as a working hypothesis that can be withdrawn in an empirical inquiry, it would be a possible thesis naturalists could adopt.

Here, I have discussed the constraints on ontological claims that can be developed within naturalism. In the next section, I will focus on one of such naturalist ontological claims, physicalism, examining its import and implications.

2.2 The Place of Physicalism as an Ontological Option

The main objective of this chapter is to explore what would be convincing ontological theses for naturalism. To prepare the ground for achieving this objective, the previous section has distinguished two ontological questions, presenting the basic framework for understanding ontological debates: 'From which set of statements should an ontological commitment be derived?' and 'What is the appropriate method of deriving an ontological commitment from the determined set of statements?' The current section attempts to elucidate the features and basis of physicalism, identifying its place within the presented framework.[15]

2.2.1 What is physicalism?: Papineau's view

Many philosophers today—especially those within the Anglophone tradition— endorse physicalism (it is not clear, however, whether they constitute a majority because the ontological views of philosophers often remain implicit). The following passages from (Crane and Mellor 1990) and (Loewer 2001) clearly outline the features of physicalism and also why it seems so attractive to the participants in this discussion:

> Many philosophers are impressed by the progress achieved by physical sciences. This has had an especially deep effect on their ontological views: it has made many of them physicalists. Physicalists believe that everything is physical: more precisely, that all entities, properties, relations, and facts are those which are studied by physics or other physical sciences. They may not all agree with the spirit of Rutherford's quoted remark that 'there is physics; and there is stamp-collecting', but they all grant physical science a unique ontological authority: the

---

[15] Physicalism is usually seen as an ontological thesis but sometimes also as having epistemological implications in addition to ontological ones. (Quine is a representative of philosophers who hold such a view, connecting ontological and epistemological implications in terms of the notion of simplicity. See [Quine 1995, 285].) Here, I will exclusively examine the ontological aspect of physicalism.

authority to tell us what there is. (Crane and Mellor 1990, 185)

> Materialism says that all facts, in particular all mental facts, obtain *in virtue of* the spatiotemporal distribution, and properties, of matter. It was, as Putnam says, "metaphysics within the bounds of science,"[16] but only so long as science was thought to say that the world is made out of matter. In this century physicists have learned that there is more in the world than matter and, in any case, matter isn't quite what it seemed to be. For this reason many philosophers who think that metaphysics should be informed by science advocate *physicalism* in place of materialism. Physicalism claims that all facts obtain *in virtue of* the distribution of the fundamental entities and properties—whatever they turn out to be—of completed *fundamental physics*. (Loewer 2001, 37, italics in original)

As these passages suggest, it is a fairly commonly held basic physicalist intuition that all facts are physical. (Henceforth I will use the term 'fact' to stand for 'a circumstance expressed by a true statement'.) However, it is rare to provide an explicit definition of physicalism that can withstand philosophical scrutiny,[17] and it is even rarer to find an explicit argument for any formulation.[18] Here, I will present a clear formulation of physicalism through Papineau's discussion, which provides some insight into its foundation. This will prepare for the examination of physicalism in the rest of this chapter.

Papineau first considers formulating physicalism in terms of supervenience on the physical. Supervenience is a general relation between properties. For example, to say that 'chemical properties supervene on physical properties' is to say that 'any two systems (or objects) cannot differ with respect to their chemical properties without differing with respect to their physical properties' or that 'if two system are identical with respect to their physical properties, then they must be identical also with respect to their chemical properties'.[19]

Now, consider how to formulate physicalism using this notion of supervenience. Where there is a supervenience relation, there exists a difference in physical properties for any difference in non-physical properties, and also there is no difference in non-physical properties without a difference in physical properties. A circumstance being described using non-physical properties that supervene on physical properties is not over and above physical facts, in the sense that it depends on and is determined by physical properties. Therefore, taking as a 'fact' a circumstance being described using non-physical properties that supervene on physical properties is

---

[16] (Putnam 1983, 210).

[17] See (Crane and Mellor 1990, 185), whose conclusion is that any formulation of physicalism either makes it false or trivially true.

[18] According to Papineau, philosophers who support a physicalist position within any field of philosophy, such as philosophy of mind, "tend simply to start with their physicalist intuitions, and try to develop a theory which fits them," rather than starting with arguments for physicalism (Papineau 1993, 9).

[19] Depending on how to interpret the modal expressions here, 'cannot' and 'must', supervenience is classified into 'strong supervenience' and 'weak supervenience', which will be discussed in section 2.3.4.

compatible with the core intuition of physicalism that all facts are physical. Next, consider non-physical properties that do not supervene on physical properties. It is possible for two systems to differ with respect to such non-physical properties even though they are completely identical with respect to their physical properties. A circumstance being described using non-physical properties that do not supervene on physical properties can be said to be over and above the realm of physical facts. Therefore, taking as a 'fact' a circumstance being described using non-physical properties that do *not* supervene on physical properties is incompatible with the core intuition of physicalism. For, in doing so, one concedes there to be some factual difference in two physically identical systems, and this amounts to acknowledging there to be a non-physical fact, a fact that goes beyond the physical.

To summarize, under the physicalist view that all facts are physical, it is legitimate to approve as facts circumstances being described using properties that supervene on physical facts, but it is not legitimate to approve as facts those circumstances being described using properties that do *not* supervene on physical facts. In this way, narrowing the range of facts using the notion of supervenience—claiming that properties that describe facts must supervene on physical properties—it is possible to articulate precisely the basic physicalist idea that all facts are physical.

The supervenience approach to the formulation of physicalism is standard in the literature on contemporary physicalism. Nonetheless, there is a problem in the formulation of supervenience presented above: 'any two systems (or objects) cannot differ with respect to their chemical properties without differing with respect to their physical properties' or 'if two system are identical with respect to their physical properties, then they must be identical also with respect to their chemical properties'. If 'physical properties' on which non-physical properties supervene are restricted to intrinsic properties of a system, a counterexample to physicalism could be easily found. Papineau uses the property of 'heaviness' as a possible counterexample. One chemical sample could be heavier than another even though their physical properties are completely identical. (Suppose that the former is on the earth and the other on the moon.) Therefore, "the heaviness of chemical systems does not supervene on their physical characteristics" (Papineau 1993, 10).

For Papineau, of course, this is not an actual counterexample to physicalism. Rather, this apparent conflict merely shows that the formulation of supervenience needs further refinement, and Papineau introduces the notion of 'relational property' here. A property of a system is relational when it depends on both the intrinsic features of the system and also on its relation to other systems. As in the above example with chemical samples, the heaviness of a chemical sample is not determined solely by the physical features inherent in the sample, but by the intrinsic features together with the external features of the sample (namely, the surrounding gravitational field). That is, the heaviness of a sample supervenes on the physical features of a comprehensive compound system, rather than on the sample plus its environment. Thus, the property of heaviness can be accounted for in terms of supervenience by construing it to be a relational property.[20]

---

[20] In addition to the 'strong-weak' distinction, there is also a distinction between a 'local'

Papineau considers supervenience formulated in this way to be a necessary condition for physicalism. If two systems differ with respect to some factual property despite their physical identity, then there would be a non-physical fact, which is incompatible with the basic physicalist intuition that all facts are physical. Thus, for physicalism to hold, there cannot be such two systems, and so supervenience is required in the proper formulation of physicalism. Indeed, supervenience is sometimes called 'minimal physicalism' in the sense that physicalists must accept at least supervenience even though they may disagree with one another on other points.[21] Based on these considerations, for the further discussion, let us define physicalism using the notion of supervenience as follows:[22]

Physicalism: all properties that are used to describe facts supervene on physical properties.[23]

2.2.2 The basis of physicalism

In what follows, I will examine the basis of physicalism as defined above. The main reason for doing so is not to evaluate the legitimacy of physicalism, but to understand

---

supervenience and a 'global' supervenience, which is concerned with the question of which system has subvening properties. The refinement through the introduction of relational properties permits a global supervenience, and so subvening physical properties do no have to exist locally. This leads to the suggestion that, as Papineau points out, "this kind of shift, from a 'local' to a more 'global' supervenience, makes room for *ad hoc* defences of supervenience, and so dilutes physicalism beyond interest" (Papineau 1993, 11f). In response, Papineau proposes a constraint that, for a non-physical property to supervene on the physical properties of a wider system, there must be some independent reason for taking the non-physical property to be relational (other than a desire to retain physicalism).

[21] See (Todayama 2003, 69) and (Stoljar 2009, section 4 "Minimal Physicalism and Philosophy of Mind").

[22] Papineau, however, maintains that supervenience is a necessary but not a sufficient condition for physicalism because he thinks that a non-physicalist view accepting supervenience is possible. Papineau shows epiphenomenalism as an example, according to which "mental states 'float above' the brain as distinct conscious phenomena, not responsible for any physical effects themselves, but nevertheless causally determined by the physics of the brain, and so incapable of varying without physical variation" (Papineau 1993, 11). According to Papineau, epiphenomenalism implies supervenience but "explicitly specifies that mental properties are quite distinct from physical ones" (ibid.), and so it is not physicalism. The proper formulation of physicalism, Papineau stresses, should thereby include a clause ruling out epiphenomenalism; the thesis of mind-body identity—the mental is in some sense identical with the physical—is required in addition to supervenience—"the mental is determined by the physical" (ibid.). (The identity relation here can be spelled out in different ways. Papineau adopts what he calls 'token congruence' to specify the relation.) See (ibid., 12).

It can be disputed, however, whether physicalism really needs to rule out epiphenomenalism (Todayama 2003, 89). Papineau also does not seem to think that all physicalists would accept his particular formulation of physicalism. In any case, on the definition of physicalism to be adopted in this book, those accepting supervenience are physicalists. It is, of course, possible to formulate different forms of physicalism by adding further clauses—just as Papineau does so by ruling out epiphenomenalism. I will also use the term 'physicalism' generally to talk about different forms of physicalism.

[23] As will be discussed in section 2.2.3, this definition of physicalism must be understood as describing the 'core' of physicalism. That is, the term 'physicalism' stands for a cluster of views with the core qualities captured by the definition, and a variety of physicalist views can be sustained by adding further clauses (further restrictions on truth and facts or specific requirements for ontological commitment).

the logic behind physicalism. (This will be important for discerning what aspect of physicalism is under attack by an objection from indeterminacy, which will be discussed in more detail in section 2.3.)

(1) The completeness of physics

Papineau introduces the 'completeness of physics' as a first premise for deriving the supervenience of factual non-physical properties on physical properties. The basic idea is that "all physical events are determined, or have their chances determined, by prior *physical* events according to *physical* laws" (Papineau 1993, 16, italics in original), and it follows from this that "we never need to look beyond the realm of the physical in order to identify a set of antecedents which fixes the chances of any subsequent physical occurrence" (ibid.).

A number of questions must be answered to clarify this notion of the completeness of physics. For one thing, it is unclear how to understand the term 'physics'. If the term is construed simply as 'what is currently taught in university physics courses', the completeness would be false, since "current physics is no doubt inadequate in certain respects, and in particular in failing to identify all the antecedents for certain physical effects" (ibid., 29). Construing the term to be an 'ideal future physics' would hardly be an improvement, since "we don't yet know what physical categories will be assumed by the ideal future physics" (ibid.), and so it is impossible to determine whether "those categories will suffice for complete explanations of all physical effects" (ibid.), that is, whether physics is complete.[24]

To overcome this problem—physics would not be complete whether the term 'physics' is construed as the 'current physics' or an 'ideal future physics'—Papineau proposes to simply *define* physics as "the science of whatever categories are needed to give full explanations for all physical effects" (ibid., 29-30). Physics so defined resolves the problem because, first, it is different from current physics, and second, though we do not yet know how it will look in the future, it obviously by definition satisfies the requirement for completeness.

Papineau's treatment of the problem may be questioned on many grounds. Two possible objections are sketched out in the Papineau article: (i) the treatment makes it extremely difficult to understand the term 'physical' in the definition; (ii) it trivially follows from the definition that physics so defined satisfies the requirement for the completeness, and no substantial thesis can be drawn from such a thesis. Papineau

---

[24] This problem is often referred to as 'Hempel's dilemma': the first horn of the dilemma is that 'currentism'—taking physical properties to be specified by current physics—makes physicalism false, and the second horn is that 'futurism'—taking them to be specified by an ideal future physics—makes physicalism to be a trivially true thesis positing no substantial claims. See (Ney 2008) for a general discussion of this dilemma as well as the 'currentism' and 'futurism' terminology. Two major approaches to the dilemma include—both based on futurism—specifying the features of physics in more detail and thereby making physicalism non-trivial (Dowell 2006) and introducing an *a priori* requirement such as that 'fundamental physical properties do not include mental properties' and thereby making physicalism non-trivial (Wilson 2006). My present purpose is, however, not to issue a final verdict on the proper formulation of physicalism but to grasp an overview of physicalism, so I will continue by relying on Papineau's treatment of the dilemma, simplifying the ensuing discussion without being distracted by unimportant details. Ney (2008) provides a comprehensive survey of formulating physicalism.

attempts to answer both objections.[25]

In response to objection (i), Papineau suggests pre-theoretically characterizing the notion of 'physical' appealing to typical physical events, such as 'stones falling'. This kind of characterization is pre-theoretic in the sense that it is committed to no theory, and so we do not yet know the details of the completed physics; but the pre-theoretic notion determines its explananda. As for (ii), acknowledging that the completeness of physics is trivial in itself—it is guaranteed by the definition of physics—Papineau claims that it entails a substantial thesis about supervenience if considered together with the empirical hypothesis that no psychological category is included in the categories assumed in the completed physics.[26] Consider the following remarks:

> ... if psychological categories are not in fact ever essential to explaining physical effects, then physics, in the sense of whatever is needed to explain physical effects, will be both complete and exclusive of psychology, and the arguments of this chapter will show that psychological states are *non*-trivially supervenient on and congruent with physical states. (Papineau 1993, 31, italics in original)

Papineau's idea expressed here is something like the following. The above definition of physics, 'the science of whatever categories are needed to give full explanations for all physical effects', leaves it open whether psychological categories are included in physics. If they are indeed included in physics, then the supervenience of mental properties on physical properties would trivially hold. (If mental properties are physical properties, then the thesis 'if two systems are identical with respect to their physical properties, then they must be identical also with respect to their psychological properties' would have to be restated trivially as 'if two system are identical with respect to their physical properties, then they are identical also with respect to a particular class of their physical properties'.) However, if no psychological category is included in the categories assumed in the completed physics, as Papineau supposes, then the supervenience of mental properties on physical properties does not trivially hold as a matter of definition. Thus, even if the completeness of physics trivially follows from the definition of physics, the supervenience of mental properties on physical properties is a substantial consequence as long as the empirical hypothesis that no psychological category is included in the categories assumed in the completed physics is correct.

Further objections, no doubt, can be raised to Papineau's responses here. The present purpose is, however, to understand the logic behind physicalism (through a particular example, the Papineau article), not to evaluate extant arguments for physicalism one by one, let alone to give any ultimate verdict on physicalism. The discussion so far has sufficiently illuminated a part of the logic behind physicalism: a premise for physicalism is the completeness of physics, and Papineau defines (the completed) physics in a way that satisfies the completeness. Let us now turn to the

---

[25] Crane (1991) brings up the second objection.
[26] Papineau defends this hypothesis based on the history of science, pointing out that the recent developments of physiology started enabling explanations of human physical activities with no reference to psychological concepts. See (Papineau 2001).

other premise for physicalism.

(2) The manifestability of the mental

The second premise Papineau presents to derive a thesis concerning supervenience is what he calls the 'manifestability of the mental', the idea that "if two systems are mentally different, then there must be some physical contexts in which this difference would display itself in differential physical consequences, or at least in differential chances for such consequences" (Papineau 1993, 17-8). Papineau combines the manifestability of the mental and the completeness of physics, discussed above, to derive the supervenience of mental properties on physical properties. The line of reasoning is summarized as follows:

> Premise (1). According to the completeness of physics, the chances of physical consequences are fixed, once physical antecedents are given. So if two systems are physically identical and in the same physical contexts, they will issue in the same physical consequences or chances thereof.
>
> Premise (2). Now add ... *the manifestability of the mental*, that if two system are mentally different, then there must be some physical contexts in which this difference would display itself in differential physical consequences, or at least in differential chances for such consequences.
>
> Conclusion. It follows that mental differences without physical differences are impossible. (1) tells us that physical identity guarantees identity of physical consequences or chances thereof. And (2) tells us that mental difference requires the possibility of different physical consequences or chances thereof. So physical identity rules out mental difference. (ibid., 17-8, italics in original)

It is now clear how Papineau derives physicalism from the two premises, the completeness of physics and the manifestability of the mental (as the argument above seems valid). Then, on what grounds is the manifestability of the mental used as a premise? Papineau defends the manifestability by stating that "a mental difference which was not physically manifestable in any way would be radically undetectable" (ibid., 19). Our sense organs—presumed to be the unique entrance of external information—"work by physical interaction with the environment ... So if two different mental states yielded exactly the same physical manifestations in all contexts, then there would be no possibility whatsoever of our ever finding out about their difference" (ibid., 20).

The discussion so far has examined the possible basis of the supervenience of mental properties on physical properties following Papineau's argument for physicalism. As is clear from Premise (2) above—the manifestability of the *mental*—the argument is only concerned with the supervenience of mental properties on physical properties. However, extending the argument to the supervenience of factual properties in general would be feasible. The proposed justification for the manifestability of the mental is that "our sense organs work by physical interaction with the environment" (ibid., 19-20), and so it would seem applicable to different types of properties as well.[27] On the basis of Papineau's formulation of the manifestability of the mental, let us define the manifestability of factual properties in general as follows:

> The manifestability of factual properties in general: If two systems are different with respect to their non-physical factual properties, then there must be some physical context in which this difference would display itself in differential physical consequences, or at least in differential chances for such consequences.

I generalize Papineau's argument for supervenience as discussed here to factual properties in general by replacing the manifestability of the mental with this type of manifestability. That is, it is justifiable to assume that factual properties in general supervene on physical properties. Let us now proceed with this assumption in mind.

2.2.3 The implications of physicalism on ontological debates

The preceding part of this section has pointed out that the basic intuition of physicalism—all facts are physical—can be captured in terms of the supervenience of factual properties on physical properties, and that supervenience is based on the completeness of physics and the manifestability of the mental. In what follows, to deepen our understanding of physicalism as an ontological thesis within naturalism, I will examine physicalism relying on the basic perspective for ontological debates, proposed in section 2.1.2 and repeated here:

> The basic perspective for ontological debates
>
> The set of statements from which an ontological commitment is derived is determined (in other words, 'truth' is determined).
> +
> The method of deriving an ontological commitment from a statement is determined (the criterion of ontological commitment is determined).
> ↓
> A list of entities is created.

As is stated in section 2.2.1, physicalism is defined (minimally) in this chapter as the position that all properties used to describe facts supervene on physical properties. Notice that physicalism in this minimal sense poses constraints on 'truth' and 'facts', from which ontological theses about entities are to be deduced, rather than being directly concerned with ontology—or with entities themselves—even though physicalism is often referred to as an 'ontological thesis'. First, supervenience is a relation holding between types of properties, and so physicalism, evidently, advances no ontological thesis by presenting an 'inventory of entities'. Therefore, physicalism

---

[27] The general applicability of the manifestability argument has been pointed out explicitly in (Witner 1998, 84) and implicitly in the formulation of 'manifestability' in (Todayama 2003, 70).

figures in an ontological debate at either one of the earlier steps before a particular inventory of entities is developed. Next, since the minimal definition of physicalism refers only to facts and properties, not to the relation between accepted statements and commitments to entities, it is also evident that physicalism does not figure in the second step of the perspective as spelled out above, determining the criterion for ontological commitment. It follows that physicalism figures in an ontological debate at the very first stage, determining a set of statements from which an ontological commitment is to be derived.

Then, how does physicalism figure in determining a basis for an ontological commitment? To answer this question, recall that the formulation of physicalism, 'all properties used to describe facts supervene on physical properties', is intended to capture the basic physicalist intuition that 'all facts are physical'. Conversely, this intuition tells that nothing non-physical is a fact, ruling out any non-physical thing from the set of all facts. Likewise, the formulation of physicalism can also be viewed as ruling out non-factual properties by selecting what does not supervene on physical properties. In other words, according to physicalism, a circumstance being described using properties that do not supervene on physical properties is not a fact, and so statements composed of predicates standing for such properties are not included in a set of statements that is a basis for an ontological commitment. (This point can be restated using the outline of the theory of naturalism proposed in chapter 1 as follows. Naturalism requires truth, facts, and reality to be described internally within our belief system, but it also leaves open how to understand the scope of our belief system. Physicalism offers a way to determine what counts as a fact in our belief system in terms of supervenience: all properties used to describe facts supervene on physical properties.)

These considerations have laid open that, in ontological debates, physicalism defined in terms of supervenience is directly concerned with the level of determining a set of statements from which an ontological commitment is to be derived, not with the level of entities or the criterion of ontological commitment. It is, therefore, inappropriate to draw implications for entities directly from physicalism (for example, by claiming that only such-and-such class of objects exists according to physicalism). To emphasize the importance of this point, consider the discussion of ontological naturalism presented in (Todayama 2003). Todayama defines 'minimal naturalism' as the view that all factual properties supervene on physical properties (Todayama 2003, 69), with which he tries to elucidate the nature of ontological naturalism, writing as follows:

> Should physicalists accept those abstract mathematical objects as part of objects constituting the world because they are posited in an ideal physics? Doing so would probably be incompatible with the fundamental belief of physicalists that nothing causally inert exists. (ibid., 72)

Todayama in the quote assumes the ontological commitment that nothing causally inert exists to be included in the fundamental beliefs of physicalists.[28] What

---

[28] In the same article, Todayama also writes, "It is, however, controversial whether epiphenomenalism

physicalism directly implies, however, must be characterized at the level of properties —or at the level of facts or the truth that properties describe—as long as physicalism is defined in terms of supervenience. (Remember that supervenience is primarily a relation holding between types of properties.) That is, it is unjustifiable to deduce directly from physicalism, defined in terms of supervenience, an ontological thesis at the level of entities.

Of course, the point here is that the object-level thesis that nothing causally inert exists cannot be viewed as a *direct* implication of physicalism in general; it is not that the ontological thesis is incompatible with physicalist naturalism. It is possible to formulate an ontological position that acknowledges only causally efficacious objects, probably, by figuring out a suitable criterion for ontological commitment or restricting the set of statements that provides a basis for ontological commitment. (Todayama indeed seems to be aware of this [Todayama 2003, 72].) However, any auxiliary principle ruling out causally inert objects is independent of physicalism (as long as it is defined in terms of supervenience),[29] and so requires a different argument than the one discussed above—the completeness of physics and a thesis about manifestability derive supervenience. (Moreover, to justifiably say that the ontological thesis is the 'fundamental belief' of physicalists, it must be shown that the thesis is intimately connected to the basic physicalist intuition stated in section 2.2.1.)

To summarize, the thesis that only causally efficacious objects exist is (i) acceptable as a physicalist view, but (ii) ranks above a claim about supervenience, and so (iii) must be justified on different grounds than the completeness of physics and manifestability.

As I have argued earlier, it is not justifiable to establish a thesis at the level of objects or entities directly on the basis of physicalism defined in terms of supervenience. (To do so it is necessary at least to identify a criterion of ontological commitment.) Therefore, according to the terminology adopted in this book, the ontological thesis that nothing causally inert exists, what Todayama refers to as the physicalists' 'fundamental belief', should not be accepted as a general physicalist assumption, if it is an expression of a particular physicalist view (at least until it is shown that there is good reason to think otherwise and that the ontological thesis is necessary for retaining the basic physicalist intuition).

---

really does not deserve the name of physicalism (it would be, no doubt, a very weak form of physicalism), and also there are objections to Papineau's argument that since supervenience alone does not rule out epiphenomenalism, physicalism must be supplemented with the thesis that the mental is physically realized to rule out epiphenomenalism" (ibid., 89). Todayama assumes, these remarks suggest, that physicalists can take mental properties to be factual as long as they supervene on physical properties, even if mental properties have no causal efficacy. How could this assumption be compatible with the idea that nothing causally inert exists? In accepting the statement 'A has the mental state M' as true or factual, it is necessary to avoid committing to the existence of the mental state M as an entity. To establish this, Todayama would probably attempt to devise a suitable criterion of ontological commitment. Nonetheless, such a criterion would be significantly less convincing because it is arbitrarily fine-tuned for the sake of sustaining the view that nothing causally inert exists. (If the view is a necessary condition for physicalism, this approach would be less problematic, but there are several reasons to think otherwise, as will be stated later.)

[29] Such an auxiliary principle seems to be more suitably labeled a 'materialist' principle than a 'physicalist' one.

The discussion so far has fulfilled the aim of this subsection, to understand physicalism from the perspective for ontological debates proposed in section 2.1.2. In conclusion, I will also discuss the relation between physicalism and naturalism. As examined in section 2.1.3, ontological claims possibly developed within naturalism are constrained by belief system immanentism and the abandonment of foundationalism. Therefore, for physicalism to be a viable ontological option that can potentially be added to the minimal naturalism, it must satisfy the constraints from these two aspects of naturalism.

First, physicalism clearly satisfies the constraint from belief system immanentism. The reason is that physicalism is defined as the view that all properties used to describe facts supervene on physical properties, and the concept of 'physical property', which determines what facts there are, is understood internally within our belief system. (This remains the case if physical properties are provided by a future ideal physics, since it is us who will eventually construct a future physics, which cannot be part of 'reality-in-itself', something completely independent from our belief system.) Thus, physicalist claims are perfectly compatible with belief system immanentism, according to which truth and facts must be described from a perspective internal to our belief system, and they remain as claims in what Putnam calls 'metaphysics within the bounds of science'.

Next, the constraint from the abandonment of foundationalism demands that any ontological claim be treated as open to revision. Leaving some complexities aside for the moment, physicalism in accordance with this constraint is open to revision if it is asserted together with the existence of some factual non-physical properties. For example, suppose physicalism is asserted together with the existence of factual mental properties. Physicalism in this case would be refuted if mental properties turn out not to supervene on physical properties. Thus, physicalism asserted together with the existence of some factual non-physical properties can be discarded in an empirical inquiry.

2.3 Physicalism and Indeterminacy

The previous section has examined the features and basis for physicalism, an ontological option for naturalists, using the basic perspective for ontological debates. It is true that physicalism is the favorite ontological position among naturalists, but it has also attracted much criticism, such as that 'facts about qualia constitute a counterexample to physicalism'[30] and 'intentional concepts such as those of 'meaning' and 'propositional attitude' cannot be understood from a physicalist viewpoint'.[31] Among these negative assessments of physicalism, this section focuses on an objection based on the indeterminacy of translation and interpretation, which claims that the reality of meaning and propositional attitudes is incompatible with physicalism; and through the examination of the objection, I will depict the difficulties physicalism needs to overcome.[32] The reason for focusing on this particular objection

---

[30] One representative example of this criticism is Frank Jackson's (1986) 'knowledge argument'.
[31] Besides the objection from indeterminacy to be discussed below, Kripke (1982) raises this criticism.
[32] The same conclusion, the incompatibility of the reality of meaning as well as propositional attitudes

is three-fold: (i) it has a structure common to much other criticism of physicalism: 'physicalism wrongly rules out such and such from facts'; (ii) the conclusion of this argument, the incompatibility of physicalism and the reality of propositional attitudes, has significant implications; and (iii) this will pave the way towards an understanding of how 'pluralism'—to be discussed as an alternative in the next section—solves the difficulties of physicalism.

A caveat is in order before developing these themes. What follows is not intended to present a 'knock-down' argument against physicalism. The discussion of indeterminacy to be developed in the current section is certainly an objection to physicalism, but section 2.3.4 clarifies why it cannot definitely refute physicalism. (The current section, hence, does not provide a final verdict on physicalism.) The goal of this section is rather to understand clearly the dialectical situation concerning the sustainability of physicalism through an examination of the criticism it has been subjected to. Speaking from a broader perspective, this section serves to present the background for 'pluralist naturalism', the view to be ultimately defended in this book, by discussing possible motivations for it.

2.3.1 The thesis of the indeterminacy of translation and physicalism

(1) Radical translation and the thesis of the indeterminacy of translation

Now I will discuss the thesis of the indeterminacy of translation, proposed by Quine in *Word and Object* (1960), explicating Quine's argument for this thesis and its implications on physicalism. The following is Quine's formulation of the thesis:

> The thesis of the indeterminacy of translation: "manuals for translating one language into another can be set up in divergent ways, all compatible with the totality of speech dispositions, yet incompatible with one another."[33] (Quine 1960, 28)

Let us examine Quine's argument for this thesis. First, to illuminate what evidence is available in learning a language or understanding utterances of speakers of that language, Quine introduces a hypothetical situation, 'radical translation', which is defined as "translation of the language of a hitherto untouched people" (Quine 1960, 28). In the context of radical translation, there exists no extant translation manual whatsoever, such as an English dictionary, nor is there any lexicographical evidence, such as shared etymologies for many English and German words. The only type of evidence, Quine maintains, available in radical translation comprises of "native utterances and their concurrent observable circumstances" (Quine 1987, 5). Thus,

---

and physicalism, has also been defended in the literature on the question of whether connectionism is compatible with folk psychology. (The dominant approach in the literature is to eliminate folk psychology based on the plausibility of connectionism in cognitive science, however.) See (Todayama, et. al. 2003) for more details.

[33] Note that Quine formulates the thesis using the term 'speech dispositions'. Multiple translation manuals—incompatible with one another—are compatible not only with actual utterances but also with all possible utterances.

field linguists trying to translate the language of native speakers of this 'foreign language'—equipped with no background information—have to rely on nothing but their own sensory inputs.[34]

How would a linguist undertake radical translation given these restricted data? There seem to be sentences that are closely connected to circumstances; they can be translated solely on the basis of 'native utterances and their concurrent observable circumstances'. Imagine, for example, that an informant utters 'Gavagai' as a rabbit passes by, and the linguist hypothetically translates it as the sentence 'Rabbit'. This hypothesis would be supported if an informant assents every time the linguist inquisitively asks, 'Gavagai?' as a rabbit appears. Quine calls such sentences that are directly connected to circumstances 'observation sentences',[35] stating that the translations of them are uniquely determined even in the context of radical translation.[36]

At the same time, there are sentences the translations of which are hardly determined in radical translation. Consider the scenario in which a field linguist undertakes radical translation for the Japanese counterpart to 'electrons have a charge' (the sentence 'denshi-wa denka-o ninau'). In this scenario, it would be useless to appeal to evidence based on 'native utterances and their concurrent observable circumstances', since the natives (Japanese informants) would assent to the sentence in whichever circumstance. (Quine calls such sentences to which speakers react consistently across different circumstances 'standing sentences'.) Then, how could the field linguist translate any sentence apart from observation sentences? Quine's answer to this question goes as follows. First, the linguist analyzes native utterances into properly short recurring parts, creating a list of 'words' of the native language (the language the translation is from). Then, the linguist tries to match a native word with a word of the language it is to be translated into in accordance with already established translations of observation sentences. According to Quine, such hypotheses that match words of the native language and those of the language for the translation, labeled 'analytical hypotheses', enable a tentative translation of

---

[34] Quine suggests that insights gained from this thought experiment, radical translation, apply equally well to the acquisition of a first language. Here is a consequence of the indeterminacy of translation extending to one's first language: the meaning of an utterance is not determined. Some philosophers, however, have questioned this suggestion. Jerrold Katz, for example, argues that radical translation is no more than a thought experiment, the consequences of which do not necessarily apply to actual circumstances of translation. See (Katz 1990).

[35] This is an inexact formulation of observation sentences. Quine changed his views on observation sentences more than once as a result of numerous debates. The ultimate formulation of observation sentences appears in (Quine 1992, section 16), which goes as follows:
A sentence is an observation sentence for a single speaker if and only if, upon receiving particular stimuli on sensory receptors, the speaker consistently assents or dissents to the sentence.
A sentence is an observation sentence for a group of speakers if and only if it is an observation sentence for each member of the group, and whenever a member assents to it everyone else also assents to it (and the same in the case of dissenting).

[36] Later Quine partially acknowledged the theory-ladenness of observation, conceding that there are no unique translations for observation sentences taken 'piecemeal', while maintaining that observation sentences taken 'holophrastically' have a unique translation (Quine 1993, 110). This concession amounts to the view that there is no unique manual of translation even at the level of observation sentences (in some sense), which could make the thesis of the indeterminacy of translation no less plausible.

sentences other than observation sentences.

This method of translation, however, is not completely satisfactory. The problem lies in the lack of evidence; the only data available to verify analytical hypotheses comprise of, after all, linguistic behaviors of native speakers and (presumably established) translations of observation sentences. As has been pointed out already, evidence based on 'native utterances and their concurrent observable circumstances' would not be useful in translating standing sentences, and such evidence would (presumably) establish the translations of only few observation sentences; so it would "woefully under-determine the analytical hypotheses on which the translation of all further sentences depends" (Quine 1960, 72). Therefore, the translations of standing sentences, unlike those of observation sentences, cannot be determined by the available evidence alone.

Quine introduces the thesis of the indeterminacy of translation at this point, where analytical hypotheses are constructed for sentences different from observation sentences. Manuals for translating one language into another, referred to in the quoted formulation of the indeterminacy thesis above, are systems that consist of analytical hypotheses providing word-to-word correspondence relations. A system of analytical hypotheses can be uniquely determined neither by evidence comprised of native utterances and their concurrent observable circumstances nor by a comparison with already established translations of observation sentences; these are essentially inadequate for unique determinations. These considerations led Quine to the indeterminacy thesis that it is possible to build multiple systems of analytical hypotheses, namely, manuals for translating one language into another.[37]

I have so far discussed how the theoretical device of radical translation supports the thesis of the indeterminacy of translation. Now, let us briefly discuss the effectiveness of this device, the thought experiment of radical translation. The validity of the behavioristic assumptions underpinning radical translation has been sometimes questioned. As stated earlier, for Quine, the only data available to radical translators are 'native utterances and their concurrent observable circumstances', in which no internal information (such as introspective mental states) is included. This bolsters the interpretation that Quine holds a behavioristic position.[38]

---

[37] Quine does not offer a concrete example showing that translation is indeterminate—namely, that more than one translation manual is indeed possible. (One reason for this is that giving a complete translation of a language twice would require enormous time and effort.) Quine has offered three arguments for the indeterminacy of translation.
  (i) The argument from the inscrutability of reference (Quine 1960, 71-2)
  (ii) The argument from the underdetermination of theory (Quine 1970)
  (iii) Levy's argument based on hyperbolic geometries (Quine 1992, 51)
However, Quine eventually withdrew the first argument (Quine 1970), and Bechtel (1980) raised a strong objection to the second. Further, the third argument only shows that there can be multiple incompatible translations for some geometric statements; the scope of this argument is restricted to utterances of geometric statements, and so it fails to establish the indeterminacy of translation in general, which states that a multiplicity of analytical hypotheses are compatible with all possible dispositions of linguistic behavior. Therefore, it must be concluded that the legitimacy of the indeterminacy of translation thesis has not been established at this date.

[38] A number of objections have been leveled against Quine's behaviorism. For one thing, some critics have taken the implausibility of the indeterminacy of translation to constitute a *reductio* of his

Discussing what underlies this behavioristic view of language, Quine writes:

> In psychology one may or may not be a behaviorist, but in linguistics one has no choice. Each of us learns his language by observing other people's verbal behavior and having his own faltering verbal behavior observed and reinforced or corrected by others. (Quine 1987, 5)

Since no one possesses telepathic or clairvoyant abilities, perceptions of what is in the minds of others are not available in language learning. The data accessible to language learners are restricted to what is perceivable or observable. What underlies Quine's behavioristic view of language is, as these remarks indicate, the scientific knowledge of our sensory organs from which we extract information. In this chapter, I assume that Quine's behaviorism is justified to the extent that our scientific knowledge of our sensory organs is justified, and no further scrutiny will be given to this.[39]

---

behaviorism. Searle (1987) points out that the meaning of an utterance or the referent of a term is indeed determinable from a first-person perspective, arguing that absurd consequences of the indeterminacy of translation prove behaviorism—presupposed for indeterminacy—to be inadequate in providing a proper method of linguistics. For a detailed response to Searle, see (Follesdal, 1990).

[39] According to Quine, "behaviorism sees nothing uncongenial in the appeal to innate dispositions to overt behavior, innate readiness for language-learning" (Quine 1976, 58). Although Quine narrowly restricts the evidence available for determining translation to the behavioristic kind, he accepts explanations based on neurophysiology (which underlies behavior). It is difficult to make sense of this apparently conflicting attitude, about which Quine speaks as follows:

> It [behaviorism] disciplines data, not explanation. On the explanatory side my readers are familiar rather with my recourse to innate endowments. I cite instinct and hence natural selection to explain induction, and to explain also our innate subjective standards of perceptual similarity and their preestablished intersubjective harmony. All this is essential to language readiness. Behaviorism welcomes genetics, neurology, and innate endowments. It just excludes mentalistic explanation. It defines mentalistic concepts rather, if at all, by their observable manifestations in behavior. (Quine 2000, 417)

What is crucial here is the last sentence, which characterizes behaviorism as defining "mentalistic concepts rather, if at all, by their observable manifestations in behavior". If meaning and synonymy (and propositional attitudes to be discussed later) are defined in terms of their observable manifestations in behavior, then facts about meaning and synonymy are exhaustively described at the level of behavior, and "even though some of the internal factors (the brain states) can be observed, they do not tell us what people mean by what they say, they do not provide identity criteria for meanings or propositions, they do not allow the establishment of synonymy, and they do not determine translation" (Gaudet 2006, 63).

It is worth noting that in the future we may revise the idea that facts about the concepts of 'linguistic meaning' and 'synonymy' are exhaustively described at the level of behavior. Certainly, at the present moment, meanings and propositions are individuated by means of our linguistic practices —based on behavioristic data—but, as physiological sciences advance and specify law-like regularities between linguistic practice and concurring brain states, the concepts of 'meaning' and 'proposition' may be redefined in terms of such physiological states. (See Putnam's [1975] discussion of 'one-criterion words'.)

This imagined future scenario is not, however, intended to show that physicalistically acceptable evidence alone resolves the indeterminacy of translation. (This point will be important in the ensuing discussion of the validity of the inference from the indeterminacy of translation to the elimination of meaning.) It primarily depicts the following process: a translation manual is arbitrarily chosen (among other possible manuals); researchers discover law-like regularities between physiological states and meanings and propositions that are internally individuated given the chosen manual; the concepts of

(2) From the thesis of the indeterminacy of translation to the elimination of propositions

The previous part has summarized the features of and Quine's argument for the thesis of the indeterminacy of translation. What follows will examine its implications. Consider the following conclusion that Quine draws from the indeterminacy thesis: "What the indeterminacy of translation shows is that the notion of propositions as sentence meanings is untenable" (Quine 1992, 102)[40].

At a first glance it seems straightforward to understand the inference from the indeterminacy of translation to the untenability of the notion of 'propositions as sentence meanings'. If the synonymy relations between sentences—which sentences are synonymous with which—are not uniquely determined, then it would be impossible to identify the notion of 'sentence meanings' (or 'propositions'), nor would it be possible to sustain the idea that a sentence corresponds to a fixed meaning or propositional content.[41]

However, the indeterminacy of translation alone does not entail the conclusion that the notion of propositions as sentence meanings is untenable. To see this it is necessary to understand the similarities and differences between the underdetermination of theory and the indeterminacy of translation. Before doing so, let us briefly review the thesis of the underdetermination of theory. Although the essentially same idea appeared in *Word and Object*,[42] Quine formulated the underdetermination of theory explicitly for the first time (to the best of my knowledge) in the following passage:

> Theory can still vary though all possible observations be fixed. [...] In a word, they can be logically incompatible and empirically equivalent.[43] (Quine 1970, 179)

---

meaning and proposition are redefined in terms of physiological states, and the individuation conditions for meanings and propositions are also reformulated. This process should be understood as an effort to reconcile the indeterminacy of translation with the physicalist worldview, rather than as a resolution of the indeterminacy.

[40] Also consider the following remarks:
> My conjecture of indeterminacy of translation is a different sort of thing. It is that in the general interlinguistic case the notion of sameness of meaning is an objectively indefinible [sic] matter of intuition. This implies that the notion of meanings as entities, however abstract, is untenable, there being no entity without identity. I reject introspection as an objective criterion, however invaluable heuristically. (Quine 2000, 148)

[41] I have already explicated this point in section 1.4.3. See also (Quine 2000, 418). Quine's views on the indeterminacy of translation have received much criticism—partly because of its bold consequence, the rejection of the idea that a sentence corresponds to a fixed meaning or propositional content. The objections to the indeterminacy, despite their large number, largely boil down to just two: first, the objection that questions the legitimacy of the indeterminacy of translation, and second, the objection that rejects the inference from the indeterminacy of translation to the elimination of meaning, while conceding the former. Both Chomsky (1969) and Rorty (1972)—frequently mentioned as arguing against Quine's defense of the elimination of meaning—present the second type of criticism.

[42] For example, see (Quine 1960, 11).

[43] Quine writes on empirical equivalency, "the two theory formulations are empirically equivalent—that is, they imply the same observation conditionals" (Quine 1975, 319).

Observation conditionals are conditionals whose antecedents are sets of observation sentences the truth values of which are fixed by specifying their spatio-temporal coordinates ('pegged observation sentences') and whose consequents are another pegged observation sentence. Simply, an observation

'Theory' here stands for physics and other scientific theories, the validity of which is empirically tested by observations; so the main idea of the thesis is: a scientific theory to be adopted may not be uniquely determined even given all possible observations.[44]

With this characterization of the underdetermination of theory, let us now compare it with the indeterminacy of translation. The similarity between the two is apparent: the underdetermination thesis maintains that there exist multiple scientific theories compatible with all observations, whereas the indeterminacy thesis maintains that there exist multiple manuals of translation compatible with 'native utterances and their concurrent observable circumstances'. There is a parallelism between scientific theories and translation manuals; neither of them can be uniquely determined by available evidence.

The parallelism between the two theses, however, should not be emphasized too much in view of the elimination of meanings and propositions. Consider the following passages from *Word and Object*:

> It is rather when we turn back into the midst of an actually present theory, at least hypothetically accepted, that we can and do speak sensibly of this and that sentence as true. (Quine 1960, 25)

> Have we now so far lowered our sights as to settle for a relativistic doctrine of truth—rating the statements of each theory as true for that theory, and brooking no higher criticism? Not so. The saving consideration is that we continue to take seriously our own particular aggregate science, our own particular world-theory or loose total fabric of quasi-theories, whatever it may be. [...] Within our own total evolving doctrine, we can judge truth as earnestly and absolutely as can be ... (ibid., 24-5)

---

conditional expresses empirical predictions: under such-and-such conditions a so-and-so phenomenon occurs. That is, for two theories to imply the same observation conditionals is for them to be equivalent with one another with respect to empirical predictions. This is how Quine defines the notion of 'empirical equivalency'. (Quine later replaced the notion of observation conditionals with that of 'observation categoricals' in discussing empirical equivalency [Quine 1992, 9-12]. The antecedents and consequents of observation categoricals are mere observation sentences rather than pegged observation sentences. This development is not relevant to the discussion of the current chapter.)

[44] Over the years Quine had tweaked the formulation of the underdetermination of theory. The conditions for an alternative theory were ultimately characterized as follows (Quine 1975; Quine 1992, 97):
1. An alternative theory is empirically equivalent to the original theory.
2. We do not know how to reinterpret the predicates to make the alternative and original theories logically equivalent.
3. The thesis of underdetermination applies only to theories that imply an infinite number of observation conditionals and that cannot be expressed simply by means of universal quantification.

What is important here is that there is no requirement that the theories be logically incompatible with one another. The evolution of Quine's formulation of the underdetermination thesis is not directly relevant to the current discussion, so I will proceed by following the 1970 formulation of the thesis.

While acknowledging that the truth values of statements (such as 'electrons are particles with such-and-such mass') are determined internally within a particular theory, Quine regards truth as something we can treat 'earnestly and absolutely' within a theory we actually hold true, even if there are multiple theories that are perfectly compatible with observable data. (Quine's attitude here is that of belief system immanentists discussed in chapter 1.)[45] Now, let us observe if a parallel conclusion can be drawn with respect to the notion of synonymy. Consider the synonymy claim that the English sentence 'iron is harder than stone' is synonymous with the Japanese sentence 'tetsu-wa ishi-yori katai'. If there is a perfect parallelism between the underdetermination of theory and the indeterminacy of translation, then Quine would—while acknowledging that the correctness of the claim depends on a particular translation manual—regard synonymy as something we can treat 'earnestly and absolutely' within the translation manual we actually adopt, even if there are multiple possible manuals. It would follow that synonymy relations could be determined relative to translation manuals, and it would be possible to state the identity conditions for the notion of sentence meanings (or propositions). Chomsky clearly describes this consequence in the following comments revisiting the debates with Quine:

> ... when Quine asserts that there is no fact of the matter, no question of right choice, he is once again merely reiterating an unargued claim which does not become more persuasive on repetition. If the underdetermination of physical theory by evidence does not lead us to abandon the "realistic point of view" with regard to physical theory, then the comparable underdetermination of grammatical theory by evidence does not support Quine's claim that there is no fact of the matter in this domain to be right or wrong about ... (Chomsky 1975, 183)

> First, let me clear up a misunderstanding. Putnam believes, as Quine does too, that I regard the indeterminacy thesis as false; on the contrary, I regard it as true and uninteresting. [...] What is really at stake is only what Donald Hockney has called "the bifurcation thesis," that is, the thesis that theories of meaning, language and much of psychology are faced with a problem of indeterminacy that is qualitatively different in some way from the underdetermination of theory by evidence in the natural sciences. (Chomsky 1980, 15-6)

---

[45] The following is Gibson's clear exposition of the problem of how to retain the notion of 'internal truth' given the indeterminacy of theory.
> ... given all the (possible) evidence, *this* ontology [scientific theory] is warranted, *that* ontology is warranted, and so on. However, it makes no sense to say they are equally true, because we are *not* speaking from within the same theory of objects (i.e., ontology). The trouble isn't with 'equally', it is with 'true'. Such an extra-theoretical, or transcendental, usage is without meaning, for truth is an immanent notion—à la Tarski. In order for such a transcendental usage to be meaningful, there would have to be, presumably, a first philosophy, but there isn't, according to Quine. And since there is no such cosmic vantage point from which we could survey all competing equally warranted ontologies, we are destined to occupy the position of some historical theory of what there is, which settles for us, at that time, the facts of the matter, what there is. (Gibson 1986, 152)

To sum up, the thesis of the indeterminacy of translation—that more than one manual of translation is compatible with all evidence—alone does not entail the conclusion that the notion of propositions as sentence meanings is untenable. It is further required to deny a complete parallelism between scientific theories and translation manuals, rejecting the approach that tries to figure out synonymy relations absolutely within the manual we actually adopt.[46] (Following Quine's terminology in discussing the implications of the underdetermination thesis, let us call this line of approach the 'sectarian' approach.)[47]

(3) Reasons for the disparity between translational synonymy and theoretical physics

As has been already observed, there is a clear parallelism between the underdetermination of theory and the indeterminacy of translation. Then, why does Quine believe that there is a disparity between the two: scientific truth, which is determined internally within a theory, can be viewed as something absolute, whereas translational synonymy cannot? On what grounds is the disparity based?

Quine acknowledges that there is a parallelism between translational synonymy and theoretical physics in that they cannot be determined by all possible evidence, and in that to answer questions concerning something unobservable both linguists and physicists rely on their own particular systems (manuals of translation and theories, respectively).[48] According to Quine, however, the parallelism eventually breaks down:

> Where then does the parallel fail? Essentially in this: theory in physics is an ultimate parameter. There is no legitimate first philosophy, higher or firmer than physics, to which to appeal over physicists' heads. [...] So we go on reasoning and affirming as best we can within our ever under-determined and evolving theory of nature, the best one that we can muster at any one time (Quine 1969c, 302-3)

> ... the indeterminacy of translation is not just inherited as a special case of the underdetermination of our theory of nature. It is parallel but additional. Thus,

---

[46] It appears that Quine was aware of this point when writing *Word and Object*. See (Quine 1960, 75-6).
[47] See (Quine 1992, section 42).
[48] Here are Quine's remarks on the similarities:
> In respect of being under-determined by all possible data, translational synonymy and theoretical physics are indeed alike. The totality of possible observations of nature, made and unmade, is compatible with physical theories that are incompatible with one another. Correspondingly the totality of possible observations of verbal behavior, made and unmade, is compatible with systems of analytical hypotheses of translation that are incompatible with one another. Thus far the parallel holds. If you ask a physicalist a theoretical question, well out beyond the observation sentences, his answer will be predicated on his theory and not on some unknown and incompatible theory which would have fitted all possible data just as well. Again the parallel holds: if you ask a linguist 'What did the native say?', where the native's remark was far from the category of observation sentences, the linguist's answer will be predicated on his manual of translation and not on some unknown and incompatible manual which would have fitted all possible linguistic behavior just as well. Where then does the parallel fail? (Quine 1969c, 302-3)

adopt for now my fully realistic attitude toward electrons and muons and curved space-time, thus falling in with the current theory of the world despite knowing that it is in principle methodologically under-determined. Consider, from this realistic point of view, the totality of truths of nature, known and unknown, observable and unobservable, past and future. The point about indeterminacy of translation [that there are multiple translation manuals] is that it withstands even all this truth, the whole truth about nature. This is what I mean by saying that, where indeterminacy of translation applies, there is no real question of right choice; there is no fact of the matter even to *within* the acknowledged under-determination of a theory of nature. (ibid., 303)

In these passages, where theory in physics is described as 'an ultimate parameter', Quine states that there is no fact of the matter if multiple translation manuals are possible after identifying all physical truths. In other words, for Quine, the fact of the matter is restricted to physical facts, and everything that cannot be uniquely determined within the domain of physical facts falls outside of 'factual' matters.

Evidently, the idea expressed in these passages conforms to the physicalism defined in the previous section. (Quine's definition of physicalism, examined in section 1.4.3, indeed captures this idea in terms of supervenience.) Also, to repeat an earlier point, the indeterminacy of translation—that more than one manual of translation is compatible with all evidence—alone does not entail the untenability of the notion of propositions as sentence meanings. It is further required to deny a complete parallelism between scientific theories and translation manuals, rejecting the sectarian approach that tries to figure out synonymy relations absolutely within the manual we actually adopt. Then, it follows that it is physicalism that provides the grounds for rejecting the sectarian approach.

Behavioristic assumptions in radical translation perhaps make it difficult to see this role of physicalism. It is unquestionable, however, whether physicalism serves to reject the sectarian approach. If behavioristic evidence by itself can uniquely determine translation, then an actually produced manual of translation would contain synonymy relations that are factual to the standards of physicalists, insofar as the behavioristic evidence is acceptable from a physicalist viewpoint. If behavioristic evidence *cannot* uniquely determine translation—and, further, no other kind of physicalistically acceptable evidence helps doing this—then synonymy relations, asserted internally based on a particular translation manual, could not be viewed as factual. From a physicalist point of view, physics determines what facts there are, and all manuals of translations—indeterminate and incompatible with one another— are on a par in terms of this notion of 'facts'. There is no remaining fact that linguists could use to choose one manual over others, and as a matter of course nothing could be a 'fact beyond physical facts'. Behaviorism about evidence plays a crucial role in deriving the indeterminacy of translation, but it is physicalism, as an ontological view restricting the scope of facts, that serves to reject the sectarian approach to overcoming the indeterminacy of translation.

Quine had continued to appeal to physicalism, as an ontological view, to bridge an inferential gap from the indeterminacy of translation to the elimination of meaning.

For example, the following two paragraphs, written in the 1980s, clearly indicate that Quine rejects the sectarian approach on the basis of physicalist naturalism:

> I have argued that two conflicting manuals of translation can both do justice to all dispositions to behavior, and that, in such a case, there is no fact of the matter of which manual is right. The intended notion of matter of fact is not transcendental or yet epistemological, not even a question of evidence; it is ontological, a question of reality, and to be taken naturalistically within our scientific theory of the world. (Quine 1981, 23)

> Then when I say there is no fact of the matter, as regards, say, the two rival manuals of translation, what I mean is that both manuals are compatible with all the same distributions of states and relations over elementary particles. In a word, they are physically equivalent. (ibid.)

In the second quote, stating that there is 'no fact of the matter' with respect to two competing manuals of translation, Quine uses physicalism to dismiss the sectarian approach, according to which a synonymy relation is regarded as something absolute by taking a perspective internal to the manual we actually adopt. The first quote discusses the background to this claim, the naturalist constraint on the notion of facts. This clearly shows that the reason for the disparity between the underdetermination of theory and indeterminacy of translation lies in Quine's physicalist naturalism: synonymy relations, determined internally relative to manuals of translation, cannot be regarded as being absolute.

Here is a summary of the relation between the indeterminacy of translation and physicalism. First, restricting the data available to radical translators to behavioristic data, 'native utterances and their concurrent observable circumstances', Quine proposes the thesis of the indeterminacy of translation, which maintains that behavioristic data cannot uniquely determine translation. The thesis purports to prove the untenability of the notion of propositions as sentence meanings, but to do so in fact requires not only the indeterminacy of translation but also a rejection of the sectarian approach that tries to regard synonymy relations as being absolute from a perspective internal to the manual of translation we may actually adopt. This is where Quine introduces physicalism,[49] according to which the fact of matters or

---

[49] Eve Gaudet (2006) claims that physicalism must be excluded from considerations of indeterminacy, since physicalism plays no role in explaining why behaviorism entails the indeterminacy thesis and also why the indeterminacy thesis is 'additional' to the underdetermination of theory. This account, however, seems unsatisfactory because it overlooks an important goal of rejecting the notion of propositions as sentence meanings (based on the lack of identity conditions), and the indeterminacy thesis alone is insufficient for doing so. From the perspective of this book, stating that the indeterminacy of translation is additional to—and occurs independently of—the underdetermination thesis, Gaudet's account addresses only a part of the problem that the indeterminacy thesis faces. Unless Quine rejects the sectarian approach to the problem, on which synonymy relations are regarded as being absolute after selecting a particular manual among the candidates, the elimination of meaning would not follow from indeterminacy. To deduce the elimination of meaning the notion of 'facts about linguistic meaning' must be ontologically constrained, in addition to the indeterminacy

'factuality' consists exclusively of what is determinable by physical truths. The indeterminacy of translation thesis remains intact even when considered with a narrower physicalist notion of facts. Given these physicalist considerations, it is straightforward to understand Quine's view that there is 'no fact of the matter' in choosing among manuals of translations compatible with utterance dispositions.[50] That is, if all the aggregate of physical facts cannot uniquely determine a translation manual, no single manual can be described as the correct manual containing facts about synonymy, and this is what Quine means by saying that 'there is no fact of the matter'.

2.3.2 The indeterminacy of interpretation and physicalism

(1) Radical interpretation and the indeterminacy of interpretation

Donald Davidson accepted Quine's thesis of the indeterminacy of translation and transformed it into a further claim by situating it within the context of his own work; Davidson's thesis of 'the indeterminacy of interpretation' asserts that propositional attitudes are also indeterminate by examining the correlation between belief and meaning. In what follows, I will discuss the relation between the indeterminacy of interpretation and physicalism.

Davidson depicts a situation of 'radical interpretation'—analogous to Quine's thought experiment of radical translation—in which one attempts to interpret an unknown language with only the evidence of the speaker's verbal behavior and the surrounding circumstances (just as the case of radical translation).[51] After all, "behavioral grounds are all we have for determining what speakers mean" (Davidson 2001, 215).

There are several differences between radical translation and radical interpretation. For one thing, radical translation aims at elucidating the relation between two languages, whereas radical interpretation aims at understanding the target language (presupposing an understanding of the interpreter's own language). (See, for example, [Davidson 1984, 127-30] for this difference.) Another major difference is the role of what is known as 'the principle of charity'. Strictly speaking, the principle of charity is described as a combination of 'the Principle of Correspondence' and 'the Principle of Coherence', where the former "prompts the interpreter to take the speaker to be

---

thesis. Behaviorism, which is an epistemological thesis, cannot provide an ontological constraint, and so a physicalist ontology is necessary for restricting what falls under the notion of facts.

[50] Conversely, if physicalism is rejected, then it would be possible to retain meaning while accepting the indeterminacy of translation. Recall the internalist—'sectarian'—approach to the notion of truth assuming the underdetermination of theory: "Within our own total evolving doctrine, we can judge truth as earnestly and absolutely as can be" (Quine 1960, 25). If physicalism is rejected—not all facts are physical—then this sectarian approach would also apply to the indeterminacy of translation and the notion of meaning: facts about meaning can be judged absolutely within the translation manual or interpretation theory we actually hold. See (Rorty 1972) for this argument. Also, the main topic of chapter 4 is the rejection of physicalism, as a possible solution to the problem the indeterminacy of translation poses.

[51] According to Davidson, the most important insight of radical interpretation is that meanings and beliefs cannot be known independently of one another, and that the only clues to what we mean and believe are the events that caused them. See (Davidson 2001, 150).

responding to the same features of the world that he (the interpreter) would be responding to under similar circumstances" (Davidson 2001, 211), and the latter "prompts the interpreter to discover a degree of logical consistency in the thought of the speaker" (ibid.). Here, Kunihiko Kiyozuka's simpler characterization of the principle of charity would suffice, stating it to be "the principle that the interpreter should prefer an interpretation that makes the belief of the interpretee almost completely overlap with the belief of the interpreter" (Kiyozuka, 2007, 356). The principle of charity plays a limited role in Quine's radical translation, in connection with the translation of truth-functional logical connectives (negation, disjunction, conjunction, etc.).[52] For Davidson, on the other hand, the principle of charity is essential to radical interpretation. To understand this contrast it is necessary to examine the interdependence between belief and meaning. Consider the following remarks from Davidson:

> The interpreter's problem is that what he is assumed to know—the causes of assents to sentences of a speaker—is, as we have seen, the product of two things he is assumed not to know, meaning and belief. If he knew the meanings he would know the beliefs, and if he knew the beliefs expressed by sentences assented to, he would know the meanings. But how can he learn both at once, since each depends on the other? (Davidson 2001, 148)

Suppose, for example, that what is uttered is 'there is a dog'. Here there would be a number of possible interpretive pairs of belief and meaning that explain this utterance. Let me illustrate two such pairs. On one interpretation, the person believes that there is a dog in front of her (or in a relevant location), and the utterance means that there is a dog. On the other interpretation, the person believes that there is a fox in front of her (or in a relevant location)—wrongly so from the perspective of the interpreter—and the utterance means that there is a fox. The language of the speaker, however, may be peculiar in that the word 'dog' is always used to talk about a fox. What is crucial here is that the data available to the radical interpreter, verbal behavior and surrounding circumstances, cannot determine which interpretation is correct—both fit the data. The problem Davidson identifies in the quote is now apparent. Beliefs and meanings only manifest themselves by being knitted together, and hence verbal behavior and surrounding circumstances, evidence available to the radical interpreter, are essentially insufficient in attempting to determine the meaning of an utterance and the belief content.

---

[52] See (Quine 1960, section 13). The following issue probably contributes to this contrast between radical translation and radical interpretation with respect to the scope and significance of the principle of charity. Translators only aim at figuring out correspondence relations between sentences of two different languages, not at understanding the meaning of the target language. However, it is the understanding of meaning that interpreters set as their goal, and to understand meaning it is necessary to understand belief, as will be clear from the interdependence of belief and meaning, to be discussed below. The interdependence between belief and meaning poses a serious problem for interpreting others solely on the basis of limited data, linguistic behavior and surrounding circumstances. This problem highlights the methodological importance of the principle of charity.

Then, how could radical interpretation be possible? Davidson discusses how to undertake radical interpretation as follows:

> This method is intended to solve the problem of the interdependence of belief and meaning by holding belief constant as far as possible while solving for meaning. This is accomplished by assigning truth conditions to alien sentences that make native speakers right when plausibly possible, according, of course, to our own view of *what is right*. (Davidson 1984, 136, italics added)

To restate 'this method' here, the interpreter works under the assumption that the interpretee believes most of what the interpreter believes. This assumption is nothing but the principle of charity, which instructs the interpreter "to read some of his [the interpreter's] own standards of truth into the pattern of sentences held true by the speaker" (Davidson 2001, 148). The role that this principle plays in radical interpretation is that it "helps solve the problem of the interaction of meaning and belief by restraining the degrees of freedom allowed belief while determining how to interpret words" (ibid., 148-9).[53]

A consequence of applying the principle of charity to the situation of radical interpretation is a reduction of the degree of indeterminacy putatively generated from the process of interpretation. The reduction, however, does not reach all the way to uniquely determining a theory of interpretation by completely resolving the indeterminacy. In fact, Davidson writes:

> If interpretation is approached in the style I have been discussing, it is not likely that only one theory will be found satisfactory. The resulting indeterminacy of interpretation is the semantic counterpart of Quine's indeterminacy of translation. (Davidson 2001, 153)

What concrete examples can be provided to illuminate the indeterminacy of interpretation? It is in fact difficult to find cases of indeterminacy, but the following quote illustrates the grounds of Davidson's view that the principle of charity does not necessarily uniquely determine interpretation:

> I find that I very often disagree with other people over whether to call the color of some object green or blue. The disagreement is consistent: there is a fairly definite range of cases where I say green and they say blue. We can account for this difference in two ways: it may be that I (or most other people) are wrong

---

[53] Here I have focused on the methodological aspect of the principle of charity, but it also has another important role to play: it is a requirement for a phenomenon to count as either a linguistic or mental phenomenon. Simon Evnine (1991, section 6.6) clearly articulates this point, particularly, in the following part:
> Davidson, however, regards the Principle as being constitutive of the concepts it governs. The concepts of belief, desire, meaning and intentional action are defined by what the 'theory', the Principle of charity, says about them. (Evnine 1991, 113)

For the status of the principle of charity, also see (Davidson 1984, 137; 197) and (Kiyozuka 2007, 357-8).

about the color of certain objects, or it may be that I don't use the words 'blue' and 'green' in quite the way others do. There may be no way to decide between these two accounts; by making compensatory adjustments elsewhere in one's interpretation of my sentences and beliefs one can accommodate either story. But on one account certain of my pronouncements about colors are false, while on the other they are true. (ibid., 80-1)

In this example it is possible to construct a theory of interpretation attributing a false belief to the interpretee, 'I', by construing the interpretee's utterance of, say, 'this is blue' in the ordinary sense (from a viewpoint of other people). At the same time, the scenario is compatible with another theory of interpretation that attributes a true belief to the interpretee by construing the utterance in an extraordinary sense. Notice that, even if the first theory of interpretation is adopted—thereby taking the interpretee's beliefs about colors to be false—the majority of other beliefs can be held true, and so it conforms to the principle of charity.[54] Therefore, Davidson's discussion here indicates that the principle of charity does not necessarily eliminate the indeterminacy of interpretation.

(2) From the indeterminacy of interpretation to the elimination of propositional attitudes

The elimination of propositional attitudes is entailed by the indeterminacy of interpretation (via the interdependence of belief and meaning). Let me first quote at length Davidson's discussion of this consequence.

Take, for example, the interdependence of belief and meaning. What a sentence means depends partly on the external circumstances that cause it to win some degree of conviction; and partly on the relations, grammatical or logical, that the sentence has to other sentences held true with varying degrees of conviction. Since these relations are themselves translated directly into beliefs, it is easy to see how meaning depends on belief. Belief, however, depends equally on meaning, for the only access to the fine structure and individuation of beliefs is through the sentences speakers and interpreters of speakers use to express and describe beliefs. If we want to illuminate the nature of meaning and belief, therefore, we need to start with something that assumes neither. Quine's suggestion, which I

---

[54] It is clear that, at least, Davidson regards this color example as an instance of indeterminacy that remains after the application of the principle of charity. After discussing a reduction of the degree of indeterminacy due to the principle of charity, Davidson states, "There remain two important kinds of indeterminacy on which we [Quine and Davidson] agree" (Davidson 2001, 78), and this color example is one of them.

Although Davidson' principle of charity requires that the belief of the interpretee mostly overlap with the belief of the interpreter, he is not forthcoming about to what degree they can diverge without violating the principle. Davidson probably considers the color example not to violate the principle, in which some of the interpretee's utterances are false. Of course, Davidson does not necessarily have the final word on the degree to which the interpretee and interpreter can diverge in following the principle of charity, but his views on this issue must be accurately evaluated first (he is at any rate a major proponent of the principle).

shall essentially follow, is to take *prompted assent* as basic, the causal relation between assenting to a sentence and the cause of such assent. This is a fair place to start the project of identifying beliefs and meanings, since a speaker's assent to a sentence depends both on what he means by the sentence and on what he believes about the world. Yet it is possible to know that a speaker assents to a sentence without knowing either what the sentence, as spoken by him, means, or what belief is expressed by it. Equally obvious is the fact that once an interpretation has been given for a sentence assented to, a belief has been attributed. If correct theories of interpretation are not unique (do not lead to uniquely correct interpretations), the same will go for attributions of belief, of course, as tied to acquiescence in particular sentences. (Davidson 2001, 147, italics in original)

Notice that the reasoning from the situation of radical interpretation to the indeterminacy of propositional attitudes is structurally very similar to that from radical translation to the indeterminacy of translation (relations of synonymy). In the case of radical interpretation indeterminacy remains sustained, though to a smaller degree due to the principle of charity, with the result that limited evidence of verbal behavior and surrounding circumstances are unable to uniquely determine either translations or propositional attitudes attributed to speakers. It follows that, if the elimination of meaning is entailed by the indeterminacy of translation plus physicalism (as discussed in the previous section), then by the same reasoning, the elimination of propositional attitudes is also entailed by the indeterminacy of interpretation plus physicalism. Let us scrutinize this line of reasoning step by step.

First, consider the thesis of the indeterminacy of interpretation, which entails, together with the interdependency of belief and meaning, the possibility of attributing different sets of propositional attitudes to an individual. It is, however, unjustifiable to conclude from this indeterminacy alone the elimination of propositional attitudes. For, even if there is more than one theory of interpretation, a 'sectarian' approach to the indeterminacy is still available: it is possible to regard the meanings of utterances and the propositional attitudes of the interpretee as being absolute within the theory of interpretation we actually employ. At this point, introducing physicalism makes a crucial difference. According to physicalism, all facts are physical facts, and anything that is not uniquely determined by physical facts would be excluded from the set of all facts. With this restricted domain of factuality, it is unjustifiable to assert that there is exactly one correct theory of interpretation that describes facts about propositional attitudes to be attributed to the interpretee, since all possible theories of interpretation —incompatible with one another—are on a par in their compatibility with physicalistically acceptable facts, and there are no more facts that could help to choose one theory over others; there is no such thing as even one further fact obtaining beyond the scope of the physical facts. To borrow Quine's phrase, under physicalism, there is 'no fact of the matter' in the choice among theories of interpretation.

Anyone who accepts this realism about propositional attitudes faces a serious challenge from the fact that there is more than one set of propositional attitudes that can be attributed to an individual. That is, putting aside extraneous details, a theory of interpretation, A, attributes a propositional attitude a to an individual, whereas another theory of interpretation, B, attributes attitude β (distinct from a) to the same individual, where the theories of interpretation A and B are assumed to be perfectly compatible with the physical facts, and so neither is 'the correct theory' from a physicalist point of view. Consequently, it is not justifiable to maintain (under physicalism) that an individual has a unique set of propositional attitudes, since propositional attitudes to be attributed to individuals have no identity conditions for their contents within the domain of facts that are acceptable within physicalism. In this way, the elimination of propositional attitudes is entailed by accepting the indeterminacy of interpretation together with physicalism.

I have so far detailed the reasoning from the indeterminacy of interpretation to the elimination of propositional attitudes.[55] To conclude this part, it is worth pointing out that this argument for the elimination of propositional attitudes should not be attributed to Davidson. In contrast to Quine, who argues for the elimination of meaning from the indeterminacy of translation, Davidson states, "I see no way around indeterminism, but think it leaves the reality of the mental untouched" (Davidson 2001, 73). In other words, Davidson *somehow* rejects the reasoning starting from indeterminacy to eliminativism about propositional attitudes.

Before examining Davidson's defense of propositional attitudes, it must be noted that there is no need to include a discussion of Davidson's 'anomalous monism' and the 'token identity theory', which he has presented in connection with mental causation. The present topic, the indeterminacy of interpretation, has been developed in the context of radical interpretation, through which 'interpretivism' about propositional attitudes is proposed. On the other hand, the argument for anomalous monism and the token identity theory has been developed in the debates over mental causation, which goes roughly as follows: there are causal relations between mental and physical states, but causal relations only hold following strict laws of physics; therefore, mental states are at least token-identical with physical states. In short, the context of anomalous monism and the token identity theory is different from that of interpretivism—the latter interpretivism is concerned with problems such as 'How to dissolve the indeterminacy of interpretation?' At least for the moment the two contexts must be kept clearly distinct and not mixed up with one another. Moreover, it is also possible to question whether Davidson's views on these two topics are coherent. For example, Davidson takes an interpretivist approach to propositional attitudes in the context of the indeterminacy of translation, while at the same time adopting a functionalist approach to mental states in discussing token identity—the approach that attempts to understand propositional attitudes and other mental states in terms of causal relations. It is unclear whether these two approaches can be considered compatible.[56] Therefore, it is justifiable to regard Davidson's discussion of indeterminacy as independent from that of token identity; the contexts and also

---

[55] An argument for the same conclusion can be reconstructed starting with the indeterminacy of translation. For the tension between the indeterminacy of translation and the acceptance of intentional vocabulary, see (Hamano 1990).

[56] Evnine (1991) also points out, though from a different perspective that there is a tension between Davidson's interpretivism and his views on causation and explanation.

Davidson's approaches to propositional attitudes—although propositional attitudes feature in both discussions—are different from one another.

Accordingly, let us exclusively focus on Davidson's discussion of indeterminacy of interpretation, where the interpretivist approach is adopted. As noted earlier, Davidson endorses the reality of the mental while at the same time accepting indeterminacy. In a late article, "Indeterminism and Antirealism" (1997, collected in [Davidson 2001]), Davidson primarily addresses this possible conflict but fails to clearly argue for the compatibility of the indeterminacy of interpretation and realism about propositional attitudes. First, Davidson distinguishes two questions concerning the reality of propositional attitudes: 'Are attitudes entities?' and 'Does a person have a certain attitude?' (The former corresponds to the level of entities, and the latter the level of truths or facts; the distinction was taken up in section 2.1 when the basic perspective for ontological discussion was introduced.) Davidson focuses on the latter question of whether a person has a certain attitude, characterizing the question as asking "whether there are objective grounds for choosing among conflicting hypotheses" (Davidson 2001, 82), not concerned with "vagueness or borderline cases" (ibid.), where 'conflicting hypotheses' of course stand for competing theories of interpretation. The answer to this question that Davidson offers does not directly resolve indeterminacy by presenting objective grounds for a choice; his approach to the problem is expressed in the following: "Are there objective grounds for choosing among conflicting hypotheses? Especially in this case we have to ask what makes grounds 'objective'. The ultimate source (not ground) of objectivity is, in my opinion, intersubjectivity" (ibid., 82-3). Based on this approach, Davidson concludes, "if our judgements of the propositional attitudes of others are not objective, no judgements are, and the concept of objectivity has no application" (ibid., 84). Davidson's answer to the question of whether a person has a certain propositional attitude can be stated as follows. Since our judgments of the propositional attitudes of others constitute the 'ultimate source' of objectivity, there are no further objective grounds for determining the correctness of our judgments, nor are there 'objective grounds for choosing among conflicting hypotheses'. However, the fact that there are no objective grounds other than the judgments we make in fact guarantees the existence of propositional attitudes.

It is unclear how exactly this answer establishes the compatibility between the indeterminacy of interpretation and realism about propositional attitudes. One way to understand Davidson's approach would be the following: there is certainly more than one theory of interpretation that is compatible with evidence, but the theory of interpretation we actually adopt shapes the concept of objectivity; therefore, our attitudinal attributions growing from the adopted interpretation must be viewed as being 'objective'. On this construal, Davidson's approach is very nearly equivalent to the 'sectarian' approach to indeterminacy discussed earlier. Since a sectarian solution to indeterminacy is incompatible with physicalism, it would be justified to describe Davidson here as expressing an abandonment of physicalism.

Davidson also presents a distinct argument for the compatibility of the indeterminacy thesis and realism about propositional attitudes. This argument begins with the idea that the indeterminacy of translation and interpretation is analogous to the multiplicity of units for measuring temperature; theories of interpretation only appear to conflict with one another, and the apparent conflict does not threaten the existence of propositional attitudes. (This approach seems considerably different from the sectarian approach mentioned above.) Davidson first states that the ratios between measured temperatures remain invariant—whether the Centigrade or Fahrenheit scale is used—and with respect to temperature measurement invariant ratios are "facts of the matter" (Davidson 1998, 316). Analogously, in spite of multiple possible theories of interpretation, "facts are the empirical relations between a speaker, her sentences, and her environment. This pattern is invariant" (Davidson 1998, 317).

However, if this outline accurately describes Davidson's argument for realism about propositional attitudes, then it appears to be essentially insufficient. What Davidson describes as 'invariant facts of the matter'—'empirical relations between a speaker, her sentences, and her environment'—are nothing but the data on which theories of interpretation are based, and they cannot be equated with propositional attitudes that have particular contents. Even if this pattern of empirical relations is factual, the problem of indeterminacy is that there is more than one theory of interpretation that is compatible with the pattern, and this indeterminacy questions the status or reality of propositional attitudes. It is true that, in the case of temperature measurements, the indeterminacy of units would not pose a problem because we are interested not in the units themselves but in the ratios they express. In the case of propositional attitudes, however, indeterminacy raises real problems because our interests lie in what contents of propositional attitudes are attributed to individuals, not in 'invariances' that lurk behind indeterminate interpretations.[57] Therefore, I need to

---

[57] Nobuharu Tanji also questions Davidson's analogy here probably on the same grounds. Davidson fails to recognize the importance of the indeterminacy of translation by assimilating it to the indeterminacy of the units of temperature measurement, such as Centigrade and Fahrenheit. Commenting on this failure, Tanji writes:
> If anything is added at all, I would have to state that I cannot completely agree with Davidson's passage here. One reason is that how Democritus's claim is treated changes depending on whether 'translation 1' or 'translation 2' is used, even though how an object is treated would not change whether the temperature of the object is measured in Centigrade or Fahrenheit. The other reason is that in translation we inevitably need what is indeterminate (either 'translation 1' or 'translation 2') (Tanji 1997, 182).

Moreover, in fact, it is possible to recognize in Davidson's writings the idea (proposed in the discussion above) that in the case of interpretation our interests lie not in invariances but in propositional attitudes that are attributed to individuals in an indeterminate way. One example is the article "Three Varieties of Knowledge" (1991, collected in [Davidson 2001]), where Davidson develops an account of why normative mental concepts are irreducible to physical concepts (Davidson 2001, 215-7). In this article Davidson argues for the irreducibility stating that physical concepts can be supplemented or replaced with new, more refined concepts based on strict laws (replacement would not change the subject matter), whereas psychological concepts cannot be supplemented or replaced with such new concepts. The reason for the impossibility of replacing or supplementing psychological concepts with new concepts is that there is "some particular explanatory interest" (ibid., 216) in introducing a mental concept. In other words, physics aims at strict laws or laws that are as complete and accurate as possible, whereas folk psychology aims at explaining reasons for actions and belief changes; their goals are different, and therefore, the former cannot replace the latter.

What is crucial here is that to achieve the goal of explaining reasons for actions and belief changes it is necessary not merely to identify and predict behavioral patterns but also to provide more fine-

conclude here that Davidson's defense of realism about propositional attitudes, which appeals to the analogy of the multiple units of temperature measurement, is unsatisfactory, at least to the extent that propositional attitudes are regarded as having a uniquely determined content.

As the discussion so far has laid out, Davidson clearly *somehow* rejects the inference from the indeterminacy of interpretation to the elimination of propositional attitudes, but it is hard to identify on what grounds the rejection is based. (In particular, what is significantly relevant to the discussion of the current chapter is whether the rejection of physicalism provides reason for the compatibility of the indeterminacy thesis and realism about propositional attitudes. However, no clear answer is given to this question.[58]) In any case, no matter how the issues in Davdison's obscure discussion of realism about propositional attitudes are resolved, there is no reason currently in sight to reject the above argument for the elimination of propositional attitudes (the elimination of propositional attitudes is entailed by the indeterminacy thesis together with physicalism and the rejection of the sectarian approach to indeterminacy), and so there is no reason to revise this argument. Therefore, in this chapter, I will proceed retaining the basic picture that the elimination of propositional attitudes is entailed by the indeterminacy of interpretation plus physicalism, even though Davidson explicitly endorses the existence of propositional attitudes.

2.3.3 Implications of the indeterminacy theses for physicalism

Sections 2.3.1 and 2.3.2 have examined the relations between the two indeterminacy theses and physicalism, concluding that to derive eliminativism about meaning or propositional attitudes it is necessary to reject the sectarian approach to indeterminacy by adopting physicalism. This conclusion can be schematically represented as follows:

> the indeterminacy of translation + physicalism = eliminativism about meaning
> the indeterminacy of interpretation + physicalism = eliminativism about propositional attitudes[59]

---

grained psychological descriptions. Let us consider this claim within the context of the indeterminacy of interpretation. Here Davidson suggests that, in constructing and applying theories of interpretation (folk psychological practice), our interests lie, not in the invariant patterns of the utterances, behaviors, and environments of speakers, but in propositional attitudes attributed to individuals relative to theories of interpretation (that are indeterminate). Thus, although Davidson states that "it is what is invariant that is empirically significant" (ibid., 215) either in the case of temperature measurement or interpretation, when push comes to shove, he acknowledges what is indeterminate (propositional attitude attributions) as important in interpretation. It is justifiable to conclude from these considerations that Davidson himself recognizes a mismatch between the example of temperature measurement and the construction of theories of interpretation.

[58] See (Dennett, 1991; Davidson 1997, 69-84; 1998) for the debates between Davidson and Dennett concerning the relation between the indeterminacy of interpretation and realism about propositional attitudes.

[59] Of course, eliminativism about meaning can also be derived from the indeterminacy of interpretation.

The discussion so far has focused on the question of what is required to derive the intended results from the indeterminacy theses. Now, let us reconsider the conclusion above from the perspective of the question of what significance the indeterminacy theses have for physicalists. The answer to this question, suggested by the discussion so far, is that physicalists must deny the existence of meaning and propositional attitudes as long as they accept the indeterminacy theses.

Let me reformulate this answer in accordance with the discussion of section 2.2, where physicalism is its central focus. In the current chapter, physicalism is understood as the view that any property that is used to describe facts supervenes on physical properties. Conversely, this view implies, no property that does not supervene on physical properties can be used to describe facts. According to the indeterminacy theses, however, properties concerning meaning or propositional attitudes do not supervene on physical properties (recall Quine's statement that two conflicting manuals of translation are "compatible with all the same distributions of states and relations over elementary particles" [Quine 1981, 23]). It then follows that, from a physicalist point of view, the domain of facts rules out circumstances that are described using properties concerning meaning or propositional attitudes, such as that sentence a is synonymous with sentence b, and that Smith wants to drink water.

In this way, the indeterminacy theses require physicalists to deny the factuality of statements concerning meaning or propositional attitudes. What drawbacks can this result cause for physicalists? A discernible problem is that it deprives various types of discourse of factuality. For example, linguistics, history, ethics, psychology, and the like frequently refer to concepts concerning meaning or propositional attitudes, and so discourses in these fields cannot be regarded as being factual, at least in their current forms.[60]

There is also a tension between physicalist naturalism and normative epistemological naturalism, a real problem that some naturalists should not disregard.[61] As observed in section 1.3.1, many theorists trying to develop normative epistemology from a physicalist viewpoint attempt to understand epistemological normativity in terms of 'purposive rationality', describing it as 'if one's goal is P, then she ought to take the means M'.[62] If it is denied that statements about propositional attitudes are factual, then this strategy to understanding epistemological normativity would have to be insufficient. For, granting that the notion of 'purpose' or 'goal', which plays a crucial role in this approach, belongs to the category of propositional attitudes (at least at the primary level of individuals[63]), goals cannot be introduced as properties

---

[60] See (Tanji 1997, 176-7) for this point. Tanji's discussion, however, includes no explicit reference to the role that physicalism plays.
[61] Naturalists who should not overlook this tension—to be described below—are those endorsing both the project of normative epistemology and physicalism (for example, Quine and Kazuhisa Todayama are such naturalists).
[62] Quine (1986a) proposed this position, which has been further developed in works such as (Todayama 2005).
[63] Todayama, for example, has proposed a project to construct a hierarchy of goal-means relations that describe what is valued in science, and 'the ultimate value or goal' sits at the pinnacle of this hierarchy (Todayama 2005, 83-4). For naturalists, however, it is beyond doubt unacceptable to identify

acceptable for physicalists with no further support.

It must be realized here that this tension between physicalism and epistemological normativity understood as purposive rationality cannot be resolved by redefining 'having such-and-such goal' in terms of causal dispositions. Certainly, if 'having such-and-such goal' can be redefined as an instance of some kind of causal disposition, goals would be situated within the physicalist worldview, and a recognized tension between normative naturalism in general and physicalism would be resolved. However, as long as epistemological normativity is understood as purposive rationality, this redefinition would be faced with a problem, and below I will elaborate on why this is the case.

First, consider hypothetical normative statements of the form 'if one has goal P, then the person should take the means M', which are essential to normative naturalism. Quine claims that a scientific inquiry discovers which means is the most suitable for a specific goal, attempting to naturalize epistemological normativity. If the question to be asked is about which of the available means ($M1, M2, ...$) makes it most likely to realize a particular goal (P), then it is indeed through a statistical investigation and studies of the physical mechanisms underlying the available means that an adequate answer to this question can be provided. Therefore, generally speaking, a physicalist theoretical framework can account for the relations between goals and means.

However, what aspect of hypothetical normative statements does a physicalist framework illuminate? A hypothetical normative statement arguably consists of three constituents: 'having goal P', 'P is related to the means M', and 'M must be adopted'. If this analysis is on the right track, then the discussion in the previous paragraph elucidates the second constituent, namely, the relation in which P is more likely to be achieved (or more completely achieved) on the condition that M is used. It is, however, not justified to deduce a normative claim, 'one ought to do ...', exclusively from factual relations that describe likelihoods and dispositions. That is, the relations between goals and means alone are insufficient for establishing hypothetical normative statements, on which normative naturalism can be based. Rather, it is reasonable to suppose that normativity figuring in the third constituent, 'M should be taken', originates in the first constituent, 'having goal P'.[64] To summarize, the state of 'having goal P' produces a normative 'force', while (scientific) inquiry identifies the likelihood of different means for achieving P (or the degrees to which they achieve P); these two aspects constitute epistemological normativity (and this account is a genuine instance of naturalistic epistemology).

These considerations, however, cast doubt on the strategy to redefine goals in terms of dispositions. I am not suggesting here that folk psychological

---

'the ultimate goal' through *a priori* conceptual analysis. (For example, it is not justifiable to reflect on what a living creature is in an *a priori* manner and assert that the ultimate goal of living creatures is to survive.) It is likely to follow that for naturalists to identify the structure of a hierarchy of goal-means relations it is necessary to start from describing the goals of scientists by examining their activities and utterances as data, and turn to the explanation of the ultimate goal in a bottom-up fashion. If this implication is correct, then the elimination of propositional attitudes seems to pose a serious challenge to the enterprise of normative naturalism.

[64] Hamano (2002) has already pointed to this issue.

characterizations of the concept of 'goal' (if there are any such characterizations) are immune to revision; any proposal for artificially refining the characterizations and making better use of the concept of 'goal' must be seriously considered. Yet, if we adopt the proposal to understand epistemological normativity as purposive rationality, then the redefined concept of 'goal' would have to be able to yield normativity, and the new concept of 'goal' as a mere causal disposition seems to fall short of doing so.[65]

The preceding discussion by no means demonstrates that no attempt to resolve the tension between physicalism and normative naturalism will be successful. It is, however, reasonable to draw the following lesson from it. The concept of 'goal' (or that of 'purpose') is, at least as long as it is used in an account of epistemological normativity, a normative concept in the sense that it implies that an agent who has a goal *ought to* adopt a means that is effective in achieving the goal (to the best of her knowledge). Therefore, unless the concept of 'goal' is accounted for—not losing sight of (carefully retaining) its normative aspect—in terms of facts that are acceptable for physicalists, the tension between physicalism and normative naturalism will continue to hold, and as a result, physicalists must conclude that the issues in normative epistemology are not concerned with facts.

The discussion so far has elucidated the criticism of physicalism based on the indeterminacy theses, as well as the problems—the remaining tasks—for physicalism that arise due to the criticism. In what follows, I will consider possible physicalist replies (rather briefly) that will assist in an evaluation of the legitimacy of the criticism of physicalism. But before doing so, I need to stress that this kind of criticism is not able to refute physicalism itself.

The criticism of physicalism posed by indeterminacy has the following form: physicalism cannot recognize A to be a fact, where A is something that is presumably factual. This kind of criticism will never, in principle, refute physicalism itself, since physicalists could always appeal to a remedy: to stop considering A to be a fact. For example, recall that the indeterminacy theses discussed here question the compatibility of physicalism and the factuality of statements concerning meaning and propositional attitudes. If a physicalist is (sincerely) committed to the view that no statements concerning meaning or propositional attitudes describe facts, and thereby no statements in the fields appealing to such statements describe facts, then the criticism of physicalism based on indeterminacy would pose no threat to physicalism. In other words, physicalism together with realism about meaning or that of propositional attitudes can be challenged by an appeal to indeterminacy, but physicalism in itself cannot be refuted through this kind of criticism using factuality. (This is why I pointed out, at the beginning of this section, that the discussion of indeterminacy does not present a 'knock-down' argument against physicalism.)

Keeping this in mind in what follows, let us focus on physicalists who endorse the existence of meaning or propositional attitudes, evaluating their possible responses to the criticism of physicalism based on indeterminacy. A first response to be considered

---

[65] Notice that the same problem does not arise for interpretivism, according to which the constructive ideal of rationality is introduced in attributing propositional attitudes.

is to reject the theses of indeterminacy. According to Quine, the behavioral dispositions of natives and the circumstances of their utterances can constitute evidence for determining observation sentences (taken 'piecemeal'), but such behavioristic evidence is insufficient for uniquely determining a system of analytical hypotheses required to translate standing sentences and others that have a more sophisticated, complex structure. This argument by Quine seems compelling but has not been vindicated by virtue of the lack of concrete—sufficiently detailed—examples.[66] Therefore, if physicalists can show that behavioristic evidence alone uniquely determines a manual of translation or theory of interpretation, they can retain the factuality of statements concerning meaning or propositional attitudes while remaining physicalists. (However, showing that there is exactly one possible manual of translation is much more difficult than showing that there is at least one manual of translation.)

A second possible response from physicalists to the criticism of physicalism based on indeterminacy is to argue that translation or interpretation is uniquely determinable due to the development of neurophysiology, while accepting indeterminacy at the level of behavior—behavioral dispositions are indeed insufficient for a unique determination. The central idea in this response is the expansion of the scope of evidence available to translators and interpreters. By developing the theoretical device of radical translation (and also that of radical interpretation), Quine and Davidson restrict the evidence that can be available for determining meanings or propositional attitudes to the behavioral dispositions of natives and the circumstances of their utterances. This second response, on the other hand, suggests including physiological knowledge about native speakers in the available evidence for translation or interpretation. If it can be shown that physiological knowledge about speakers (or whatever is acceptable within physicalism) uniquely determines a manual of translation or theory of interpretation, then compatibility between physicalism and realism about meaning or that about propositional attitudes would be established.

Quine and Davidson, however, do not restrict the available data to the behavioristic kind for no reason. Their behaviorism is grounded in the insights into our perceptual abilities as well as in the observation that the data used in our actual language learning are comprised only of linguistic behaviors and circumstances of utterance. Thus, what physicalists need to do to avoid the criticism based on indeterminacy is not only to demonstrate that translations and interpretations are uniquely determined referring to neurophysiological knowledge (doing just so would create enormous difficulties),[67] but also explain how ordinary speakers who only employ behavioristic data become able to learn the concepts of meaning and propositional attitudes (the

---

[66] See (Quine 1992, 50-1).
[67] It must be noted here that considering propositional attitudes to be relational properties would not overcome the challenge to physicalism posed by the indeterminacy theses. As discussed in section 2.2.1, relational properties are properties that are determined depending not only on the intrinsic features of the systems to which the properties are attributed but also on the relations they have to other objects or systems. Since the indeterminacy theses state that evidence consisting of the behavioral dispositions of native speakers and the circumstances of their utterances does not

contents of which cannot be determined without using neurophysiological knowledge) and also to talk about meaning and propositional attitudes. Moreover, if it turns out that a translation manual determined by neurophysiological knowledge—over and above behavioristic evidence—differs from our customary manual (which is one of many manuals compatible with behavioristic evidence), then physicalists would also have to explain why our customary manual is deemed false. In any case, unless these problems are fully addressed, the criticism of physicalism based on the indeterminacy theses remains as a serious challenge, at least, for physicalists who endorse the existence of meaning and propositional attitudes.

The discussion so far has examined two responses to the criticism of physicalism based on indeterminacy that can be raised by physicalists who endorse the existence of meaning and propositional attitudes. No physicalist, however, has actually spelled out either one of the responses: the indeterminacy of translation is claimed to be false or neurophysiological knowledge is brought up to determine a unique manual of translation. For this reason, at least in this chapter, let us accept the legitimacy of the indeterminacy of translation and interpretation as well as the Quine-Davidson view that our actual understanding of meanings and propositional attitudes are based on behavioristic evidence, thereby assuming the criticism of physicalism from indeterminacy to be compelling. With this assumption—that physicalists must deny the existence of meaning and propositional attitudes—I will discuss physicalism further below.

2.3.4 What aspect of the defense of physicalism do the indeterminacy theses conflict with?

Now, the reader must be sufficiently familiar with the difficulty the indeterminacy theses pose to physicalism: meaning and propositional attitudes cannot be integrated into the physicalist worldview. Considering statements concerning meaning or propositional attitudes to describe facts, Papineau and many other physicalists have tried to incorporate such statements into the physicalist worldview through a variety

---

uniquely determine the meaning of an utterance or the propositional attitude to be attributed to a speaker, the physical properties of external objects or systems are already referred to there. Therefore, introducing the concept of 'relational properties' and employing the physical features of another system—say the external environment—would not solve this problem of indeterminacy.

Moreover, I have to point out that appealing to the goal of surviving in the effort to resolve indeterminacy would merely postpone the problem and fail to provide a genuine solution. This is because it is unclear whether the property of 'having goal A' can be determined within physicalism. Any property of a system can be claimed to be factual in the physicalist framework only if the property is ultimately determinable within physicalism, whether the property is determined by the intrinsic features of the system or accounted for as a relational property referring to the properties of external systems. Thus, unless the property of 'having goal A' in itself is a physical property, it must be shown to supervene on physical properties. Put differently, the question of what goal a system possesses has to be answered solely on the basis of physicalistically acceptable facts. Nonetheless, it seems enormously difficult to identify the goal of an organ—a brain or any physiological system—solely based on the type of evidence that is acceptable within physicalism. Also, introducing the goal of a human agent would give rise to an obvious circularity (because the goal of an agent is a clear instance of propositional attitudes).

of approaches (appealing to type-identity, token-identity, functional explanation, supervenience, and others.). The indeterminacy theses maintain that none of such approaches will be successful. In other words, the indeterminacy theses entail the conclusion that realism about meaning and propositional attitudes contradicts physicalism.

However, as has been stated repeatedly, physicalism is currently a widely accepted position and also the standard view among naturalists (some even think that it is 'evidently' correct.) This situation may lead to doubts about whether the conflict between the indeterminacy theses and physicalism really undermines physicalism; and given the plausibility of physicalism, it may be reasonable to suspect that this conflict demonstrates the falsity of the indeterminacy theses rather than anything else.

To extirpate this suspicion completely, in what follows, alluding to the logic behind physicalism discussed in section 2.2.2, I will scrutinize exactly what aspect of physicalism directly conflicts with the indeterminacy theses. The suspicion above stems from the assumption that physicalism is very convincing. I will argue that this assumption is not supported as well as it may appear.

As is clear from Quine's statement concerning indeterminacy that two conflicting manuals of translation are "compatible with all the same distributions of states and relations over elementary particles" (Quine 1981, 23), indeterminacy seems to conflict directly with physicalism, assuming that there are facts about meaning and propositional attitudes. This comes about as, in this chapter, physicalism is characterized as the view that any properties used to describe facts supervene on physical properties, and this characterization entails the thesis that two things cannot differ with respect to factual non-physical properties without differing with respect to physical properties.

Depending on the interpretation of the modality included in supervenience, this thesis about physicalism and supervenience has different implications. The standard approach to the modality of supervenience is to distinguish 'weak' and 'strong' supervenience. On the 'weak' understanding of supervenience, the above supervenience thesis states that, for any possible world, two systems do not differ with respect to factual properties in that world without differing with respect to physical properties in that world. On the 'strong' understanding of supervenience, the thesis states that two systems do not differ with respect to factual properties without differing with respect to physical properties, whether they are in the same possible world or in different possible worlds; that is, two physically identical systems are, whether in the same or different possible worlds, identical with one another with respect to their factual properties. We may then ask which understanding of the modality should be employed in characterizing physicalism, the weak or the strong as detailed here.

It is not easy to answer this question. For example, Papineau initially stated that supervenience relations that are derived based on the manifestability of the mental must be understood as strong supervenience.[68] However, recognizing the criticism by Steward (1996), Papineau later modified this position by reinterpreting the

---

[68] See (Papineau 1993, 20-1; 1995, 230).

supervenience relations of his views of physicalism as weak supervenience (Papineau 1996). This development suggests that physicalism can be defined using either one of the two types of supervenience, and that different types of supervenience lead to different formulations of physicalism.[69] The present purpose is, however, not to figure out the best formulation of physicalism, but to precisely understand the conflict between the indeterminacy theses and physicalism. For this purpose, it will be sufficient for now to consider whether the criticism of physicalism based on indeterminacy is adequate for both types of supervenience.

If there is a strong supervenience relation, then two systems that are physically identical with one another are also identical with respect to their factual properties, whether they are located in the same possible world or in different possible worlds. Suppose that strong supervenience is claimed to hold together with realism about propositional attitudes. This claim would obviously be inconsistent with the indeterminacy of interpretation. To make sure that this is the case, consider an individual X in a possible world and the counterpart X' in a different world, where X' is physically identical to X (including the surroundings of both).[70] According to the formulation of physicalism with strong supervenience, the propositional attitudes that X and X' have would not be different. However, if the thesis of the indeterminacy of interpretation is considered correct, then it would be possible to use two different theories of interpretation for interpreting X and X'. As a result, it would also be possible to attribute two different sets of propositional attitudes to X and X'. In this way, the indeterminacy of interpretation becomes inconsistent with strong supervenience.

Next, let us turn to weak supervenience, according to which two systems in the same possible world cannot differ physically without differing with respect to factual properties. At first sight it is perhaps tempting to suppose that this formulation of physicalism based on weak supervenience does not conflict with indeterminacy. For the indeterminacy of interpretation states that, for *one and the same speaker*, there is more than one theory of interpretation, and on the other hand, weak supervenience implies that, for *two different individuals* (in the same possible world), their psychological properties are identical if their physical properties are identical. However, the following considerations will illustrate how weak supervenience also conflicts with indeterminacy. Suppose that two individuals—inhabiting the same world—are physically identical with one another (down to every aspect of their surroundings).[71] Also suppose that there are two different interpreters constructing two different theories of interpretation for the two individuals. Now, weak

---

[69] See (Loewer 1995) for an example of the approach to characterizing physicalism in terms of strong supervenience.
[70] Here, I describe the scenario using Lewis's counterpart theory, but counterpart theory is not essential for sketching a circumstance that is proper to the context of the current discussion; I could also have used the Kripkean notion of 'transworld identity'.
[71] These two individuals may exist at two different times, so alternatively, the reader can imagine the scenario in which one individual is in the same physical state at two different times. This may be the proper scenario to be considered because, given the structural differences of the brains of individuals, it is probably extremely difficult to have two distinct, yet physically identical, individuals inhabiting in the same world, so that we can evaluate weak supervenience.

supervenience implies that (unless properties concerning propositional attitudes are not factual properties) the two individuals have the same propositional attitudes, whereas the indeterminacy of interpretation permits the applications of two different theories of interpretation to the individuals, thereby making it possible to attribute two different sets of propositional attitudes to them. Therefore, even if weak supervenience is adopted, indeterminacy yields a problem for physicalism.

I have so far attempted to elucidate how physicalism can be challenged by indeterminacy whether physicalism is characterized in terms of strong supervenience or weak supervenience. To understand the details of this criticism of physicalism based on indeterminacy more adequately, however, I need to go one step further in examining the nature of the conflict between indeterminacy and physicalism. As discussed in section 2.2.2, Papineau's argument for supervenience has two premises: the completeness of physics and the manifestability of factual properties. If these two premises provide the logical basis for physicalism (and if the indeterminacy theses are incompatible with physicalism), then it is reasonable to suppose that either of the two premises is under attack when physicalism is criticized on the basis of indeterminacy.[72]

One of the premises, the completeness of physics, is characterized as the idea that "all physical events are determined, or have their chances determined, by prior *physical* events according to *physical* laws" (Papineau, 1993, 16, italics in original), or that "we never need to look beyond the realm of the physical in order to identify a set of antecedents which fixes the chances of any subsequent physical occurrence" (ibid.). These characterizations of the completeness are concerned with relations among physical properties and do not directly conflict with the indeterminacy theses, which are concerned with properties of meaning and propositional attitudes. Therefore, it would be justified to assume that the criticism of physicalism based on indeterminacy does not present a sustainable attack on the completeness of physics.[73]

The other premise for physicalism, the manifestability of factual properties in general (or of the mental, for Papineau), states that "if two systems are mentally different, then there must be some physical contexts in which this difference would

---

[72] Strictly speaking, it is also possible to question the inference from the completeness of physics and the manifestability of the mental to physicalism (the validity of Papineau's argument for physicalism can be questioned). As noted in section 2.2.2, however, the inference itself seems to leave no gap (the overall argument seems valid). (As typical of analytic philosophers, Papineau must have constructed the premises in such a way that they logically entail the intended conclusion.) This is why I will not examine the validity of the argument.

[73] As the ensuing discussion will show, the criticism of physicalism based on indeterminacy in this section targets, not the completeness of physics, but the 'monopolization of facts' by physics. In my view there is enormous difficulty in criticizing physicalism by targeting the completeness of physics, since physicists always develop and modify physical theories to accommodate any discovered anomalies—phenomena the occurrences of which cannot be explained by the current theories even though the phenomena are considered to be physical facts. Put differently, physics is a discipline that is fundamentally designed to be 'complete'. Thus, claiming there to be physical facts that cannot be explained by a complete physics (if there is any such thing) creates what seems to be an oxymoron. (Phenomena that cannot be explained by a complete physical theory would simply be excluded as non-physical facts.) Therefore, unless the possibility of physics as a discipline designed to be complete is refuted for some reason, it would be difficult to criticize physicalism by targeting the completeness of physics.

display itself in differential physical consequences, or at least in differential chances for such consequences" (Papineau 1993, 17-8). If this thesis is correct and any difference in non-physical properties must yield a difference in physical properties, two systems differing from one another with respect to specific properties concerning meaning or propositional attitudes must display some difference in their physical consequences. It then follows that there are no differences in meaning or in propositional attitudes that cannot be discerned using data acceptable to physicalists. Since this result is obviously incompatible with the indeterminacy theses, the criticism of physicalism based on indeterminacy is intended to undermine this thesis about the manifestability.[74]

The discussion so far has identified that the criticism of physicalism based on indeterminacy is intended to undermine the manifestability of factual properties in general, one of the premises of the argument for physicalism. As noted in section 2.3.4, the perception that physicalism is very convincing creates the suspicion that the indeterminacy theses are in fact false because they are incompatible with physicalism. Whether this perception is actually correct depends on the plausibility of the manifestability thesis. It is, however, difficult to find sufficient arguments for the manifestability thesis.[75] Several philosophers have defended supervenience physicalism on the basis of the manifestability thesis, but none seems to have argued exhaustively and convincingly for the manifestability itself. For example, Loewer defends supervenience physicalism using the manifestability thesis, while at the same time presenting no argument for the manifestability. (What Loewer does is, noting that properties such as the spin of an electron and acidity are physically detectable, simply state that if intentional predicates express properties, those properties are plausibly detectable as well.[76]) By contrast, Papineau presents a more thorough

---

[74] To corroborate this diagnosis of the criticism of physicalism, it is reasonable to draw on Papineau's remarks, quoted below, in which the manifestability of the mental is acknowledged not to obtain if the modality in the thesis is given a 'strong' interpretation:
> In particular, it [the manifestability of the mental] won't hold good if we take some physical state which fixes some mental state in this world, and then go to another physically possible world in which that physical state fixes a different mental state. This mental difference—between the two mental states fixed in different worlds by this physical state—clearly won't show itself in any differential physical consequences. Yet these two worlds can both be physically possible, since no physical laws need vary between them, but only physical-mental bridge laws. (Papineau 1996, 688-9)

Here, Papineau notes that physical laws can be separated from physical-mental bridge laws, and also that the physical laws (plus the initial physical conditions) do not uniquely determine the physical-mental bridge laws. That is, the manifestability of the mental does not hold without fixing not only the physical laws but also the physical-mental bridge laws. (The remarks following the quote above also illustrate the same point: "the "manifestability premise" only remains plausible as long as we stick to worlds in which the physical-mental laws, as well as the physical laws, stay constant" [ibid., 689].) However, fixing the physical-mental bridge laws, a necessary condition for establishing the manifestability of the mental, directly contradicts the indeterminacy theses, since these theses imply that, even in the same world, physical properties alone cannot uniquely determine mental properties. Therefore, the diagnosis of the indeterminacy-based criticism of physicalism proposed in this book—that it is the manifestability thesis that is under attack—appears to be correct.

[75] By contrast, Witmer (1998) and others have pointed to the inadequacies of the discussion motivating the manifestability.

[76] See (Loewer 1995, 221). Note that Loewer uses the term 'physical detectability' rather than

discussion in favor of the manifestability thesis (Papineau 1993, 19-20). Yet that discussion is still rather brief (consisting of ten sentences, just one paragraph) and fails to provide a sufficient examination of the thesis. This discussion is, however, still the only explicit, if only somewhat detailed, defense of the manifestability thesis, and I will examine the validity of that discussion more closely below.

In defense of the manifestability thesis, Papineau supports the idea that "a mental difference which was not physically manifestable in any way would be radically undetectable" (ibid., 19) on the basis of the knowledge that our sense organs through which external information is taken in "work by physical interaction with the environment" (ibid., 20), and this idea is considered to entail the manifestability thesis. The main force of this argument is in the fact that the source of the information on which our cognition of the external world is based is limited to our sense organs physically interacting with the environment. That is, since the source of information about the external world is limited to physical interaction, any difference in mental properties will be detectable by tapping into the sense organs physically interacting with the environment.[77]

At first sight, this argument seems to hold, but the line of reasoning contains a critical leap (gap). Below is an outline of Papineau's line of reasoning (where mental differences are generalized into factual differences):

(ⅰ) Our sources of information are limited to the sense organs physically interacting with the environment.

(ⅱ) A difference that cannot be manifested physically in any way is undetectable by the sense organs.

Manifestability: if two systems are different in non-physical factual properties, then there must be some physical contexts in which this difference would display itself in differential physical consequences.

Now, nothing worrisome is found in the inference from (i) to (ii); certainly any difference that cannot be manifested physically would not be detectable by the sense organs that collect information only through physical properties. However, there is a logical leap in the reasoning from point (ii) to the manifestability thesis, since (ii) is compatible with the existence of factual non-physical differences that are undetectable by the sense organs—because the sense organs only detect physical differences. To bridge the gap in the reasoning, the following implicit assumption appears to be needed:

'manifestability', and on the same page, also states that he is "not offering physical detectability as a conceptually or metaphysically necessary condition for the existence of a property" (ibid.). This reservation, however, seems to make it impossible to defend Loewer's position that for mental properties to be genuine properties they must satisfy strong supervenience.

[77] As noted earlier, Papineau does not devote much space to examining the grounds for the manifestability of the mental, presenting no details of an argument for its manifestability, and so the discussion here is considerably expanded from Papineau's own discussion.

(iii) A difference that is not detectable by the sense organs — a non-physical difference — is not a factual difference.

Without this implicit assumption, which would bridge the gap between detectability and factuality, it would be unjustified to move on from point (ii), the statement about the detectability of differences by the sense organs, to the manifestability thesis, the thesis about the conditions for being a factual property.[78]

Let us take stock of the discussion so far. What has been made clear is that to support the manifestability thesis it is necessary to assume (iii) in addition to (ii). However, the constraint on the sources of information to be only those allowing acqusition by the sense organs, namely (i) — which is explicitly presented by Papineau — can only entail (ii), the statement about the detectability of differences by the sense organs; (i) does not entail (iii), the statement constraining the domain of facts. Therefore, Papineau's argument for the manifestability thesis is not fully convincing because it is formulated solely using (i) and disregarding (iii). Also, given that physicalism is based on the completeness of physics and the manifestability of factual properties, it is reasonable to conclude that physicalism is not as well grounded as it may appear without providing further discussion to bridge the gap between (ii) and the manifestability thesis.[79]

In conclusion, the current section, 2.3.4, began with the suspicion that the conflict between indeterminacy and physicalism may demonstrate the falsity of the indeterminacy theses given the apparent plausibility of physicalism, and closely examined the point of conflict between indeterminacy and physicalism, scrutinizing

---

[78] The following formulas describe the presented analysis of Papineau's argument for the manifestability thesis:

$D(x, y) =_{def}$ x and y are different in such a way that the difference is detectable by the sense organs
$E(x, y) =_{def}$ x and y are equivalent in their physical consequences in all physical contexts
$F(x, y) =_{def}$ x and y are factually different

(i) $\forall x \forall y (D(x,y) \rightarrow \neg E(x,y))$
(ii) $\forall x \forall y (E(x,y) \rightarrow \neg D(x,y))$
(Manifestability) $\forall x \forall y (F(x,y) \rightarrow \neg E(x,y))$
(iii) $\forall x \forall y (\neg D(x,y) \rightarrow \neg F(x,y))$

I owe the discussion here to Kasaki Masashi and Tora Koyama, and I wish to thank them for helping me clarify this analysis.

[79] The premises of Papineau's argument for the manifestability, (i) and (iii), essentially state that if there are factual differences, their consequences must be detectable as physical differences by the sense organs. In my view Papineau's argument can be best understood as constraining the uses of our concepts and claiming that there are no factual concepts that express more detailed information than the physical information acquirable by the sense organs (also see section 3.2.6 for this point). However, we may then ask on what grounds Papineau advances the claim that the information given to the sense organs exhausts the whole domain of facts. Rather than being grounded in any reason, this claim seems to be a mere expression of a naive form of empiricism, which is also incompatible with our actual uses of concepts. It is true that our sense organs function by physically interacting with the environment, and that our cognition always *begins with* the inputs of external information that are recognizable to us. However, working on the limited information by employing some conceptual apparatus, we have developed far more complicated ways of describing facts than the extent to which the limited information allows articulating.

the justifications for physicalism the proponents of this thesis have presented. As a result, it has been discovered that the plausibility of physicalism—on which this suspicion concerning indeterminacy is based—is not as convincing as it appears to be. This result should prompt physicalists to consider seriously a variety of objections leveled against physicalism and to conduct a reevaluation of the grounds they think they have for physicalism.

Now, I have completed the evaluation of the criticism of physicalism based on the indeterminacy theses. The discussion of this section has identified the problems for physicalism and also made it clear that they are problems the proponents of physicalism need to overcome. In the next section, with the discussion here as the background, I will start exploring ontological theoretical options that may be able to replace physicalism.

2.4 Pluralism as an Alternative to Physicalist Monism

As discussed in the previous section, the criticism of physicalism based on the indeterminacy points out a difficulty in accepting the existence of meaning and propositional attitudes; and the difficulty arises from the standard dictating that existence is determined only through evidence acceptable within physicalism.

Now, it is worth considering this criticism from a naturalist viewpoint, rather than from the viewpoint of physicalism. Physicalism is certainly the most commonly accepted ontological position that is available to naturalists and it has a great many virtues. As observed in chapter 1, however, physicalism and naturalism are not conceptually inseparable. In other words, naturalists can take a physicalist position, but it is not necessary for them to be committed to physicalism. Considering this, in the effort to overcome the criticism of physicalism based on indeterminacy, it would not be unreasonable to entertain the possibility of discarding physicalism to sustain realism about meaning and propositions.

For this we may ask what alternative ontological views are available in place of physicalism. In this section will focus on 'pluralism' as a theoretically possibile alternative to physicalism, discussing its features and functions.

2.4.1 A preliminary formulation of pluralism

This subsection aims at formulating 'pluralism' as an ontological alternative to physicalism. As a key to formulating pluralism, consider the comments on Quine's physicalism made by Putnam, which characterize Quine's position as (i) distinguishing a 'first-grade' and a 'second-grade conceptual system', and (ii) asserting that "only our first-grade conceptual system represents an account of what the world contains that we have to take seriously" (Putnam 2004a, 61).[80] Putnam then goes on to contrast the views of theorists often proclaimed as 'naturalists' and his own position as follows:[81]

---

[80] The idea stated here is that only the first-grade conceptual system is identified with the set of statements from which an ontological commitment is to be derived (see section 2.1.2).

[81] Here, Putnam uses quotation marks around "naturalism" (and also around "naturalists"), and of course, what they stand for is different from the naturalism defined in chapter 1. Assuming that

While other "naturalists" would draw the line between the first-grade and the second-grade elsewhere (no two "naturalists" seem to draw it in the *same* place), what is common to most versions of "naturalism" is that those conceptual resources and conceptual activities that do not fit into the narrow scientific first-grade system are regarded as something less than *bona fide* rational discourse.

The heart of my own conceptual pluralism is the insistence that various sorts of statements that are regarded as less than fully rational discourse, as somehow of merely "heuristic" significance, by one or another of the "naturalists" ... are *bona fide* statements, "as fully governed by norms of truth and validity as any other statements," as James Conant has put it. (Putnam 2004a, 61, italics in original)

Quine's physicalism certainly plays a role in drawing the line described in this passage. For Quine, whether something is an objective fact of the matter depends on whether it can be accounted for within physicalism, and this criterion obviously illustrates the above distinction between the first- and second-grade systems. It must be emphasized, however, that such a distinction is merely a hypothesis that can be submitted within the framework of minimal naturalism and is not forced upon naturalists as an unavoidable criterion. After stating explicitly that there are numerous specialized fields in our scientific activities, and that even the question of whether there is a fact of the matter unifying all specialized fields is a question internal to science, Quine continues as follows:

Naturalism can still respect the drive, on the part of some of us, for a unified, all-purpose ontology. The drive is typical of the scientific temper, and of a piece with the drive for simplicity that shapes scientific hypotheses generally. Physicalism is its familiar manifestation, and physicalism is bound to have had important side effects in the framing of more special hypotheses in various branches of science; for physicalism puts a premium on hypotheses favorable to close integration with physics itself. We have here a conspicuous case of what I touched on earlier: scientific hypotheses which, though not themselves testable, help to elicit others that are. (Quine 1995, 285)

On the bases of these quotes from Putnam's and Quine's writings, I will now formulate what 'pluralistic naturalism' is, the main theme of this section. Drawing on Quine's remarks above, let us characterize 'monism' as the view that there is a fact of the matter that unifies all branches of science, and that a single overarching discourse represents an 'all-purpose ontology' that unifies (or ought to unify[82]) diverse scientific

---

many contemporary naturalists adopt natural scientism or physicalism, Putnam puts quotation marks around the term(s) to indicate that the term 'naturalism' implies natural scientism or physicalism. Also, as these quotation marks suggest, Putnam criticizes the current use of the term 'naturalism'. See also (Putnam 2002, 130-1).

[82] I use both 'unifies' and 'ought to unify' because I do not wish to rule out either the descriptive or normative way of understanding the formulation of monism. Quine states that "[t]he naturalistic

activities.[83] Then, physicalism can be understood as a monistic view in which physics is an overarching discourse representing an all-purpose ontology and plays a particularly important role in the unification of the sciences. On this understanding all branches of science will be (or ought to be) unified (as they will be revised in the future) in such a way that they approach closer and closer to the course of the development of physics. (This process of unification or conversion involves, for example, transforming non-physical concepts that resist physicalist explanation—explanation in terms of, say, supervenience—into concepts that admit of physicalist explanation and also eliminating non-physical concepts, where attempts towards physicalist explanation are abandoned.[84]) To put this monistic view differently, from the perspective of what constitutes a fact, physics determines an objective fact of the matter or delineates the scope of facts, and nothing that is not uniquely determined by the physical facts can be a fact.[85] On the other hand, pluralism—to be contrasted with monism—can be understood as a rejection of the idea that an overarching discourse representing an all-purpose ontology will (or ought to) unify diverse scientific activities. It would also be possible to focus on the question of what constitutes a fact and describe pluralism as opposing any single criterion of factuality—a particular discourse determining what facts there are. To borrow Putnam's phrases above,[86] pluralism denies the distinction between a first-grade conceptual system, which supposedly represents the facts constituting the world, and a second-grade conceptual system, which is merely heuristically important. Given these considerations, let us tentatively define pluralism in this chapter as follows (a more detailed and concrete formulation of pluralism will appear in the next chapter):

---

epistemologist settles for what he can learn about the strategy, logic, and mechanics by which our elaborate theory of the physical world is in fact projected, or might, or should be, from just that amorphous neural intake" (Quine 1995, 281).

[83] It must be noticed here that in this passage Quine glosses over the distinction between the notion of 'fact of the matter' and that of 'all-purpose ontology': the former is understood at the level of truths or facts, whereas the latter is understood at the level of objects or entities. This omission creates a problem because, even if the set of all true statements is determined, it is possible to fail to identify the criterion for deducing entities from the set of true statements—the criterion of ontological commitment—without which an ontology would have no substantial claim in it, and so these two notions—and the two different levels—must be clearly distinguished (see section 2.1.2). Of course, since Quine explicitly states that an indispensability argument constitutes the criterion of ontological commitment, in accordance with which entities are to be deduced from truths, he should not be blamed for failing to distinguish one notion from the other. Yet, since we have understood in section 2.1.2 that there are different criteria of ontological commitment, it is necessary for us to distinguish them. Moreover, the focus of the discussion here is physicalism, and as observed in section 2.2.3, physicalism is an ontological claim at the level of truths (rather than at the level of objects or entities or being concerned with ontological commitment). Thus, for the ensuing discussion I formulate monism narrowly as a view concerning the level of truths by referring to a single overarching discourse presenting an all-purpose ontology.

[84] Of course, a monistic view can be formulated without using physics. It is logically possible that branches of science will converge on a discipline other than physics, such as psychology—forming 'psychological monism'.

[85] This understanding of physicalism is in perfect agreement with the formulation of physicalism presented in section 2.2.1—the view that any properties used to describe facts supervene on physical properties.

[86] These phrases originally come from (Quine 1969a, 24), however.

Pluralism: the view that denies accepting a particular discourse as the criterion of factuality.

Pluralism formulated in this way obviously conflicts with physicalism defined as the view that any properties used to describe facts supervene on physical properties. Also notice that pluralism conflicts with, besides physicalism, any form of monism that employs a particular discourse as the criterion of factuality. It must be further noted, as is clear from the above formulation focusing on the criterion of factuality, that the point of conflict between physicalist monism and pluralism, as an ontological theory to be adopted, is concerned with truths or facts; they do not vie with one another over issues about entities or criteria of ontological commitment (see section 2.2.3).

This subsection has laid out a basic understanding of pluralism, which will be discussed in more detail in the rest of this chapter. In what follows, I will consider the significance of pluralism by contrasting it to physicalism.

2.4.2 Pluralism as an ontological option for naturalists and its significance

This subsection first briefly discusses the places of physicalist monism and pluralism, two competing ontological options, within the framework of naturalism, and then spells out how pluralism overcomes the problems of physicalism taken up in the previous section.

To begin with, let us recap the basic perspective for ontological debates to better understand the role of ontology in naturalism.

The basic perspective for ontological debates

The set of statements from which an ontological commitment is derived is determined (in other words, 'truth' is determined).
+
The method of deriving an ontological commitment from a statement is determined (the criterion of the ontological commitment is determined).
↓
A list of entities is created.

As stated earlier in section 2.4.1, the point of conflict between physicalist monism and pluralism, as an ontological theory to be adopted, is concerned with truths or facts, and they do not vie with one another over issues about entities or criteria of ontological commitment. To accommodate this, the discussion below focuses on the level of truths or facts.

It must be noted first that belief system immanentism, one of the basic assumptions for naturalism, gives rise to a first constraint on truths or facts. Belief system immanentism asserts that truths or facts must be accounted for internally within a belief system. In other words, it is our belief system that illuminates what truths or facts there are.[87] The difference between physicalist monism and pluralism depends on whether any further constraint is imposed on naturalism in addition to that of belief system immanentism, a basic assumption for naturalism. That is, the notion of what constitutes a truth or fact changes depending on whether physicalism is added to belief system immanentism (the core thesis of naturalism). To state it more concretely, according to physicalist naturalism all facts are physical facts (that are described only in terms of physical properties and properties supervening on physical properties), and no other kind of circumstance can constitute a fact. However, if physicalism is not adopted, every circumstance that is accepted within our belief system would be endorsed as a fact.[88]

This was a brief discussion of the places of physicalist monism and pluralism, two competing ontological options, within the framework of naturalism. Next, considering the criticism of physicalism based on indeterminacy, I will examine how pluralistic naturalism can overcome the difficulties faced by physicalist naturalism.

First, as an example, let us quickly review the line of reasoning starting from the indeterminacy theses to the conclusion that no statements about propositional attitudes are factual. A consequence of the indeterminacy of interpretation is that it is possible to attribute different sets of propositional attitudes to a single individual. This consequence alone does not entail eliminativism about propositional attitudes. For, even if there is more than one acceptable theory of interpretation, one could appeal to the 'sectarian' approach, in which the meanings of utterances and the propositional attitudes of interpretees (speakers) are accounted for absolutely within the theory of interpretation we employ. However, physicalism can be introduced at this point, and according to physicalism the notion of 'facts' is restricted to physical facts and anything that is not uniquely determined by physical truths is excluded from the set of all facts (all facts are physical facts). If the scope of facts is restricted in this way, it would be unjustifiable to assume that there is a single, correct theory of interpretation that describes the facts about propositional attitudes, which are to be attributed to an interpretee. It follows that propositional attitudes attributed to individuals do not have identity conditions for what they are in terms of facts that are acceptable within physicalism, and therefore, statements about propositional attitudes do not describe facts.

Thus, by endorsing physicalism and thereby restricting the scope of facts, from the indeterminacy theses it becomes possible to conclude that no statements about meaning and also those about propositional attitudes are factual. This conclusion would motivate objections to physicalism such as that physicalists would have to deny statements held factual in a variety of disciplines (statements held true in linguistics, history, ethics, psychology, etc.), and that normative naturalism is

---

[87] Of course, our belief system may be expected to be revised in due time. For the compatibility of belief system immanentism and the transcendence of truth, see section 2.1.3.
[88] Here, physics is not an overarching discourse governing the entirety of our belief system, but this does not imply that there are no norms on the basis of which the correctness of statements is evaluated. Statements belong to different discourses, each of which independently owns a set of norms; the correctness of statements is evaluated in accordance with the norms of the discourses to which they belong.

incompatible with physicalism (see section 2.3.3). Now, consider what would be entailed if physicalism is not adopted. If there are no physicalist constraints on the scope of facts (such as that all facts are physical facts, and that there is no objective fact of the matter with respect to the subject that is not uniquely determined by the physical facts), then it would be unnecessary to discard statements about meaning and about propositional attitudes as being nonfactual, even on the assumption that the indeterminacy of translation and interpretation is correct. This is the advantage of adopting pluralism in place of physicalist monism.

Let us pursue this point in more detail. The crucial step in the above reasoning towards the thesis that no statements about meanings or propositions are factual is the rejection of the sectarian approach to indeterminacy. Physicalists do not accept this approach because, for them, all facts are physicalistically determinate. Non-physicalists, however, can accept the sectarian approach, in which the meanings of utterances and the propositional attitudes of interpretees are accounted for absolutely within the theory of interpretation we employ, and thereby synonymy statements and statements concerning propositional attitudes can be considered factual. That is, by denying any single discourse treated as the criterion of facts, pluralists can acknowledge synonymy claims and propositional attitude attributions as being factual *without submitting them to the verdict of the physical facts*.

If statements about meaning and also about propositional attitudes can be acknowledged to be factual, then the problems pointed out in section 2.3.3 would be resolved altogether. As a result, we could rest assured that many statements, like those held in linguistics, history, ethics, psychology, as well as in normative naturalism, are indeed factual. (This relaxed treatment of facts is in agreement with the characterizations that Putnam gave to his own version of pluralism, namely that, "various sorts of statements that are regarded as less than fully rational discourse, as somehow of merely 'heuristic' significance, by one or another of the 'naturalists' ... are *bona fide* statements ... [that are] fully governed by norms of truth and validity as any other statements" [Putnam 2004a, 61].)

Pluralistic naturalism is the position formulated by adding the pluralist ontology to minimal naturalism. Different from physicalist naturalism—the dominant view among contemporary naturalists—pluralistic naturalism has been by far less studied, and many of its aspects have been left underdeveloped: this includes an exact formulation of the position, its implications, and a critical examination of its sustainability.[89] As has been argued so far, however, pluralist naturalism is greatly advantageous to enabling the acceptance of the legitimacy of Quine's argument for the transition to naturalism without being committed to the problematic aspects it poses: Quine labels 'nonfactual'

---

[89] Having said that, it is false to say that no contemporary thinker endorses pluralistic naturalism. In my view, Goodman and Putnam must be classified as pluralistic naturalists. They are, first, classified as naturalists by virtue of rejecting the idea of reality-in-itself, which is completely independent from our belief system, and from abandoning the epistemological project of infallible foundationalism. Second, they are classified as pluralists by virtue of rejecting physicalist monism. (Putnam does not call himself a naturalist, however, possibly because of his dissatisfaction with the current usage of the term 'naturalism'.)

or 'second-grade' concepts that are difficult to account for in the physicalist worldview and also discourses in which such concepts appear. (In particular, I think that it is necessary to adopt pluralism to account for epistemological normativity in a naturalistic way.) Therefore, it is worth pursuing a clearer formulation of pluralist naturalism and elucidating its implications and scope. (As an effort to achieve these goals, in chapter 3, I will develop a particular formulation of pluralist naturalism addressing more detailed issues, and present my replies to what I anticipate to be objections to this developed form of pluralist naturalism.)

The discussion so far has provided an overview of pluralist naturalism and given a basic understanding of its significance. To conclude the current chapter, I wish to comment on the consequence that statements about propositional attitudes can be acknowledged to be factual, one of the important advantages pluralist naturalism offers over physicalist monism. As the discussion in section 2.3.2 suggests, I assume in this book that an account of propositional attitudes from the perspective of pluralist naturalism will be formulated broadly based on Davidson's idea of a 'theory of interpretation'. According to Davidson, a theory of interpretation is constructed by employing the behavior of a speaker (including utterances made) and the surrounding environment as empirical data (see [Davidson 1984, 135]). What this indicates is that a theory of interpretation is an empirical theory, and hence the attribution of a propositional attitude to an agent can be conducted within the framework of minimalist naturalism.[90]

Despite this apparent compatibility of naturalism and Davidson's theory of interpretation, there are theorists who argue against their compatibility. For example, Mikael Janvid (2004) argues that since the epistemological status of the principle of charity, which is constitutive of a theory of interpretation, is special—it is an *a priori* principle and immune to revision—the principle of charity is incompatible with Quine's 'gradualism', which is one of the core theses of naturalism. If this argument is sound, then it would be required to start over and redo the project of pluralistic naturalism in a form in which the factuality of statements about propositional attitudes is secured by means of removing the physicalist constraints on the scope of facts.

In my view, however, Janvid's understanding of a theory of interpretation is misguided. First, the principle of charity is immune to revision only within the

---

[90] Moreover, the fact that it is possible to attribute a propositional attitude to an agent within the framework of minimalist naturalism also entails the possibility of accounting for a certain kind of normative statement within the framework of minimalist naturalism. This is because, as Quine states about epistemological normativity, naturalists can paraphrase normative statements as instrumental normative statements (that is, as hypothetical normative statements with respect to a particular, fixed goal). Since 'having a such-and-such goal' can be understood as a kind of propositional attitude, if propositional attitudes can be accounted for within the minimalist naturalist framework, then normative statements could also be accounted for within the minimalist naturalist framework (although they would have to be paraphrased into the form of hypothetical normative statements).

I have developed these considerations concerning the compatibility of naturalism and interpretivism as well as the possibility of a naturalistic account of normative statements in response to the comments given by Hiroyuki Hattori at the meeting of the Philosophical Association of Japan in 2006 (at Tohoku University). I wish to thank him for the comments.

framework of a theory of interpretation (or within the project of folk psychology), the objective of which is to understand human beings in terms of concepts such as those of 'belief' and 'desire'. If a theory of interpretation or folk psychology is abandoned as empirical studies advance (as could happen by virtue of the lack of efficacy), then the principle of charity, a constitutive ideal of a theory of interpretation, could also be abandoned (together with the whole project). It is true that no naturalists can accept a proposition that can never be abandoned as a result of any empirical inquiry. However, since the principle of charity is not immune to revision in an empirical inquiry (if not directly refutable), the construction of a theory of interpretation with help from the principle of charity is compatible with naturalism.

These considerations show that a theory of interpretation and naturalism are compatible with one another, and that those who endorse pluralistic naturalism can rest assured that statements about propositional attitudes are factual. Moreover, since the principle of charity and the leading idea in this principle, that an agent must be rational are constitutive of a theory of interpretation, the concept of propositional attitudes can be considered a normative concept from the viewpoint of a theory of interpretation, and thereby it becomes possible to develop normative naturalism. (Recall the point discussed in section 2.3.3 that as long as we attempt to understand epistemological normativity as purposive rationality, the concept of 'goal' (or that of 'purpose'), to be redefined in such an attempt, must be able to produce normativity.) In this way, it is possible to retain a number of advantages that are attributed to pluralistic naturalism by virtue of removing the physicalist constraints on the scope of facts.

Chapter 3

Towards the Development of Pluralistic Naturalism

In chapter 2 I have discussed ontological options available to naturalists. In particular, the focus has been on the most dominant and extensively studied naturalistic view in recent years, physicalist monism, and its problems have been identified. In conclusion, I proposed to adopt pluralism in place of physicalist monism in order to overcome the problems faced by physicalism while retaining naturalism.

However, pluralist monism has not yet been studied as extensively as physicalist monism, with respect to which different formulations of the view have been proposed and the problems it confronts have been examined (as a result of active research in areas such as philosophy of mind and philosophy of science). (To illustrate this point, recall that in section 2.4.1 pluralism is defined as a view that denies accepting any particular discourse as the criterion of factuality. This would make it natural to ask how one should understand the scope of 'discourse' in the definition, the multiplicity of which gives rise to pluralism, and also what identity conditions a discourse has. For pluralism to be put forward as a sophisticated position that can withstand critical scrutiny, such questions must be answered clearly.) The reason for this contrast between pluralism and physicalist monism is that there are a small number of philosophers who explicitly endorse pluralism, and as a result there are only few particular models or formulations of pluralism. Therefore, what has to be done to establish pluralistic naturalism is to propose a model of pluralism in an as detailed and clear way as possible (so that the formulation would contribute to the further critical discussion).

To achieve this goal, this chapter is devoted to formulating pluralistic naturalism as clearly as possible. More specifically, first, I will examine Putnam's discussion of conceptual relativity and conceptual pluralism as presenting a model of pluralism (section 3.1), and then turn to Carnap's semantic project (section 3.2). Through examining these ideas, I will develop a particular form of pluralism, spelling out its characteristics.

3.1 Putnam's Pluralistic Model: Conceptual Pluralism and Conceptual Relativity

The approximate formulation of pluralistic naturalism presented in chapter 2 rests on Putnam's idea of 'conceptual pluralism'. In the current chapter I aim at articulating a model of pluralism that is clearer than this approximate formulation, and I begin (again) with the philosophy of Putnam, who is representative of contemporary philosophers explicitly endorsing pluralism and who has developed an interesting account of the plurality of linguistic schemes in the recent book *Ethics without Ontology* (Putnam 2004a), in connection with 'conceptual relativity', which is a thesis distinct from 'conceptual pluralism'. In this section, I will focus on the conclusions that Putnam reaches in *Ethics without Ontology*, examining his pluralistic views.[1]

3.1.1 Conceptual relativity and conceptual pluralism

First, let us consider the phenomenon Putnam refers to as 'conceptual relativity': "the fact that in certain cases what exists may depend on which of various conventions we adopt" (Putnam 2004b, 36). An instance of conceptual relativity, Putnam notes, is the choice as to whether mereological sums are to be included in the inventory of entities.[2] In a mereological framework, for any two things, there is a sum of those two things, which is a new thing to be added to the inventory of entities.[3] (For example, Putnam mentions "the sum of my nose and the Eiffel Tower" as a "perfectly good object in mereology" [Putnam 2004b, 36].) Now, imagine the world consisting of three particulars, x_1, x_2, and x_3, (they permit no further decomposition). In terms of our standard logical apparatus, there are three objects in this world. In a mereological framework, by contrast, they become total of seven objects: x_1, x_2, x_3, x_1+x_2, x_1+x_3, x_2+x_3, and $x_1+x_2+x_3$.[4] What this example shows is that the concept of

---

[1] Putnam's pluralistic views have been presented on various occasions prior to the publication of *Ethics without Ontology*, but as Putnam himself acknowledges, there have been unclear parts in the previous discussion of pluralism. In *Ethics without Ontology*, Putnam clarifies his pluralistic views (to some extent), a refinement triggered by (Case 1997). One can also consult (Case 2001) and (Putnam 2001) for details of this.

[2] For other instances of 'conceptual relativity' that Putnam describes, see (Putnam 2001, 432-3).

[3] Strictly speaking, this does not hold in all theories of mereology, which is the study of part-whole relations. A different theory of mereology can be constructed by adding axioms to the following three basic axioms:

(P1) Pxx Reflexivity
(P2) $(Pxy \& Pyx) \rightarrow x=y$ Antisymmetry
(P3) $(Pxy \& Pyz) \rightarrow Pxz$ Transitivity

Depending on which axioms are added to these basic axioms, the resulting systems are stronger or weaker than others with respect to provability. (Further, even the three basic axioms have been challenged on the basis of the use of the natural language phrase 'is part of'.) Now, in mereology the axiom for deriving the existence of a mereological sum from the existence of two objects is given as follows:

$Uxy \rightarrow \exists z \forall w(Owz \leftrightarrow (Owx \lor Owy))$

(where $Uxy =_{def} \exists z(Pxz \& Pyz)$, and $Oxy =_{def} \exists z(Pzx \& Pzy)$). However, as the conditional form of this additional axiom suggests, it alone does not entail the theorem that, for any two objects, there is a mereological sum of the two. To derive this statement as a theorem it is necessary to add another axiom,

$\exists z \forall x(Pzx)$.

Moreover, there are axiomatic systems in which '$Uxy \rightarrow \exists z \forall w(Owz \leftrightarrow (Owx \lor Owy))$' is adopted as an axiom but '$\exists z \forall x(Pzx)$' is not. Therefore, it is false to state with no qualification that in mereology there is a mereological sum for any two objects. (The discussion in this footnote relies on [Varzi 2003].)

[4] However, if the axiom,

'existence' and the usage of the predicate 'exist'—or at least the extension of the existential predicate—change depending on which logical framework is in use.

The discussion so far has illustrated a typical way to substantiate conceptual relativity. There are two important points to be noted here for an accurate understanding of conceptual relativity. One is that the choice between frameworks or schemes is a matter of convention, and the question of which framework or scheme is correct has no objective answer supported by facts. The other point to be noted with respect to conceptual relativity is that the instances it incorporates are given as the possibilities of 'optional language' (the notion of which will be introduced immediately below). Let me quote, now, Putnam's passages that illustrate each point:

> I have taken the view that while we can indeed speak as Leśniewski taught us to speak—we can say that there are such as mereological sums, we can tell which mereological sums are identical and which are not identical, we can say that mereological sums are not identical with sets, etc.—to ask whether mereological sums *really exist* would be stupid. It is, in my view, a matter of *convention* whether we say that mereological sums exist or not. (Putnam 2004b, 37, italics in original)
>
> Conceptual relativity, as I already indicated, holds that the question as to which of these ways of using "exist" (and "individual," "object," etc.) is *right* is one that the meanings of the words in the natural language, that is, the language that we all speak and cannot avoid speaking every day, simply leaves open. Both the set theory that developed in the nineteenth (and early twentieth) century and the mereology that Leśniewski invented are what I will call *optional languages* (a term suggested by Jennifer Case), in the sense that one may count as a master of the (English or German or Polish ...) language without leaning these particular sublanguages. The optional language of set theory and the optional language of mereology represent possible *extensions* of our ordinary ways of speaking. (ibid., 43, italics in original)

Consider, first, the second passage that illustrates the point concerning 'optional languages'. As Putnam succinctly explicates, the acquisition of an optional language is not necessary for counting as a speaker of a natural language. Optional languages are linguistic parts, and we may choose whether to adopt any one of them.[5] By introducing the notion of 'optional language', Putnam makes a significant distinction between the parts of languages that must be accepted by the speakers of the languages (the 'cores' of the languages, so to speak) and the parts of the languages that are genuinely optional.[6] What is crucial here is that the mereological example of

---

$\exists z \forall x (Pzx)$,

is added to the axiomatic system of mereology, then it would follow from the axioms that there is also the 'null entity', which is part of every object, and so there are a total of eight objects in a world consisting of three particulars, x_1, x_2, and x_3.

[5] For the notion of 'optional language', see (Case 1997, 11) and (Case 2001, 420f).

[6] Putnam raises the following example of the distinction:

conceptual relativity discussed above is concerned only with optional languages. That is, according to the idea of conceptual relativity, there is more than one optional language that is 'a possible extension of our ordinary ways of speaking'; an optional language is an extension of a natural language in the sense that it can be incorporated with the use of a natural language without giving rise to any particular contradictions.

Conceptual relativity is a thesis about the possibility of multiple optional languages. This point leads to the other point to be kept in mind for an accurate understanding of conceptual relativity: the choice between frameworks or schemes is a matter of convention. All possible optional languages—they constitute instances of conceptual relativity—can by definition be integrated with the use of a natural language without causing any particular contradictions, and so the question of which among optional languages is correct has no specific answer determined by appealing to the meaning of a natural language; in other words, the question of which optional language is correct cannot be solved by examining how we actually use language. On the basis of this point, Putnam maintains that any choice between optional languages will be a matter of convention and dismisses the question as to which is correct as an irrelevant question (see [Putnam 2004b, 37]).

The discussion so far has laid out matters related to a basic understanding of the idea of conceptual relativity. According to Putnam, an acceptance of conceptual relativity leads to 'conceptual pluralism': the view that different discourses or conceptual frameworks (schemes) can be used equally, where there is no need to reduce them into "some single fundamental and universal ontology" (Putnam 2004b, 49). In expounding the gist of conceptual pluralism, Putnam brings up two different ways of describing "the contents of a room" (ibid., 48), which can be a description in terms of fundamental physics as well as in everyday terms such as 'table', 'chair', and 'lamp'. Conceptual pluralism is the view "[t]hat we can use both of these schemes without being required to reduce one or both of them to some single fundamental and universal ontology" (ibid., 48-9).

Now it becomes important to consider the relation between conceptual pluralism and the aforementioned conceptual relativity. Putnam states that "conceptual relativity implies pluralism" (ibid., 49). To more fully understand his views of this implication relation and also of the differences between conceptual pluralism and relativity, I quote at length from *Ethics without Ontology*:

> In *Representation and Reality*[7] I counted the fact that we might describe "the contents" of a room very differently by using first the vocabulary of fundamental physical theory and then again the vocabulary of tables and chairs and lamps and so on as a further instance of conceptual relativity, and this, I now think, was a mistake, although it *is* an instance of a related and wider phenomenon I should

---

> We are not, given the material and social worlds in which we live, genuinely free not to quantify over tables and chairs, for example. But we are free to employ the conceptual scheme of mereology or not, even in mathematics, even in empirical description, even, for that matter, in philosophy. (Putnam 2001, 434)

[7] Putnam (1988).

have called *conceptual pluralism*. The fact that the contents of a room may be partly described in two very different vocabularies cannot be an instance of conceptual relativity in the sense just explained, because conceptual relativity always involves descriptions which are cognitively equivalent (in the sense that any phenomenon whose explanation can be given in one of the optional languages involved has a corresponding explanation in the other), but which are incompatible if taken at face value (the descriptions cannot be simply conjoined). But the fact that the contents of a room may be partly described in the terminology of fields and particles and the fact that it may be partly described by saying that there is a chair in front of a desk are not in any way "incompatible," not even "at face value": the statements "the room may be partly described by saying there is a chair in front of a desk" and "the room may be partly described as consisting of fields and particles" don't even *sound* "incompatible." And they are not cognitively equivalent (even if we do not bar the fantastic possibility of defining terms like "Desk" and "table" in the language of fundamental physics, the field-particle description contains a great deal of information that is not translatable into the language of desks and chairs). That we can use both of these schemes without being required to reduce one or both of them to some single fundamental and universal ontology is the doctrine of pluralism; and while conceptual relativity implies pluralism, the reverse is not the case. (ibid., 48-9, italics in original)

In examining this passage it is primarily important to heed that Putnam identifies two conditions for there to be an instance of conceptual relativity: cognitive equivalency and incompatibility. It is also important to be alert to the need for a one-way entailment relation between conceptual relativity and conceptual pluralism: namely, according to Putnam's discussion, instances of conceptual relativity are subsumed under instances of conceptual pluralism—the latter covering broader phenomena—and so anything that instantiates conceptual relativity also simultaneously instantiates conceptual pluralism.

Let me provide a brief summary of the preceding discussion of conceptual relativity and conceptual pluralism:

Conceptual relativity: the view that there is more than one linguistic rule governing the use of a concept, and that it is impossible to determine a unique, 'correct' rule on the basis of how the concept is used in natural language. An instance of conceptual relativity has to satisfy the following two conditions.

1. Cognitive equivalency: for a group of optional languages under consideration, every phenomenon that can be explained in terms of one optional language can also be explained in terms of any other optional language in the group.

2. Incompatibility: it is impossible to simply conjoin two descriptions of two different optional languages (the resulting conjunction would be contradictory

if literally interpreted[8]).

Conceptual pluralism: the view that different discourses or conceptual frameworks (schemes) can be used equally, where there is no need to reduce them to a single ontology that is fundamental and universal. Conceptual relativity is subsumed under conceptual pluralism.

3.1.2 How to counter Davidson's criticism of conceptual schemes

The previous section has sketched Putnam's pluralistic position and how it relates to conceptual relativity. There is, however, a serious challenge to Putnam's pluralism discussed above: pluralism is based on conceptual relativity, which implies that the truth of sentences and also ontologies are relative to optional languages; however, this relativist view is rejected as an unintelligible idea in Donald Davidson's article "On the Very Idea of a Conceptual Scheme" (collected in [Davidson 1984]), and it is becoming commonly accepted that Davidson's rejection of relativism is compelling. Therefore, I need to demonstrate that Putnam's pluralism is be able to counter Davidson's criticism of conceptual schemes in order to sustain pluralism as a viable option, at least as an option deserving consideration that remains in play. In what follows, for this reason, I will first present an outline of Davidson's criticism of conceptual schemes, and then, I will turn to determining the scope of this criticism, showing that Putnam's conceptual relativity indeed falls outside its scope.

(1) An outline of Davidson's criticism of conceptual schemes

Although Davidson's discussion in the article "On the Very Idea of a Conceptual Scheme" is convoluted, the outline below sketches the basic line of reasoning, and keeping this logical structure in mind, let us scrutinize the details of Davidson's argument against relativism.

> The identity conditions of conceptual schemes are given (tentatively) on the basis of translatability: two speakers have the same conceptual scheme if and only if their languages are translatable from one into the other.
> ↓
> Two kinds of failure of translatability are distinguished: complete and partial failures of translatability. For each kind of translation failure, it is examined whether there can be two different conceptual schemes.
> ↓
> For both kinds of translation failure, it would not be meaningful to say that there

---

[8] It is possible to eliminate contradictions by making relativization explicit. For example, the following conjunction is not contradictory: the statement 'there are three objects in the domain in question' is true in a non-mereological optional language, and it is false in a mereological optional language. In this way, statements can include explicit reference to optional languages (linguistic rules and conceptual schemes). According to Putnam, it is not the statements, but the conventions that are incompatible with one another (Putnam 2004b, 46).

are two different conceptual schemes.
↓

This shows that it is impossible to talk meaningfully about 'different conceptual schemes', and so there is no criterion of individuation that distinguishes one conceptual scheme from another. It is, hence, concluded that the very idea of a conceptual scheme would become unintelligible, and thereby conceptual relativism—resting on the idea of a conceptual scheme—would also become unintelligible.

Conceptual schemes are usually understood as "networks of concepts that articulate and organize our perceptions and thoughts." (Hiromatsu, et al. 1998, 211r). According to Davidson, conceptual schemes "are ways of organizing experience; they are systems of categories that give form to the data of sensation; they are points of view from which individuals, cultures, or periods survey the passing scene" (Davidson 1984, 183). Also, conceptual scheme relativism (or conceptual relativism) is characterized as the view that truth and reality are relativized to conceptual schemes, and what is true or real according to one scheme may be false or unreal according to another. Davidson begins the criticism of conceptual relativism with identifying conceptual schemes as "sets of intertranslatable languages" (ibid., 185).[9] On this criterion of identity, if German and English are intertranslatable—the sentences of one language can be translated into those of the other—then these two languages would present different ways of expressing the same conceptual scheme. (For example, consider the case in which the speech of a German physicist is translated into English and the speech of an English counterpart is translated into German.) The following will assume the validity of this criterion of identity for conceptual schemes. For conceptual relativism to be established, distinct conceptual schemes must be shown to exist (or, at least, possibly exist). It follows that it must be made clear under what conditions two conceptual schemes are different from one another, in addition to clarifying the criterion of identity for conceptual schemes.

At first glance, given the identity criterion above, it appears justifiable to propose that two individuals speaking two different languages that are not intertranslatable have two different conceptual schemes. Despite the initial plausibility this proposal may have, however, Davidson argues that the proposed condition for two different conceptual schemes fails to make the idea of different conceptual schemes meaningful. In the argument for this claim, Davidson first distinguishes two types of cases: (A) cases in which translation completely fails and (B) cases in which translation partially

---

[9] To illustrate this identification, suppose that Japanese words such as 'wabi' and 'sabi' cannot be appropriately translated into English words. Then, one may as well claim there to be concepts that are not shared by the English and Japanese languages. This kind of case would motivate the idea that two different languages that cannot be translated from one into the other embody two different conceptual schemes. Further, there are reasons to think that two different languages do not necessarily have two different conceptual schemes. For example, it is easy to conceive a circumstance in which Japanese and American physicists are committed to the same physical theory constructed from the same range of concepts, while speaking different languages. These considerations seem to corroborate and support Davidson's initial step, the idea that intertranslatable languages embody the same conceptual scheme.

138   Chapter 3 Towards the Development of Pluralistic Naturalism

fails,[10] and then attempts to show that either type of case fails to provide the grounds for assuming different conceptual schemes. In what follows, I will trace this logical structure of Davidson's argument against conceptual schemes, reconstructing the argument step by step.

(A) Does the complete failure of translatability prove the existence of different conceptual schemes?

To simplify this question, let the target language to be translated be the language we speak. Since we have already accepted the above criterion of identity for conceptual schemes (conceptual schemes are identified with sets of intertranslatable languages), for question (A) to be answered positively, at least the following idea must be considered meaningful: there is a kind of activity that is completely untranslatable into our language but still counts as a linguistic activity. It is natural to question, however, whether there can really be any such kind of activity. Of course, there is no problem with the idea that an activity translatable into our language in some way counts as a linguistic activity. Yet, it is much more difficult to grasp the idea that a completely untranslatable activity can count as linguistic. The question becomes in what sense an activity is considered to be in any way linguistic if it cannot be expressed in our language?

To counter this worry and establish the meaningfulness of the idea that there is a kind of activity that is completely untranslatable into our language but still counts as linguistic, it is necessary to provide a criterion for a language that is independent of translatability. A promising approach to this goal, Davidson suggests, is the "dualism of scheme and content" (ibid., 189), which proposes a dichotomy between a scheme (what is organizing or fitting) and a content (what is organized or fitted). For example, one may suppose that our languages organize the stream of unarticulated experience prior to conceptualization; this supposition contrasts languages—what organizes experience—and experiences prior to conceptualization—what is organized by languages—and thereby it is an instance of the scheme-content dualism.[11] As this instance illustrates (as also Davidson explicitly notes), the languages we are considering now are on the side of leaning towards 'scheme' in the scheme-content dualism. That is, on the scheme-content dualism, if there is a criterion for a scheme

---

[10] According to Davidson, 'complete failure of translatability' stands for a circumstance in which "no significant range of sentences in one language could be translated into the other" (Davidson 1984, 185), whereas 'partial failure' a circumstance in which "some range could be translated and some range could not" (ibid.).

[11] It is of great importance to notice that Davidson assumes the dualism between scheme and content to necessitate the existence of something that is commonly accounted for by all schemes—what is organized must be unconceptualized and independent from all schemes. This assumptions is clearly present in the following remarks:

> ... the common relation to experience or the evidence is what is supposed to help us make sense of the claim that it is languages or schemes that are under consideration when translation fails. It is essential to this idea that there be something neutral and common that lies outside all schemes. This common something cannot, of course, be the *subject matter* of contrasting languages, or translation would be possible. (ibid., 190, italics in original)

independent of translatability, it would also count as an independent criterion for a language that does not appeal to translatability. Consequently, it would be possible to establish the meaningfulness of the idea that there is a kind of activity that is completely untranslatable into our language but still counts as linguistic.

Now, whether this dualist approach to different conceptual schemes succeeds depends on how we are able to identify conceptual schemes, in particular, whether we can identify conceptual schemes independently from the notion of translatability. Since there are different variants of the dualism between scheme and content—and also different relations between scheme and content, accordingly—a criterion of identity for schemes must be proposed for each variant. In "On the Very Idea of a Conceptual Scheme," Davidson examines the following three variants of the scheme-content dualism:

(A-1)   A scheme organizes reality.
(A-2)   A scheme organizes experience.
(A-3)   A scheme fits experience.

Let us first consider Davidson's discussion of (A-1), which defines a scheme or a language as something that organizes reality. Organizing something amounts to classifying and categorizing the constituents of that something. Then, two organizing schemes are not intertranslatable just in case the concepts or predicates used in the schemes for classification and categorization are extensionally different. However, to say that there is no predicate in our language the extension of which matches that of a predicate in a different language, we would have to be able to identify the extension of that predicate. In conveying this point Davidson writes as follows:

> A language may contain simple predicates whose extensions are matched by no simple predicates, or even by any predicates at all, in some other language. What enables us to make this point in particular cases is an ontology common to the two languages, with concepts that individuate the same objects. (Davidson 1984, 192)

Thus, to say that a conceptual scheme organizes reality in a different way than the way in which our own conceptual scheme does, a significant chunk of the scheme must be translatable (at least to the extent that its basic ontology and the concepts used to describe the ontology can be translated). Therefore, no criterion for a scheme or a language independent from translatability can be supplied using the condition of organizing reality. Given these considerations, Davidson concludes that this kind of scheme-content dualism, (A-1), fails to establish the meaningfulness of the idea of a language being completely untranslatable.

Next, consider the second approach to a criterion for a scheme or a language, (A-2), which rests on the condition of 'organizing experience'. In this approach what is being organized is experience. Here, it will still be necessary to individuate the constituents of the experience to be organized and describe how these constituents are arranged in order to say that a scheme organizing the experience is different from ours.

However, in individuating the constituents of the experience to be organized, we would have to appeal to a familiar and customary way of doing so. As a result, the supposedly distinct language (or scheme) that organizes the individuated constituents of experience would always closely resemble our own language (at least the ways the constituents of the experience are individuated would be equivalent). Therefore, using the condition of organizing experience would fare no better in achieving the goal of establishing the meaningfulness of the idea that there is a kind of activity that is completely untranslatable into our language but still counts as linguistic.

Finally, let us examine the third approach to a criterion of a language (or a scheme), (A-3), which rests on the condition of 'fitting experience'. A common way to implement this approach is to consider a set of sentences or a theory that fits the evidence of sensory experiences. A theory agreeing with all of sensory experience "successfully faces the tribunal of experience, predicts future experience, or copes with the pattern of our surface irritations" (ibid., 193), altogether making it a theory that 'fits experience'. On this understanding of 'fitting experience', Davidson states, a theory fitting experience can be described as 'being true'.[12]

> In a common course of affairs, a theory may be borne out by the available evidence and yet be false. But what is in view here is not just actually available evidence; it is the totality of possible sensory evidence past, present, and future. We do not need to pause to contemplate what this might mean. The point is that for a theory to fit or face up to the totality of possible sensory evidence is for that theory to be true. (ibid., 193)

If 'fitting experience' can be paraphrased as 'being true', as noted here, then from the third variant of the scheme-content dualism (A-3) the criterion for a scheme that is different from ours would be given as follows: a different scheme is a set of sentences (or a theory) that is "largely true but not translatable" (ibid., 194). According to Davidson, however, this kind of criterion would be unintelligible. To understand why, first, note that this criterion requires determining whether the sentences that a theory is made up from are largely true, and to do so, it is in turn required to determine the extension of the predicate 'being true' with respect to those sentences. Yet, if the extension of the truth predicate is provided in terms of Tarski's theory of truth, then it would be impossible to determine whether the truth predicate applies to the sentences that are not translatable into our language. This comes about as Tarski's theory of truth determines the extension of the truth predicate depending on translation relations, as Davidson writes, "we do not understand it [the notion of truth] independently [of the notion of translation] at all" (ibid., 194).

For this reason, there is no way to determine whether the untranslatable sentences comprising a theory are true, and as a result, the idea of sentences being 'largely true

---

[12] Hacker (1997, 297) points out the tension between Davidson's claim here and the thesis of the underdetermination of theory. I will not discuss this tension here because it is not directly relevant to the problem of Davidson's criticism of conceptual schemes to be raised in this chapter.

but not translatable' would remain unintelligible.[13] Therefore, Davidson concludes, this approach in which a scheme is identified with what 'fits experience' fails to establish the meaningfulness of the idea of a language being completely untranslatable.

According to Davidson then, overall, the dualism between scheme and content is inadequate for making the idea of a completely untranslatable language meaningful: in all of the three different forms of the scheme-content dualism, (A1-A3), such an idea is shown not to be sustainable. Recognizing any form of activity as 'organizing' or 'fitting' for something presupposes that the activity is translatable into our language at least to some extent, and a clear recognition of this would defeat the possibility of a criterion for a language employing no notion of translation; the scheme-content dualism is unable to establish the meaningfulness of a language that is completely untranslatable. We can make the same point from the opposite direction by imagining a form of activity that we have no way (are entirely unable) to translate into our language. Such an activity "that cannot be interpreted as language in our language" (ibid., 185-6) will never be understood as any kind of linguistic activity or as expressing a conceptual scheme. Therefore, Davidson concludes, cases of complete failure of translation do not justify positing the existence of a different conceptual scheme.

(B) Does partial failure of translatability prove the existence of different conceptual schemes?

Let us now turn to cases of partial failure of translatability. To consider this type of failure of translatability, Davidson begins with an overview of how translation is conducted (here it must be noted that Davidson spends by far less space discussing partial failure of translatability than is occupied by the prior discussion of complete failure of translatability).

First, let us start with the question as to what kind of evidence is employed in translating or interpreting a language. Following Quine, Davidson considers the evidence available to us comprising solely the attitudes of a speaker accepting sentences as true or the assenting and dissenting attitudes towards sentences.[14] This kind of evidence, however, does not alone enable an adequate translation of a speaker's sentences. For there is more than one way to account for the speaker's positive or negative attitude towards a sentence by referring to the speaker's meaning and belief (for example, recall the 'dog' and 'fox' example in section 2.3.2). The positive or negative attitude a speaker takes towards a sentence can be

---

[13] What is crucial here is that the criterion of a scheme 'largely true but not translatable' has to be concerned with complete untranslatability. Otherwise—if a theory is merely partially untranslatable—it would be possible to determine the truth conditions of some class of sentences in the theory on the basis of the sentences that are translatable into our language, and consequently the theory could be judged largely true.

[14] Of course, there would be different types of evidence available in cases where the translator and the speaker of the language to be translated share some background knowledge, perhaps due to a preexisting transmission of cultural knowledge. However, the discussion here presupposes cases of radical translation or radical interpretation to focus on the problem of partial failures of translation, ignoring the distracting details.

described as the sum of two vectors, so to speak—it is the output of combining the semantic content of the sentence in question and the belief of the speaker—and so it is impossible to determine the semantic content and the speaker's belief solely on the basis of the attitude that the speaker has towards the sentence.

As also noted in section 2.3.2, to overcome this challenge Davidson introduces the notion of the principle of charity as a methodology necessary for translation and interpretation.[15]

> The principle of charity: assume that there is a general agreement concerning what is believed to be true in constructing a theory of meaning. The theory of meaning on this assumption is a first approximation of the final theory to be obtained.

The principle of charity requires that the beliefs of the interpreter largely agree with those of the interpretee. According to Davidson, in addition to a large degree of agreement between the beliefs of the interpreter and interpretee, it also follows from the principle of charity that there is a large degree of agreement between their conceptual schemes. Davidson writes on this further point as follows:

> We make maximum sense of the words and thoughts of others when we interpret in a way that optimizes agreement (this includes room, as we said, for explicable error, i.e. differences of opinion). Where does this leave the case for conceptual relativism? The answer is, I think, that we must say much the same thing about differences in conceptual scheme as we say about differences in belief: we improve the clarity and bite of declarations of difference, whether of scheme or opinion, by enlarging the basis of shared (translatable) language or of shared opinion. (ibid. 197)

Davidson's claim here is compelling, since beliefs are individuated using concepts, and if the beliefs of the interpreter and interpretee are largely in agreement, then the concepts used to individuate their beliefs would be largely in agreement as well.

In this way, if the principle of charity—a necessary part of the methodology for interpretation—requires there to be a massive agreement with respect to both beliefs and concepts, it would be unjustifiable to suppose that others possess a set of beliefs or concepts that are *radically* different from our own. From this, Davidson concludes that "the attempt to give a solid meaning to the idea of conceptual relativism, and hence to the idea of a conceptual scheme, fares no better when based

---

[15] As I have repeatedly emphasized, what is crucial here is that the principle of charity is not merely heuristically effective but also inevitably required for translation and interpretation. To illustrate this point, consider the following passage by Davidson:
> Since charity is not an option, but a condition of having a workable theory, it is meaningless to suggest that we might fall into massive error by endorsing it. Until we have successfully established a systematic correlation of sentences held true with sentences held true, there are no mistakes to make. Charity is forced on us; whether we like it or not, if we want to understand others, we must count them right in most matters. (Davidson 1984, 197)

on partial failure of translation than when based on total failure" (ibid., 197).

(2) The scope of Davidson's criticism of conceptual schemes

As has been explicated above, Davidson's main complaint against conceptual schemes is that the underlying idea of different conceptual schemes proves incoherent under close scrutiny; there is no way to make sense of the idea that two languages that are untranslatable into one another express two different conceptual schemes. In arguing for this claim, Davidson examines two types of cases in which translation fails: complete and partial failures of translation. Davidson argues that the former type does not prove the existence of different conceptual schemes because no form of activity that is completely untranslatable into our language can be viewed as a linguistic activity, while the latter type of translation failure presupposes the principle of charity, a methodology necessary for interpretation that requires a global agreement on beliefs and concepts between the speaker and interpreter, effectively ruling out the existence of two different conceptual schemes.

Davidson claims that these considerations point to the unintelligibility of the notion of conceptual scheme. Below is the second last paragraph of "On the Very Idea of a Conceptual Scheme":

> It would be wrong to summarize by saying we have shown how communication is possible between people who have different schemes, a way that works without need of what there cannot be, namely a neutral ground, or a common coordinate system. For we have found no intelligible basis on which it can be said that schemes are different. It would be equally wrong to announce the glorious news that all mankind—all speakers of language, at least—share a common scheme and ontology. For if we cannot intelligibly say that schemes are different, neither can we intelligibly say that they are one. (ibid., 197-8)

The conclusion about conceptual schemes here, however, does not validly follow from Davidson's discussion of translatability. Notice that Davidson offers different treatments for complete and partial failures of translation, and his objections to a different conceptual scheme are not equally strong with respect to the two types of translation failure. The problem with the conclusion above is that the idea of a different conceptual scheme is considered no more intelligible in the case of a partial translation failure than in the case of a total translation failure; it is wrong to conclude that all attempts to establish the intelligibility of conceptual relativism—and thereby to establish the intelligibility of the idea of a conceptual scheme—fail equally.

In my view, the difficulty pointed out for a failure of partial translation is, at least, much less severe than that for a failure of complete translation. Davidson's diagnosis of the latter seems correct: it is unjustifiable to deduce a different conceptual scheme from a form of activity that is completely untranslatable, since such an activity cannot be viewed as an instance of language, theory, or conceptual scheme. On the other hand, the difficulty Davidson presented for partial translation failures is nothing more than the following: since the principle of charity requires there to be a substantial agreement on beliefs and concepts (meanings), it is unjustifiable to acknowledge the existence of a radically different conceptual scheme. This difficulty must be clearly distinguished from the former point that it is impossible to conceive of a completely untranslatable activity as expressing a conceptual scheme. For a form of activity in which translation partially fails may be understood as an instance of language, theory, or conceptual scheme by appealing to the partial translatability of the activity. It is important to realize that the principle of charity may eliminate the possibility of any existence of a radically different conceptual scheme, but not the possibility of a partially and moderately different conceptual scheme. In short, according to the principle of charity, although two conceptual schemes cannot be radically different from one another, they can be partially different.

Now, the situation can be described as follows. Davidson is correct with respect to *radically* different conceptual schemes. No attempt to make sense of the idea of a radically different conceptual scheme will work whether it appeals to a partial or complete failure of translation—the former is no better than the latter. (It follows that if conceptual scheme relativism requires the existence of schemes that are radically different from one another, then Davidson's discussion here sufficiently refutes conceptual scheme relativism.[16]) However, since a partial difference is a difference, the idea of a different conceptual scheme is sustainable as long as the idea of conceptual schemes that are partially different from one another is intelligible; there is no need to demonstrate the possibility of a radically different conceptual scheme. Since Davidson's discussion of conceptual schemes in "On the Very Idea of a Conceptual Scheme," though showing the unintelligibility of a radically different conceptual scheme, fails to disprove the intelligibility of a partially different conceptual scheme, it is still reasonable to retain the notion of a conceptual scheme while accepting the major part of Davidson's criticism of conceptual schemes.[17]

Drawing on these considerations, let us revisit the original question as to whether Putnam's conceptual relativity can counter Davidson's criticism of conceptual schemes and remain as a sustainable view. It now seems obvious that this question can be answered in the positive. As already stated, Putnam's conceptual relativity maintains that there is more than one optional language—a partial language that is incorporated with a natural language to extend its use. That is, for Putnam, different languages have a shared component; for example, consider a language that is extended by adding the optional language of set theory and also a language extended

---

[16] I disagree with the claim that conceptual scheme relativism requires the existence of radically different conceptual schemes. Also, Putnam's thesis of conceptual relativity imposes no such requirement, as will be discussed below.

[17] It is, however, left open whether Davidson intended to criticize the idea of a partially different conceptual scheme in this article, besides criticizing that of a radically different conceptual scheme. Consider the following two passages in the article:
> Different points of view make sense, but only if there is a common co-ordinate system on which to plot them; yet the existence of a common system belies the claim of *dramatic incomparability*. What we need, it seems to me, is some idea of the considerations that set the limits to conceptual contrast. (ibid., 184, italics added)
>
> We may identify conceptual schemes with languages, then, or better, allowing for the possibility that more than one language may express the same scheme, sets of intertranslatable languages. (ibid., 185)

by adding the optional language of mereology. These two languages would harbor different implications for what entities exist, but would be accommodating to similar ordinary usages of the predicate 'exist', which is a part of their shared component. It must be clear that the example here illustrates, not the idea of having two radically different conceptual schemes, but the idea of having partially different conceptual schemes. Therefore, Davidson's criticism of conceptual schemes, which only refutes the intelligibility of the idea of a radically different conceptual scheme, fails to undermine Putnam's thesis of conceptual relativity.[18]

The idea of a conceptual scheme is certainly very attractive, but it is questionable if it is possible to expand this idea unrestrictedly and claim that there possibly exist conceptual schemes that are radically different from our own and completely unintelligible to us. Davidson objects to such uncritical expansion by arguing that only what is intelligible from our perspective to a certain degree is justifiably regarded as a conceptual scheme; it validly follows from this objection that the idea of a conceptual scheme that is radically different from our own is unintelligible. However, if Davidson goes one step further and argues that the idea of a conceptual scheme itself is unintelligible, then this step would be questionable, since Davidson's criticism of conceptual schemes does not eliminate the possibility of a partially different conceptual scheme. As long as having two conceptual schemes that are different from one another makes sense, if the difference is merely a partial one, it is possible to sustain the idea of a conceptual scheme. In short, here I have pointed out both the significance and limitations in Davidson's criticism of conceptual schemes.

3.1.3 The remaining problems for Putnam's model of pluralism

The discussion so far has shown that Davidson's criticism of conceptual schemes poses no serious threat to Putnam's conceptual relativity. This does not imply, however, that Putnam's views of conceptual relativity and conceptual pluralism are the last word here, since from a perspective independent of Davidson's criticism, it is possible to point to several problems and obscurities in the justifications and implications of these theses. In what follows, I will raise two issues that seem particularly problematic for Putnam and discuss them closely one by one.

(1) Is an ontological indeterminacy entailed by the indeterminacy in descriptive semantics?

The first issue I wish to discuss is concerned with an inferential leap between

---

[18] In this section, I have developed a defense of Putnam's thesis of conceptual relativity by revealing a weakness in Davidson's criticism of conceptual schemes (the weakness that it is unable to eliminate the possible existence of a partially different conceptual scheme). There are, however, other ways to develop a defense of the thesis. We can mention for example Case's (1997) defense based on the differences between Davidson's and Putnam's notions of a conceptual scheme and also Putnam's (1990) own response to Davidson, which maintains that a radical interpreter already possesses multiple conceptual schemes. In particular, it is worth examining the Case discussion, which is more plausible and simpler than Putnam's, if the primary aim is to defend conceptual relativity. Also, Nagasawa (2001) and Namisato (2001) present defenses of the idea of a conceptual scheme arguing against Davidson, independently of the context of Putnam's discussion of a conceptual scheme.

conceptual relativity and the conclusion Putnam intends to deduce from it. As discussed earlier, to illustrate the thesis of conceptual relativity Putnam brings up a world consisting of three particulars, x_1, x_2, and x_3, and asks how many objects there are in this world, pointing out that more than one legitimate answer is available to this question depending on what logical apparatus we adopt (such as set theory or mereology). Moreover, as for mereological sums he writes, "It is *literally* a matter of convention whether we decide to say they exist" (Putnam 2004b, 43, italics in original), and the justification for this claim is that it is impossible to determine uniquely a correct logical apparatus appealing to the usage of the natural language expression 'exist'.

It is, however, questionable if it is valid to employ the condition of 'being compatible with the uses of natural language expressions' as the sole criterion for evaluating different answers to ontological questions. For example, we may be currently unaware of a more appropriate way to use the word 'exist', which is not reflected in our current usage of the word as well as in our overall linguistic activities. It seems it would also be possible that we have developed a wrong usage of the word 'exist', one that is incompatible with a usage that is more appropriate. Given these possibilities— namely, the possibilities in which our current uses of natural language expressions are not the optimally best—it must be concluded that Putnam's observation that our current usage of 'exist' is compatible with a number of ontological views does not straightforwardly entail the indeterminacy of ontology. Even if there is a question that cannot be answered through analysis of ordinary language, we may arrive at meaningful answers by using a variety of criteria such as explanatory power, coherency with other beliefs, parsimony, etc. (Suppose, for example, that a mereological system can be incorporated with our use of a natural language. In this case, according to Putnam, there would be no reason to rule out mereological schemes. Suppose further that a mereological system has shown itself to be impractical and without any real use in any forms of inquiries. Then although Putnam would still find no reason to exclude mereological schemes, it is reasonable to conclude that there is no particular need to adopt a mereological scheme, nor is there any reason to argue for the existence of mereological sums.)

To illustrate this point in more detail, it is worth introducing Carnap's distinction between descriptive and pure semantics.[19] Descriptive semantics aims at constructing a semantic theory for a historically given language, a 'description of facts', and so descriptive semantics can be seen as an empirical science.[20] In pure semantics, on the other hand, we construct our own semantic rules, and a resulting system of semantic rules may be "in close connection with a historically given language or freely invented" (Carnap 1942, 11-2). Thus, in descriptive semantics (as well as descriptive syntax) it is necessary to theorize on the basis of pragmatic facts, how various expressions are actually used, whereas in pure semantics (as well as pure syntax) it is

---

[19] For this distinction, see (Carnap 1942, section 5).
[20] Carnap's main suggestion here is that a semantic system developed in descriptive semantics is evaluated depending on whether it fits pragmatic facts. It is important not to attribute to Carnap the view that a semantic system in descriptive semantics is a mere description of facts about a particular language. See section 3.2.2 for this point.

not necessary to employ pragmatic facts. Let me quote two relevant passages:

> Descriptive semantics and syntax are indeed based on pragmatics. Suppose we wish to study the semantical and syntactical properties of a certain Eskimo language not previously investigated. Obviously, there is no other way than first to observe the speaking habits of the people who use it. (ibid., 12)

> With respect to pure semantics and syntax the situation is different. These fields are independent of pragmatics. Here we lay down definitions for certain concepts, usually in the form of rules, and study the analytic consequences of these definitions. In choosing the rules we are entirely free. Sometimes we may be guided in our choice by the consideration of a given language, that is, by pragmatical facts. But this concerns only the motivation of our choice and has not bearing upon the correctness of the results of our analysis of the rules. (ibid., 13)

Now, in *Ethics without Ontology*, Putnam maintains that the question as to whether mereological sums exist "is one that the meanings of the words in the natural language, that is, the language that we all speak and cannot avoid speaking every day, simply leaves open" (Putnam 2004b, 43); this quote elucidates the nature of conceptual relativity that Putnam has in mind. His claim here implies, however, only that it is impossible to determine a unique, correct scheme from the perspective of descriptive semantics (which aims at describing the rules governing particular linguistic activities). It by no means supports the claim that we are unable to determine which of the optional languages in question (set theory and mereology) is more advantageous from the perspective of pure semantics as well (which aims at building a useful scheme regardless of whether it fits any particular existing linguistic activities). In other words, if conceptual relativity only implies that it is impossible to determine whether the extension of the predicate 'exist' should include mereological sums by using the condition of 'being compatible with the uses of natural language expressions', then no particular significant ontological claim can be made to follow from conceptual relativity alone.

(2) Is the Putnam position about the relation between conceptual relativity and conceptual pluralism valid?

In the discussion so far, there seems to be an inferential leap between conceptual relativity and the conclusion Putnam wishes to deduce from it. Whether there is a solution to this, Putnam still needs to deal with a problem in the relation between conceptual relativity and conceptual pluralism.

Putnam states that conceptual relativity implies conceptual pluralism, where instances of the former are subsumed under instances of the latter. It is clear that both theses argue for the multiplicity of linguistic schemes that are designed to define concepts and introduce entities, and that conceptual relativity requires two further conditions that need not be observed in instances of conceptual pluralism (cognitive equivalency and incompatibility), so making the relation between conceptual relativity and conceptual pluralism that Putnam has described seem superficially plausible.

Closely scrutinizing the presented examples of these two theses, however, it becomes clear why the Putnam description of the relation between the two is inadequate.

First, compare conceptual relativity and conceptual pluralism in terms of what they really involve. In conceptual relativity, the truth of a statement is relativized to an optional language. As has been stated, conceptual relativity maintains that there is more than one artificial and regimented language that can be incorporated with a natural language—something that we must accept—without this causing any particular contradiction. (An important characteristic of conceptual relativity is that whether an optional language is compatible with the uses of natural language expressions is irrelevant in adjudicating between multiple optional languages.) Since natural languages are different from optional languages, to which the truths of statements are relativized, conceptual relativity is not concerned with natural languages.

By contrast, the examples Putnam brings up to illustrate conceptual pluralism are irrelevant to optional languages: we may describe the contents of a room in terms of fundamental physics as well as in ordinary terms ('table', 'chair', etc.). The plurality in conceptual pluralism indicated by these examples is not a plurality of optional languages, which are incorporated with natural languages. At least, ordinary terms such as 'table' and 'chair' and an ordinary discourse constituted by such vocabulary do not make up optional languages, but belong to natural languages. In fact, in the following passage Putnam clearly acknowledges that conceptual pluralism is not advocating for the plurality of optional languages:

> Moreover, as Case notes, conceptual relativity is only a special case of the wider phenomenon she calls (and I should have called) *pluralism*. The fact that the contents of a room may be partly described in two very different vocabularies cannot be an instance of conceptual relativity in my sense, because (as just noted) *that* phenomenon involves descriptions that are cognitively equivalent in the sense just described, but which are incompatible if taken at face value. But the fact that the contents of a room may be *partly described in the "optional language"* of fields and particles and the fact that it may also be partly described (*in natural language*) by saying that there is a chair in front of a desk are not in *any* way "incompatible" ... (Putnam 2001, 437, italics added)

As suggested by these considerations, conceptual relativity and conceptual pluralism are different with respect to the plurality of what they are concerned with. Conceptual relativity is only concerned with the plurality of optional languages—there are multiple ways to expand the uses of natural language expressions (such as 'exist' and 'object')—whereas conceptual pluralism is free from such constraints, maintaining the plurality of a variety of discourses.[21]

To better elucidate this contrast between conceptual relativity and conceptual

---

[21] It follows that if we use Putnam and Case's terminology, in which a 'conceptual scheme' refers only to an optional language (an auxiliary partial language to be distinguished from a natural language), pluralism must not be formulated in terms of conceptual schemes. However, I will not further discuss this consequence to avoid complicating our discussions.

pluralism, it may be helpful to introduce the 'vertical-horizontal' pluralism distinction.[22] According to Lynch, 'vertical pluralism' is the view that the world contains different types of fact, and so a variety of discourses describing facts at different levels may not be reduced to a fundamental discourse,[23] while 'horizontal pluralism' is the view that, within a single discourse, there may be facts at the same level that are incompatible with one another. Comparing conceptual pluralism and conceptual relativity using this distinction, first, conceptual pluralism becomes classified as a form of vertical pluralism, since Putnam characterizes it as the view that multiple discourses or conceptual schemes may be used with no requirement for a reduction to a fundamental and invariant ontology. (Also, physicalism, the main opponent of conceptual pluralism, is accordingly classified as a form of 'vertical monism'.) On the other hand, conceptual relativity becomes classified as a form of horizontal pluralism, since it is characterized as the view that there may be more than one optional language for figuring out how to expand a concept in ordinary language. It follows that, although Putnam offers conceptual pluralism and relativity as implying the plurality of linguistic schemes, they are concerned with linguistic schemes along two different dimensions.

These considerations have revealed that conceptual relativity and conceptual pluralism are different with respect to not only the conditions of cognitive equivalency and incompatibility—discussed by Putnam in *Ethics without Ontology*—but also in the plurality of what they are actually dealing with. Now, keeping this contrast between the two theses in mind, let us revisit the main theme of conceptual pluralism. We are now in a position to understand more clearly the problem with Putnam's description of the relation between conceptual relativity and pluralism (that the former implies the latter, and that instances of the former are subsumed under instances of the latter). According to Putnam, the heart of conceptual pluralism is that it counters a number of monistic views that contemporary naturalists have proposed (see [Putnam 2004a, 61]). Put differently, conceptual pluralism is intended to be the antithesis to any (vertical) monistic view that draws a 'first- versus second-grade' distinction between conceptual schemes and discourses available to us, and takes only the first-grade schemes to represent the facts of the world and reality. (It follows that instances of conceptual pluralism become incompatible with monism.) The instances of conceptual relativity, however, cannot be viewed as opposing monism. For, as I will argue in what follows, conceptual relativity is compatible with at least certain forms of (vertical) monism. If this understanding of conceptual relativity is correct, then Putnam would be inaccurate in viewing instances of conceptual relativity as special cases of conceptual pluralism.

To illustrate this point further, let us consider the relation between metaphysical realism and physicalist monism, the latter of which was also taken up earlier (see section 2.4.1). According to Putnam, metaphysical realism has the following three characteristics:

---

[22] See (Price 1992, 389-90) and (Lynch 1998, 6). Price's discussion centers around 'vertical pluralism', and Lynch focuses on 'horizontal pluralism'.

[23] In this book, unless otherwise noted, the term 'reduction' is to be understood, not in a normal sense as 'type-type reduction', but as a broader notion including supervenience.

- The world consists of some fixed totality of mind-independent objects.
- There is exactly one true and complete description of 'the way the world is'.
- Truth involves some sort of correspondence relation between words or thought-signs and external things and sets of things. (Putnam 1981, 49)

As pointed out by Case (2001, 424-5), metaphysical realism characterized in this manner is incompatible with conceptual relativity, since the second characteristic directly contradicts the idea that whether there are mereological sums included in the extension of the predicate 'exist' depends on which convention we choose—as well as the idea that there is no objective answer to this question other than appealing to conventions. Therefore, conceptual relativity can be viewed as the antithesis to metaphysical realism.[24]

By contrast, it would be wrong to assume that physicalist monism is incompatible with conceptual relativity. Consider again the mereological example of conceptual relativity: whether mereological sums exist cannot be determined. The property of 'being a sum of A and B' can be regarded as a property supervening on physical properties as long as both A and B are physicalistically acceptable. Just as physicalists have no difficulty in accepting the property of 'being the center of gravity of A', which supervenes on physical properties, accepting the property of 'being a sum of A and B' would cause no trouble for physicalists. It is not, at the same time, required for physicalists to accept the existence of mereological sums.[25] For example, if physicalists have no reason whatsoever to appeal to the concept of a center of gravity—though a center of gravity is a perfectly acceptable object within physicalism—they would not concern themselves with having to accept such an object. This becomes clear as physicalism requires that, for any entity accepted by a physicalist, the set of sentences deducing the entity must fulfill specific conditions, and it is not required in physicalism that physicalists must accept every entity deduced by the set of sentences fulfilling such specific conditions. Likewise, if there is no reason to appeal to mereology, then physicalists would not necessarily have to accept mereological sums.

As is clear from the discussion so far, the question of whether mereological sums are included in the extension of the predicate 'exist' is independent from the question of whether to adopt physicalist monism,[26] and it is at least obvious that the acceptance

---

[24] Putnam famously attacked metaphysical realism through the 'model-theoretic arguments' in the article "Models and Reality" (collected in [Putnam 1983]). Nonetheless, as noted in the following passage, since *Realism with a Human Face* (Putnam 1990) he argues against metaphysical realism emphasizing more on conceptual relativity:
 Indeed, it might be said that the difference between the present book and my work prior to *The Many Faces of Realism* is a shift in emphasis: a shift from emphasizing model-theoretic arguments against metaphysical realism to emphasizing conceptual relativity. (Putnam 1990, xi)
See also (Putnam 1990, 96) for the conflict between conceptual relativity and metaphysical realism.

[25] This would not be the case if an axiomatic system of mereology is included in the foundations of physics.

[26] These questions are, however, not completely independent of one another. Suppose that the property of 'being a sum of A and B' does not supervene on physical properties. Then anyone who adopts physicalism would have to deny the existence of a sum of A and B. Thus, the relation

of physicalist monism can never determine whether to acknowledge mereological sums as entities. Here, it is important to realize that, unlike metaphysical realism, physicalist monism does not require any unique inventory of entities. (In this sense, physicalist monism may be said to be 'weaker' than metaphysical realism.) What physicalist monism requires in ontology is that the set of sentences from which entities are derived must include only those properties that supervene on physical properties. As long as this requirement is fulfilled, physicalists will find no difficulty in accepting the consequence that there is no unique inventory of entities as well as instances of conceptual relativity.

I have previously stated that conceptual relativity is compatible with at least some form of (vertical) monism, and so it will be wrong to conclude prematurely that instances of conceptual relativity are special cases of conceptual pluralism. The arguments above clearly establish the rationale behind this. It is true that instances of conceptual relativity constitute counterexamples to metaphysical realism, according to which there is exactly one true and complete description of the way the world is. However, as the examination of how physicalist monism relates to the ontological question concerning mereological sums here has shown, the mere fact that there is no unique, determinate inventory of entities does not refute monism in general.[27] Therefore, the existence of an instance of conceptual relativity does not necessarily entail conceptual pluralism.

To ease the complexity of the current discussion, let me recapitulate the problem for Putnam that has been pointed out here, part (2). First, Putnam's claim that conceptual relativity implies conceptual pluralism should not be accepted unquestioningly, since these theses are concerned with a plurality of linguistic schemes at two different levels (horizontally and vertically arranged schemes), the acceptance of horizontal pluralism does not necessarily imply the acceptance of vertical pluralism. Second, it is overly simplistic to view instances of conceptual relativity as special cases of conceptual pluralism, since the main lesson of conceptual pluralism is the rejection of monism. Certainly, conceptual relativity implies a plurality of linguistic schemes (thereby constituting the antithesis to metaphysical realism), but for Putnam it is an instance of horizontal pluralism, concerning only a plurality of optional languages. Therefore, no instance of conceptual relativity can be an instance of pluralism, in which there are multiple linguistic schemes in the vertical arrangement. (For this reason, it is wrong to use the mereological example above—

---

between conceptual relativity and monism varies depending on how the scope of monism is set and what instance of conceptual relativity is under consideration. Summing up, the discussion above has shown that there is, at least, a case in which conceptual relativity and monism are compatible. Moreover, given that Putnam most frequently uses the example of mereology in discussing conceptual relativity and that he takes physicalist monism endorsed by 'naturalists' to be the main opponent of conceptual relativity, the discussion above is fully sufficient for refuting his way of characterizing the relation between conceptual relativity and conceptual pluralism.

[27] If metaphysical realism is construed as the monistic view that draws a first- and second-grade distinction by appealing to the possibility of reduction to a fundamental discourse—namely, one true and complete description of the way the world is—then it must be acknowledged that the acceptance of conceptual relativity implies the rejection of a (very strong) form of monism. This is why, in the above, I stated that conceptual relativity is compatible with *at least some form* of (vertical) monism.

whether to acknowledge the existence of mereological sums is not determined—to support conceptual pluralism.)

In short, the relation that Putnam describes does not hold between conceptual relativity and conceptual pluralism. Attempting to establish a close relation between these two theses seems to create a potential source of numerous misunderstandings. In particular, conceptual pluralism must be separated from conceptual relativity when the focus is on the conflict between monism and pluralism, rather than on evaluating metaphysical realism.

The current subsection has pointed out that there are at least two problems with Putnam's views of conceptual relativity and conceptual pluralism. Now, it must be kept in mind that the main goal of this chapter is to provide a clear formulation of pluralism. The problem discussed here in (2), however, would appear to present a serious obstacle to achieving this goal. For, if there is no close connection between conceptual relativity and conceptual pluralism (for example, an implication relation) like Putnam suggests, it would be unjustifiable to broaden the understanding of conceptual relativity to encompass conceptual pluralism, where the instances of the former are clearer than those of the latter because the identity conditions of linguistic schemes—the plurality of which is asserted—are explicitly provided.

Let me elaborate on this point a little further referring to a concrete example. In what sense is conceptual relativity clearer than conceptual pluralism? As Putnam states (Putnam 2001, 432-3), optional languages, to which the truths of statements are relativized, are regimented partial languages, and their identity conditions can be specified by referring to rule systems. On the other hand, as also noted earlier, the instances of conceptual pluralism are not described in terms of optional languages, which have explicit identity conditions. An instance of conceptual relativity, which Putnam brings up, involves the contrast between a description of the world in terms of fundamental physics and a description of the world in terms of ordinary language such as 'table' and 'chair'. At least, the latter description belongs to the natural language that we speak every day—the language we commonly have to use—rather than to an optional language that is a regimented partial language incorporated with a natural language.

The fact that conceptual pluralism involves natural languages is problematic for the goal of this chapter: to provide a clear formulation of pluralism, since natural languages and concepts used in them are not likely to have clear identity conditions, unlike optional languages, the linguistic rules of which are made explicit or provided formally. Therefore, if the example in the previous paragraph represents conceptual pluralism, pluralism would have to be formulated in terms of a 'discourse', a 'conceptual framework', or something of that kind (their identity conditions are not very clear). (This issue creates a further problem. It is unclear whether the example above that Putnam uses to illustrate conceptual pluralism is really an instance of pluralism. Suppose that the pair of descriptions above—the descriptions of the world in terms of fundamental physics and using ordinary everyday language—are presented as a counterexample to physicalist monism. In order for this pair of descriptions to refute physicalist monism, it would have to be the case that properties such as 'being a table' and 'being a chair' do not supervene on physical properties.

However, because of the lack of clarity arising with the use of natural language, it remains unclear whether this can be argued to be the case. In other words, when multiple linguistic schemes are presented by referring to concepts or descriptions in natural languages, it cannot be simply evaluated whether such schemes really instantiate pluralism.)[28]

3.2 The Carnapian Model of Pluralism

One problem with Putnam's conception of conceptual pluralism is that the identity conditions of discourses and conceptual frameworks, which constitute pluralism, cannot be clearly specified. If Putnam were correct in taking conceptual relativity to imply conceptual pluralism, then the understanding of the former would have been likely to enable understanding of the latter—instances of conceptual relativity would then be easier to understand because it is possible to explicitly specify what the truths of statements are relativized to. As I have argued above, however, if the focus is on the conflict between monism and pluralism, then conceptual pluralism must be separated from conceptual relativity, and so the clarity in instances of conceptual relativity does not extend to instances of conceptual pluralism.

The main reason for denying a close connection between conceptual relativity and pluralism (in contrast to Putnam's claim) is that Putnam narrowly defines relativity as a phenomenon on the horizontal level, a conflict between optional languages. If he imposes no such constraint on conceptual relativity, then the understanding of its cases may be extended to cases of conceptual pluralism, yielding a clearer picture of pluralism. These considerations point to the possibility of building a model of pluralism that takes advantage of both the clarity of conceptual relativity and a rejection of monism, which is the original motivation for holding pluralism. In my view, Carnap's views on pluralism—where a number of similarities to Putnam's are

---

[28] In chapter 2, I have discussed the sectarian approach that attempts to reconcile the indeterminacy theses and realism about meaning and propositional attitudes. According to this approach, despite indeterminacy, we regard a translation manual and theory of interpretation that we adopt as providing facts about meaning and propositional attitudes. In the current section, I have brought up the lack of clarity presented by natural language and argued that Putnam's pluralist model suffers from the problem of ambiguity when considering the subject matter of pluralism. However, one may counter this criticism by arguing that the sectarian approach, discussed in chapter 2, is applicable to the matter of lack of clarity in natural language, and then there would be no difficulty in viewing natural languages as among linguistic schemes that make up instances of pluralism.

If a Davidsonian theory of interpretation provides a semantic system for a natural language and the sectarian approach overcomes the indeterminacy theses, then it would indeed be unproblematic to consider the semantic system of a natural language to belong among linguistic schemes for pluralism. This reply to my argument against Putnam, however, overlooks an important issue. Here, what is included among linguistic schemes is not a natural language itself, but a semantic system constructed by us to fit the uses of the natural language in question. As will be discussed further in section 3.2.1, in descriptive semantics, where the aim is at constructing a semantic system for an existing natural language, the resulting semantic system must be distinguished from the natural language itself. They are not identical with one another; instead, the resulting system is created in such a way that it is compatible with pragmatic facts about the target natural language. (For these thoughts I benefited greatly from discussion with Shunsuke Yatabe. I wish to express my gratitude to him.)

observed—have already pursued that possibility to a certain extent.[29]

Accordingly, in this section, I will attempt to extract a clearer formulation of pluralism from Carnap's discussion of pluralism. First, in section 3.2.1, I will provide an outline of Carnap's semantic project, formulating the 'Carnapian model of pluralism', the main theme of this section. Next, in section 3.2.2, I will examine the relation between this Carnapian model of pluralism and Carnap's philosophy, arguing that the pluralist view embraced by the Carnapian model should not be attributed to Carnap himself. Then in section 3.2.3, I will turn to Quine's criticism of analyticity, which has been (and still is) considered a major threat to Carnap's philosophy. I will argue that the Carnapian model can overcome Quine's criticism of analyticity, allowing it to remain as a viable theoretical option. In section 3.2.4, I will closely examine the characteristics of the Carnapian model of pluralism by comparing it with Putnam's views of pluralism. In section 3.2.5, I will argue that the Carnapian model is compatible with naturalism, and finally in section 3.2.6, I will discuss how our conceptual activities are to be depicted using the Carnapian model.

3.2.1 Carnap's semantic project: pure semantics and pragmatism

As already stated in section 3.1.2, Carnap's semantic studies are divided into two parts: descriptive semantics and pure semantics. What follows presents an outline of Carnap's semantic project by describing the basics of how a semantic system is constructed, first, in descriptive semantics and, second, in pure semantics.

According to Carnap, in any study of a language, the 'object-language' must be distinguished from the 'metalanguage', where the former is the subject matter of the study while the latter is the language in which the results of the study are formulated (the object- and metalanguage distinction is important in both descriptive and pure semantics). Suppose that we undertake a descriptive semantic inquiry into an unknown language B, spoken by a specific population, and use English as the metalanguage of the inquiry.[30] In pursuing this inquiry, we would first observe linguistic activities of the population in question and collect data about what and how the population use words and sentences ('pragmatics' in Carnap's sense). Based on these pragmatic observations, next, we would formulate a system of rules establishing referential and other semantic relations ('semantics'). It is worth noting here that Carnap does not think that the pragmatic observations of a language uniquely determine a system of semantic rules for that language. For example, imagine that our pragmatic observations discovered that "the word 'mond' of B was used in 98 per cent of the cases for the moon and in 2 per cent for a certain lantern" (Carnap 1939, 6). In this scenario, according to Carnap, "it is a matter of our decision whether we construct the rules in such a way that both the moon and the lantern are designata of 'mond' or only the moon" (ibid.). If we formulate a semantic system in the former

---

[29] Putnam acknowledges that his views on pluralism are similar to Carnap's, and some theorists consider Putnam to be a 'neo-Carnapian'. See (Putnam 1994, 248-9; 1990, 102-3; Eklund 2006a, 8).
[30] The ensuing exposition is a reconstruction of Carnap's (1939) discussion of descriptive and pure semantics. Carnap (1939) is the earliest publication after he started working on semantic theory, and it presents a brief overview of how to construct a system of semantic rules.

way, the use of 'mond' to talk about the lantern would be a correct application of the word; if we create a semantic system in the latter way, it would be a wrong application of the word. For Carnap, whether a use of a word is 'right' or 'wrong' can only be answered relative to a semantic system. On this point, he writes as follows:

> A question of right or wrong must always refer to a system of rules. Strictly speaking, the rules which we shall lay down are not rules of the factually given language B; they rather constitute a language system corresponding to B which we will call the *semantical system B-S*. The language B belongs to the world of facts ... The language system B-S, on the other hand, is something constructed by us ... (Carnap 1939, 7, italics in original)

Of course, the semantic system B-S is not constructed in a completely arbitrary way; it is rather developed based on an empirical constraint—in accordance with the collected pragmatic facts about the language B (this constraint essentially characterizes descriptive semantics). At the same time, however, the pragmatic facts about B do not uniquely determine a semantic system for B.[31] Also, the semantic system B-S, proposed in a descriptive semantic inquiry, is not a natural language itself but an 'imitation' of a natural language, which is constructed to be compatible with pragmatic facts about the uses of a given natural language. It is possible to construct more than one such imitation for a single natural language.

I have so far outlined how a semantic system is constructed in descriptive semantics and also discussed some of the implications. Now, I turn to the other half of Carnap's semantic project, pure semantics. Pure semantics is free from the constraint that a resulting system must be compatible with pragmatic facts about the language in question, and where more leeway is permitted in formulating a semantic system. Consider the following remarks by Carnap:

> If we are concerned with a historically given language, the pragmatical description comes first, and then we may go by abstraction to semantics and) either from semantics or immediately from pragmatics) to syntax. The situation is quite different if we wish to construct a language (or rather a language system, because we lay down rules), perhaps with the intention of practical application, as for making communications or formulating a scientific theory. Here we are not bound by a previous use of language, but are free to construct in accordance with our wishes and purposes. (ibid., 24)

> The task is not to decide which of the different systems is "the right logic" but to examine their formal properties and the possibilities for their interpretation

---

[31] In the later article "Meaning and Synonymy in Natural Languages" (collected in [Carnap 1956]), Carnap makes the same point, that pragmatic facts do not necessarily determine a unique extension of a predicate in descriptive semantics. (Though not directly related to the current discussion, in the same article Carnap made a response to Quine's "Two Dogmas of Empiricism.") This claim that pragmatic facts do not uniquely determine a semantic system is closely analogous to the thesis of conceptual relativity formulated in (Putnam 2004b). See section 3.2.4.

and application in science. It might be that a system deviating from the ordinary form will turn out to be useful as a basis for the language of science. (ibid., 28-9)

As suggested by the quote here, pure semantics develops its systems independently of pragmatic facts as presented by existing languages. To illustrate this point further, consider the following example that Carnap presents in the article "Meaning Postulates" (1952, collected in [Carnap 1956]). Let B, M, BL, and R stand for 'being a bachelor', 'being married', 'being black', and 'being a raven', respectively. Now, let us construct a semantic system in which the sentence 'if Jack is a bachelor, then he is not married' ($Bj \to \neg Mj$) is true by virtue of the meanings of the words making up the whole of the sentence. An obvious instance of a sentence that is true by virtue of the meanings of the words that make it up is a logical truth. The truth of the sentence in question, however, would not be guaranteed by merely defining the list of logical constants and their behavior, unlike the cases presenting a logical truth, such as 'Fido is black or Fido is not black' ($BLf \lor \neg BLf$). (If the behavior of the logical connectives in a semantic system is defined in accordance with classical logic, '$BLf \lor \neg BLf$' would be proven as a logical truth in that system.) So appealing to the notion of logical truth does not enable making the sentence true by virtue of the meanings of the words in it.

Then, what can we do to make '$Bj \to \neg Mj$' true in this semantic system by virtue of the meanings of its constituent words? Carnap's solution to this problem is to introduce 'meaning postulates' as rules in a semantic system. For example, the meaning postulate

P1: $\forall x(Bx \to \neg Mx)$

provides sufficient information to derive the truth of '$Bj \to \neg Mj$' (namely, the incompatibility of the properties expressed by B and M), even though it determines neither the extensions of B and M nor the truth values of the sentences in which these predicates appear (doing so would require an empirical inquiry). As a result, by stipulating this postulate, '$Bj \to \neg Mj$' becomes a sentence that is true by virtue of a semantic rule concerning the predicates B and M.

Here, we would ask whether it is legitimate to introduce a postulate like P1 into a semantic system. (In other words, on what grounds is the introduction of P1 justified?) According to Carnap, whether to introduce a meaning postulate is a matter for us to decide, and it is a moot point whether its inclusion is legitimate. Consider the following passages:

> Suppose that the author of a system wishes the predicates 'B' and 'M' to designate the properties Bachelor and Married, respectively. How does he know that these properties are incompatible and that therefore he has to lay down postulate P1? *This is not a matter of knowledge but of decision.* His knowledge or belief that the English words 'bachelor' and 'married' are always or usually understood in such a way that they are incompatible may influence his decision if he has the intention to reflect in his system some of the meaning relations of English words. (Carnap 1956, 224-5, italics added)

> Suppose he wishes the predicates 'Bl' and 'R' to correspond to the words 'black' and 'raven'. While the meaning of 'black' is fairly clear, that of raven is rather vague in the everyday language. There is no point for him to make an elaborate study, based either on introspection or on statistical investigation of common usage, in order to find out whether 'raven' always or mostly entails 'black'. *It is rather his task to make up his mind whether he wishes the predicates 'R' and 'Bl' of his system to be used in such a way that the first logically entails the second.* If so, he has to add the postulate
> (P2) '$(x)(Rx \supset Blx)$'
> to the system, otherwise not. (ibid., 225, italics added)

What is crucial here is that in pure semantics we may introduce an arbitrary meaning postulate into a semantic system, and there is no external constraint precluding or forcing the introduction of any such meaning postulate. If it is decided to introduce the meaning postulate P2 into a system, then the system is subject to the constraint on predicate R that it cannot apply to any object outside the extension of predicate BL, and the possibility of discovering an R that is not BL is excluded *a priori*. If, on the other hand, P2 is not introduced into a system, then the existence of an R that is not BL is not excluded *a priori* in that system—though a non-black raven would be probably a little surprising. It is important to note that the decision to introduce the meaning postulate P2 into a semantic system would be made by those who construct the system *independently* of pragmatic facts about how predicates are used in preexisting natural languages. According to Carnap, "They [those who construct a system] are free to choose their postulates, guided not by their beliefs concerning facts of the world but by their intentions with respect to the meanings, i.e., the ways of use of the descriptive constants [the predicates used in descriptions]" (ibid., 225).

As illustrated by this example, in pure semantics theorists may construct a variety of semantic systems as they see fit, and a semantic system created in this manner is not expected to mimic the uses of a particular natural language. Now, it is then reasonable to ask what purpose the creation of a semantic system in pure semantics serves and how semantic systems should be evaluated. According to Carnap, the answers to these questions are provided in terms of the 'principle of tolerance' and the 'criterion of pragmatic efficacy' (or 'pragmatic efficiency'). Consider the following remarks:

> The acceptance or rejection of abstract linguistic forms, just as the acceptance or rejection of any other linguistic forms in any branch of science, will finally be decided by their efficiency as instruments, the ratio of the results achieved to the amount and complexity of the efforts required. To decree dogmatic prohibitions of certain linguistic forms instead of testing them by their success or failure in practical use, is worse than futile; it is positively harmful because it may obstruct scientific progress. The history of science shows examples of such prohibitions based on prejudices deriving from religious, mythological, metaphysical, or other irrational sources, which slowed up the developments for shorter or longer

periods of time. Let us learn from the lessons of history. Let us grant to those who work in any special field of investigation the freedom to use any form of expression which seems useful to them; the work in the field will sooner or later lead to the elimination of these forms which have no useful function. *Let us be cautious in making assertions and critical in examining them, but tolerant in permitting linguistic forms.* (Carnap 1956, 221, italics in original)

Towards the end of this quote, Carnap endorses the idea that theorists are allowed to construct any semantic system (and certainly so in the development stage of an inquiry)—a principle that has been termed the 'principle of tolerance'. In other words, those who construct a system may design any form of semantic system ignoring requirements that could arise from a range of sources—for example, the requirement that the resulting system must fit the pragmatic facts about existing natural languages, that it must not deny the existence of God, or that it must exclude the existence of an abstract object occupying no particular space. Different systems of semantic rules are designed for different inquiries, each intended to function as a useful tool in a particular inquiry. The legitimacy of a system is determined on the basis of the pragmatic criterion of whether the system is useful in the inquiry for which it is designed. (The fact that the criterion of pragmatic efficacy is used in pure semantics implies that the criterion of correspondence to 'reality in itself'—existing independently of us—isn't used in pure semantics to evaluate a semantic system.[32]) Therefore, whether to adopt a semantic system as constructed depends on the result of the inquiry for which it is used, not on the similarities to any particular language, and a system of rules deviating from the actual usages of some language may turn out to be effective in achieving the goals of an inquiry. To summarize, pure semantics is primarily characterized by the principle of tolerance and the criterion of pragmatic efficacy.

The discussion so far has presented an overview of Carnap's semantic project sketching its two components: descriptive semantics and pure semantics. Carnap's views on pure semantics, in particular the principle of tolerance and the criterion of pragmatic efficacy, open up the possibility of developing a plausible formulation for pluralism, the main topic of this chapter (although Carnap's views on pure semantics do not logically imply pluralism—see section 3.2.2 for details of this qualification). Now, drawing on Carnap's semantic project, I will develop a pluralistic view that could appropriately be named the 'Carnapian model of pluralism' or 'conventionalist pluralism based on pragmatism'. The following four theses characterize this Carnapian model of pluralism (sections 3.2.4 and 3.2.6 provide a detailed examination of its characteristics and implications):

(ⅰ) The Carnapian model of pluralism is pluralism for systems of semantic rules. Conceptual schemes are specified in terms of semantic systems—they are individuated using the similarities and differences of semantic rules that are

---

[32] See (Carnap 1956, 205-21). It may be worth noting that Carnap and Quine are in complete agreement about this idea (see Quine 1953, 78-9).

established for concepts.

(ii) Systems of semantic rules are conventionally established, and there is no need to construct them in such a way that they mimic the uses of existing languages.

(iii) Systems of semantic rules are evaluated from a pragmatic viewpoint in terms of efficacy to achieve the goal of the inquiry at hand.

(iv) Different semantic systems are constructed and employed for different inquiries that have different goals. Further, there is no fundamental semantic system that derivatively justifies all other systems.

In pursuing the objective of this chapter, to formulate a clearer and more convincing form of pluralism, it is important to specify what this particular form of pluralism sees pluralism to be about and how it is an antithesis to monism (section 3.1.3 has pointed out that Putnam's pluralism fails to specify these aspects of pluralism adequately). To address these two aspects of pluralism, I will elaborate theses (i) and (iv) above in the remainder of this subsection.

First, consider thesis (i), according to which the Carnapian model of pluralism is a pluralism of semantic systems that are individuated in terms of semantic rules established for concepts. Let me illustrate this by way of example. Suppose that in pure semantics we wish to develop a semantic system for artificial languages L1 and L2, each of which includes three descriptive predicates.[33] (Note that L1 and L2 include expressions that appear to be words in English or German, but L1 and L2 are not natural languages.) Let the following specify the semantic rules for each language:
A fragment of a semantic system for L1[34]

(a) The sentence of L1 'x is black' is true if and only if the referent of 'x' is black.

(b) The sentence of L1 'x is a bird' is true if and only if the referent of 'x' is a bird.

(c) The sentence of L1 'For all x, if x is a raven, then x is a bird' is true.

(d) The sentence of L1 'For all x, if x is a raven, then x is black' is true.

---

[33] Here, I use an example in pure semantics because it simplifies the current discussion abstracting away from the constraint that a resulting system must fit pragmatic facts. Of course, I could have used an example in descriptive semantics to draw the same conclusion, where a semantic system must fit the pragmatic facts about existing languages.

[34] Although L1 and L2 include only three descriptive predicates (with the rules as specified here), the system of semantic rules for each language has many other rules including those specifying the behavior of logical constants.

160   Chapter 3 Towards the Development of Pluralistic Naturalism

A fragment of a semantic system for L2

(e) The sentence of L2 'x ist schwarz' is true if and only if the referent of 'x' is black.

(f) The sentence of L2 'x ist ein Vogel' is true if and only if the referent of 'x' is a bird.

(g) The sentence of L2 'Für alle x, wenn x ein Rabe ist, dann ist x ein Vogel' is true.

Assuming that these semantic systems correspond to conceptual schemes—networks of concepts that segment and organize our perceptions and thoughts—then at least L1 and L2 are associated with different conceptual schemes, since the rules for L1 that define the uses of the predicate 'raven' are clearly different from the rule for L2 that defines the uses of the predicate 'Rabe'. Strictly speaking, the two languages have to be associated with different conceptual schemes, although they can be said to be similar to one another due to the overlapping semantic rules that govern their behaviors.[35] (For example, the semantic system for L1 includes the meaning postulate (d), ruling out the possibility of discovering an object that the predicate 'raven' (in L1) is true of but is not black, whereas the semantic system for L2 has no such meaning postulate that rules out the possibility of a non-black object that the predicate 'Rabe' is true of. As a result, there is no concept in L2 h that is exactly like the concept 'raven' in L1.)

Now, let us consider a different semantic system for L2 (or its fragment), which is exactly like the one above except for the following additional meaning postulate:

(h) The sentence in L2 'Für alle x, wenn x ein Rabe ist, dann ist x schwarz' is true.

In this system the rules for the descriptive predicates in L2 'schwarz', 'Vogel', and 'Rabe' are exactly the same as those in the system for L1 (the rules for the predicates in L1 'black', 'bird', and 'raven'). Therefore, the semantic system for L1 and the new system for L2 are, despite their different vocabularies, not distinguished from one another in terms of the function of a conceptual scheme—to segment and organize our perceptions and thoughts. In this chapter, accordingly, let us say that for two semantic systems, if they are equivalent to one another regardless of their vocabularies, then they express one and the same conceptual scheme. (This formulation of a conceptual scheme follows Davidson's basic idea that two languages that are mutually translatable express one and the same conceptual scheme.) The discussion here has clarified the identity criterion for conceptual schemes, and the Carnapian model of pluralism is a pluralism of conceptual schemes.

---

[35] Lynch has developed an interesting idea of concept identity, which may be relevant to the current discussion. I will not, however, delve into Lynch's discussion of concepts to avoid further complications.

I have so far argued that the subject matter of pluralism is clarified in the Carnapian model; the identity criterion for conceptual schemes can be articulated in terms of the equivalency of systems of semantic rules (apart from their vocabularies). Let us now turn to thesis (iv), in particular, the view that there is no fundamental semantic system that justifies all other systems. Thesis (iv) is intended to be an antithesis to a monistic view. To understand exactly how this can be so, it seems helpful to begin by stating a monistic position, considering how semantic systems are to be constructed from a monistic viewpoint. For this reason, the following will discuss physicalism, a prototypical monistic position, examining the constraint it imposes on the construction of a semantic system.

In this book, physicalism is characterized as the view that every property that is used to describe a fact supervenes on physical properties (see section 2.1.1). Physicalism characterized in this way imposes a constraint, not only on 'properties' (which appear in this formulation of physicalism), but also on 'predicates', linguistic counterparts of properties. For example, physicalists may tolerate a semantic system that includes a descriptive predicate expressing a property that does not supervene on physical properties. They cannot, nevertheless, accept the sentences of such semantic systems as expressing facts. This is because, according to physicalism, for a sentence to express a fact all the properties or predicates in the sentence have to supervene on physical properties. In other words, from a physicalist viewpoint, a semantic system containing physicalistically unacceptable properties or predicates is considered a second-grade conceptual system and excluded from the scope of a factual discourse.

The preceding discussion describes how semantic systems are to be constructed under physicalist monism, and it became clear now how exactly thesis (iv) functions as an antithesis to a monistic view. A monistic view distinguishes first-grade and second-grade semantic systems—or factual and non-factual systems—by using a criterion that refers to a special and fundamental semantic system, whereas thesis (iv) denies the existence of such a special and fundamental system. It is true that the principle of tolerance in the Carnapian model permits the constructions of a variety of semantic systems, and that they are evaluated in accordance with the pragmatic criterion of efficacy for the goal of a particular inquiry. This criterion for evaluating semantic systems, however, by no means appeals to a fundamental system that a monistic view requires. That is, in the Carnapian model, monism and pluralism are different in terms of how to evaluate semantic systems—whether to appeal to a fundamental system or to pragmatism. (It is important here not to overlook that the role of (iv) is quite distinct from the role that the principle of tolerance plays. For, as will be discussed in section 3.2.2, the principle of tolerance is a principle operating at the point of *introducing hypotheses* about linguistic forms, not at the point of giving a final verdict on those hypotheses. By contrast, in the Carnapian model, the conflict between monism and pluralism emerges in the context of evaluating semantic systems, which are freely constructed given the principle of tolerance—in other words, in the context of determining whether a semantic system can be considered a factual discourse. Therefore, the principle of tolerance itself supports neither monism nor pluralism.)

In this subsection, I have elucidated the subject matter of the Carnapian model of pluralism—it is a pluralism of semantic systems—as well as the identity criterion for semantic systems, discussing the main characteristics of the model. I have formulated this Carnapian model of pluralism based on Carnap's semantic project, but—as is clear from the discussion so far—it does not necessarily follow that Carnap himself held any pluralistic views suggested by the model, nor do I intend to claim so. To avoid unnecessary objections and confusions, I will discuss the details of this point of interpretation in the next subsection.

3.2.2 Carnap's philosophy and pluralism

A number of authors have interpreted Carnap's semantic project, and in particular, the principle of tolerance (one of the core theses in the project) as implying relativism or pluralism (see [Eklund 2006a] and [Putnam 1990, 99]). It would be a mistake, however, to conclude hastily from the principle of tolerance alone that Carnap's project of pure semantics logically implies a pluralistic position or that Carnap is a pluralist. In what follows, I will examine this interpretation of Carnap's semantic project by addressing some of the interpretive issues in Carnap's philosophy, although not all of these are directly relevant to the present purposes.

First, I will show that Carnap's semantic project does not logically imply a pluralistic position. Many theorists maintain otherwise, primarily on the basis of the principle of tolerance. It is, hence, worth clarifying in what context this principle can be invoked. Let me quote again the relevant passage from Carnap's writings.

> Let us grant to those who work in any special field of investigation the freedom to use any form of expression which seems useful to them; the work in the field will sooner or later lead to the elimination of these forms which have no useful function. *Let us be cautious in making assertions and critical in examining them, but tolerant in permitting linguistic forms.* (Carnap 1956, 221, italics in original)

As this quote indicates, the principle of tolerance operates at the point of introducing hypotheses about linguistic forms, not of passing a final verdict on such hypotheses. In other words, this principle states that we may construct and experiment with any system, without stating anything about what system is to be ultimately adopted. Therefore, the principle of tolerance alone does not imply any form of pluralism.

For Carnap, various hypotheses must be evaluated according to the pragmatic criterion of efficacy for the goal of the inquiry at hand. This pragmatic criterion also does not logically imply pluralism. For example, like Carnap, Quine rejects the idea of evaluating conceptual schemes by a comparison with 'reality in itself', something independent of any scheme, explicitly stating that he instead adopts a pragmatic criterion for conceptual schemes. At the same time, however, Quine maintains that there is a unique, universal goal for all inquiries in terms of which all conceptual schemes must be evaluated, as is clear from the following remarks: "the purpose of concepts and of language is efficacy in communication and in prediction" (Quine 1953, 79); "As an empiricist I continue to think of the conceptual scheme of science as a tool, ultimately, for predicting future experience in the light of past experience" (ibid., 44). This idea of a unique and universal criterion led Quine to taking the normative ideal of simplicity as a special criterion and eventually to endorsing physicalist monism.[36] Of course, unlike Quine, Carnap explicitly supports no particular view of the goal of science,[37] and so Carnap seems to remain neutral at least on the meta-level question of what criterion must be used to evaluate semantic systems. At the very least, regardless of Carnap's own views of the goal of science, the above example from Quine demonstrates that accepting the pragmatic criterion of efficacy for the goal of inquiry does not imply pluralism. Therefore, it must be concluded that the core theses of Carnap's semantic project—the principle of tolerance and the criterion of pragmatic efficacy—do not imply pluralism by themselves, even if they provide the groundwork for a pluralistic position.

Second, consider another reason for why it would be a mistake to attribute a pluralistic position to Carnap, namely, his commitment to natural scientism and empiricism. The model of pluralism derived from Carnap's philosophy in this chapter embraces the following views: a variety of linguistic forms must be developed, including a language in which propositions about physical objects are basic propositions in empirical science, a language in which the phenomenal propositions for each individual are fundamental, a realist language in which numbers and classes exist, a nominalist language that denies the existence of such abstract objects, and so on; such languages are evaluated exclusively from the viewpoint of pragmatic efficacy for the goal of a particular inquiry, and it is meaningless to assert that one of these languages corresponds to 'extra-linguistic facts' or 'reality existing independently of our belief system'. Nevertheless, it would be problematic to identify Carnap's philosophy with a position that only investigates meta-level questions concerning linguistic forms and philosophical theses without endorsing particular forms or theses. For, though this position does capture an aspect of Carnap's philosophy, in many places, Carnap clearly indicates that he is also committed to natural scientism and an extreme version of empiricism. (For example, it is an undisputed fact that Carnap was a main proponent of logical positivism, a position attempting to unify all scientific inquiries by taking natural science to be an ideal of intellectual inquiry and introducing its methodology—and so logical positivism advanced a form of natural scientism. Also, Carnap adopted many theses that epitomize reductionism and foundationalist empiricism, such as the verifiability principle of meaning and confirmationism.[38])

---

[36] See (Igashira 2005).

[37] Nevertheless, Carnap exceptionally requires empiricism, according to which there has to be an objective criterion for the validity of a claim.

[38] Carnap earlier proposed 'verifiability' as the condition for the meaningfulness of a sentence—that a sentence can in principle be verified or refuted definitely—and eventually replaced it with 'conformability'—and that the sentence entails a sentence that only includes observational predicates. He also introduced 'testability'—that the sentence is not only confirmable by observable events but also the method of intentionally bringing about such events is identifiable—but this condition is not adopted as the criterion for meaningfulness. See (Carnap 1936; 1963, 56-9).

164 Chapter 3 Towards the Development of Pluralistic Naturalism

It may also be important to bear in mind that this duplicity between meta-philosophical pluralism and the commitment to natural scientism as well as empiricism observable in Carnap's writings has caused some difficulty in understanding Carnap's philosophy. Theorists who are sympathetic to Carnap tend to emphasize the pluralistic and neutral aspect of Carnap's philosophy, whereas those critical of Carnap tend to emphasize natural scientism and his extreme version of empiricism. These theories often talk at cross-purposes when depicting different visions of Carnap's philosophy. For example, Thomas Ricketts, sympathetic to Carnap, emphasizes the neutral aspect of Carnap's philosophy (by referring to the principle of tolerance, etc.); and while Putnam approves Ricketts's interpretation of Carnap to some degree, shows the following reservation:

> Yet I am not ready to admit that my criticisms of Carnap were based on misreadings, or that my charges of conventionalism and empiricism were completely unfounded. Ricketts's Carnap, the Carnap who holds no doctrines but only asks for "clarification," without any substantive position on what clarification consists of, is just not the Carnap I knew and loved.
>
> Re Carnap's empiricism: the fact is that Carnap wrote *Der Logische Aufbau der Welt*. And while readings of that work which resemble Ricketts's reading of the *Logical Syntax* have been offered, they depend on playing down both the massiveness of the construction presented in that work—if Carnap just wanted to give an example of the possibility of alternative, equally correct "bases" for the reconstruction of the language of science, it is striking that he choose to work so hard to provide a phenomenalistic, indeed a solipsistic, reconstruction—and the explicit statement in that work that the solipsistic (*Eigenpsychisch*) basis is epistemologically primary.[39] (Putnam 1994, 281)

Several respondents have also pointed out this tension between Carnap's commitment to particular philosophical theses (such as natural scientism and empiricism) and his pluralistic, neutral attitude towards meta-level questions about how to evaluate semantic systems.[40] It follows from this tension that even if some form of pluralism can be developed from the principle of tolerance together with the criterion of pragmatic efficacy, it would be unjustifiable to attribute such a view to Carnap.

This tension in Carnap's philosophy, however, results in no particular contradictions, nor is it a problem for the model of pluralism that this book has been developing. This is because Carnap's project of pure semantics is separable from his acceptance of natural scientism and empiricism, since the project is concerned with meta-level questions about these particular theses. Consider, for example, the following remarks on empiricism by Carnap:

> It seems to me that it is preferable to formulate the principle of empiricism not in the form of an assertion—"all knowledge is empirical" or "all synthetic

---

[39] See (Carnap 1936, 423-4) for the gist of his 'methodological solipsism'.
[40] See, for example, (Hookway 1988, 61-2).

sentences that we can know are based on (or connected with) experiences" or the like—but rather in the form of a proposal or requirement. As empiricists, we require the language of science to be restricted in a certain way; we require that descriptive predicates and hence synthetic sentences are not to be admitted unless they have some connection with possible observations, a connection which has to be characterized in a suitable way. (Carnap 1936, 33)

This may be summed up as that Carnap uses the project of pure semantics as a backdrop—characterized by the principle of tolerance and the criterion of pragmatic efficacy and also admits of pluralism—and makes a particular proposal based on that backdrop—he proposes a linguistic form that supports empiricism and natural scientism, the most plausible and effective from his own perspective (more specifically, the proposal is a constraint on semantic systems).[41] These two separate steps create no contradiction.[42] Thus, upholding Carnap's semantic project neither conflicts with nor necessitates a commitment to natural scientism or empiricism. Depending on how to interpret the purpose and goal of an inquiry, there may be cases in which no empirical scientific constraint should be imposed on the introduction of a linguistic form (consider, for example, history in which empirical testing is not required to defend a claim). Therefore, adopting Carnap's semantic project is independent of proposing particular theses on the basis of it.

Given these considerations, this chapter will distinguish Carnap's views on meta-level questions, which are constituted by the principle of tolerance and pragmatism,

---

[41] Carnap considers this linguistic form to be 'effective' probably in the sense that it enables objectively evaluating the validity of a claim. For, in his biography Carnap states, "there seemed hardly any chance of mutual understanding, let alone of agreement, because there was not even a common criterion for deciding the controversy" (Carnap 1963a, 44-5) in debates over traditional metaphysical questions, and this situation partially motivated Carnap to introduce scientific methods into philosophy.

[42] The following discussion by Ricketts is a good elucidation of the claim that Carnap's empiricism was proposed as a linguistic form:

> Throughout his career, when he disparages philosophy as entangled in pseudo-problems, he [Carnap] is contrasting philosophy with science. After the adoption of the principle of tolerance and the shift to logical pluralism, he tries to clarify this, to him, intuitive difference as a difference in language. Scientific theorizing is formalizable in languages in which investigated hypotheses are observationally confirmable. The exacting use of a language whose indeterminate sentences have this feature, is, Carnap suggests, what distinguishes science from traditional philosophy: it is through the employment of these empiricist languages that scientists avoid the fruitless squabbles evident among traditional philosophers. Carnap endorses the evidential standards captured by these empiricist languages and advocates that in so far as we enquire after sentences that are not L-determinate, we should restrict our enquiries to claims formulated in empiricist languages. This advocacy of empiricism is advocacy of the use of a range of languages, not the affirmation of a sentence within a particular language. Empiricism is not a theoretical matter; there is no right or wrong to it, for in logic there are no morals. Carnap's advocacy is backed up only by his endorsement of the evidential standards, the language use, that he believes typify science. It is in this sense, then, that Carnap's application of the criticisms "pseudo-problems" and "nonsense" is ultimately ad hominem. (Ricketts 1994, 194-5)

That is, as stated in the previous footnote, Carnap adopted an empiricist position to clarify the criterion for the validity of a claim, and he proposes a linguistic form that precisely specifies the criterion (that also excludes sentences impossible to clarify).

from his particular theses developed against the background of such meta-level views (empiricism and natural scientism). On this understanding of Carnap's philosophy, his commitment to particular philosophical theses (such as an empiricist claim of the verifiability principle of meaning) are interpreted as linguistic forms that can be developed in a variety of ways, and we are able to resolve the tension that was pointed out between such a particular commitment and Carnap's semantic project, which accepts pluralism.

Let us take stock here. First, it has been argued that Carnap's semantic project—constituted by the principle of tolerance and the criterion of pragmatic efficacy—does not by itself imply a pluralistic view. This conclusion follows from the fact that Carnap's principle of tolerance operates at the point of introducing a linguistic form, not at the point of passing a final verdict on it, together with the fact that the acceptance of the criterion of pragmatic efficacy alone does not imply pluralism. Further, this conclusion provides a reason to reject attributing a pluralist position to Carnap. Second, this subsection has examined the tension between the pluralistic model derived from Carnap's semantic project in this section and the empiricist and natural scientism aspect of Carnap's philosophy. On closer scrutiny, it has been shown that this tension can be resolved by distinguishing Carnap's particular philosophical commitment from his meta-level claims. This examination has also brought to light that it would be wrong to attribute a pluralistic view to Carnap solely on the basis of the fact that his meta-level claims concerning semantics are compatible with a pluralistic view. Certainly, Carnap's semantic project—characterized primarily by the principle of tolerance and pragmatism—can be separated from various forms of empiricism that Carnap expressed as well as from natural scientism, and it can be evaluated independently of such issues. Irrespective of this, the resulting view abstracting away from the commitment to particular theses is not (as Putnam has pointed out) what Carnap had in mind. Therefore, the 'conventionalist pluralism based on pragmatism', proposed in section 3.2.1, is to be called the 'Carnapian model' of pluralism, not the 'Carnap model'.

Drawing on this result, in what follows, I will discuss the Carnapian model of pluralism somewhat independently of Carnap's own views on pluralism; the ensuing discussion of pluralism will substantially rely on Carnap's views but nevertheless diverge from them when necessary. Although Carnap's philosophy definitely contains many insights useful in developing a pluralistic view, this strategy will be most productive for the purpose of this chapter, which is not an exegesis of Carnap, but an attempt to provide a clearer formulation of pluralism.

The discussion so far has sufficiently clarified interpretive questions concerning Carnap's philosophy. Now, I will turn to the Carnapian model of pluralism itself. The next subsection, 3.2.3, will discuss whether this model faces insurmountable difficulties, and the main focus will be on Quine's criticism of analyticity.

3.2.3 A Solution to Quine's criticism of analyticity based on the Carnapian model of pluralism

As the previous discussion has elucidated, the Carnapian model of pluralism—the main theme of this section—is largely based on Carnap's semantic project, abstracting away from some of its details. The overall philosophy of Carnap including his semantic project, however, has been the target of much criticism. In particular, it is often assumed in historical discussions of twentieth century analytic philosophy that Quine, a student of Carnap, presented an insurmountable challenge to Carnap's philosophy and effectively ended any further attempt to develop it. For this reason, to revive the Carnapian model of pluralism as a viable option that has contemporary significance and implications, it is necessary to show that Quine's seemingly insurmountable challenge can be overcome.

The focal point of the following discussion is the criticism of analyticity Quine presented, since the concept of analyticity is indispensable to Carnap's semantic project (as will be discussed below), and the Carnapian model of pluralism incorporates almost all aspects of the semantic project, even though it has jettisoned the commitment to empiricism and natural scientism, which Carnap himself embraced. In what follows, I will examine Quine's criticism that the concept of analyticity is unintelligible together with Carnap's replies to this charge, scrutinizing the validity of the Quine criticism. To state the conclusion in advance, the root of the disagreement between Carnap and Quine lies in whether the aim is in 'describing existing linguistic activities' or in 'making proposals about future linguistic activities'. Quine objects to Carnap's semantic project construed as pursuing the former goal, and so the objection fails to undermine the semantic project that in fact pursues the latter goal (and by extension, it also fails to undermine the Carnapian model of pluralism). This is the diagnosis I will propose in this section.

(1) The criticism of analyticity in "Two Dogmas of Empiricism"

In "Two Dogmas of Empiricism," Quine criticizes the concept of analyticity by examining and refuting seemingly satisfactory characterizations of analytic statements. Here, I will identify which characterization of analyticity examined by Quine is the point of contention between Carnap and Quine. In "Two Dogmas," the following three characterizations of analyticity are examined:

(i) Analytic statements are first classified into logical truths and statements that can be transformed into logical truths, and they are characterized using the concepts of logical truth and synonymy.

(ii) Analytic statements are characterized as statements that are true by virtue of semantic rules.

(iii) Analytic statements are characterized as statements that are confirmed under any circumstances.

Quine attacks characterization (i) for failing to explain analyticity adequately due to the lack of clarity in the concept of synonymy. Whether this attack is successful, raising an issue with synonymy is not directly relevant to Carnap's theory of language. An example of an analytic statement Carnap brought up, 'one thing cannot be red and blue at the same time', clearly illustrates this point. As will be discussed below, Carnap's characterization of analyticity does not rest on the concept of synonymy. Therefore, this characterization of analyticity based on synonymy, (i), is not a point of contention between Carnap and Quine.

How about characterization (iii)? Claiming that no statements are in principle immune to revision, Quine judges (iii) to be an implausible approach to analyticity. If Carnap were defining analyticity following this approach, then his semantic project would be inherently problematic. In *The Logical Syntax of Language* (originally published in 1934 and translated into English in 1937), however, Carnap made it explicit that even logical statements constituting a linguistic framework are subject to revision.[43] This clearly indicates that Carnap does not characterize analytic statements as statements that are confirmed under any circumstances. Therefore, as far as the disagreement between Carnap and Quine is concerned, characterization (iii) only raises an extraneous point.

Now, we are left with the characterization of analyticity in (ii), 'truth by virtue of semantic rules'. It is indeed this characterization that Carnap used to account for analyticity, and it thereby became the point of contention between Carnap and Quine. Consider the following remarks by Carnap:

> My proposals for the explication of analyticity have always been given for a formalized (codified, constructed) language L, i.e., a language for which explicit semantical rules are specified that lead to the concept of truth ... The explication [of analyticity] is given by additional rules, essentially by a list of meaning postulates (A-postulates) and, based upon them, a definition of "A-true" (which I use as a technical term for the explicatum). (Carnap 1963b, 918)

Meaning postulates, mentioned here, as already noted in section 3.2.1, are parts of the semantic rules of a language (or 'semantical' rules in Carnap's terminology). Analyticity is characterized as a truth that is determined solely on the basis of semantic rules including meaning postulates ('A-true').

The discussion so far has identified a key to understanding the debates between Carnap and Quine over analyticity. The issue to be addressed is whether the characterization of analyticity 'truth by virtue of semantic rules' is justifiable. We have to keep this in mind while examining the arguments of both sides. Below I will first present an overview of Carnap's treatment of semantic rules, and then turn to the debates between Carnap and Quine over the characterization of analyticity 'truth by virtue of semantic rules'.

(2) Carnap's treatment of semantic rules

As has already been stated (sections 3.1.3 and 3.2.1), Carnap's semantic project is split into two parts: descriptive semantics and pure semantics, the former of which constructs a semantic theory for a historically given language while the latter freely constructs a linguistic system according to our desires and goals. To understand the

---

[43] See (Carnap 1937, 317-8). Also, a similar remark can be found in (Carnap 1963b, 921).

idea of semantic rules in Carnap's semantic project, it must be noted that the rules that a semantic system consists of are different from the rules held true for a particular natural language.

With respect to pure semantics, it will be easy to grasp this point about semantic rules. (For the goal of constructing a semantic system in pure semantics is neither to describe naturally occurring linguistic activities nor to build a system fitting such activities.) It may be surprising, however, to discover that the same point holds with respect to descriptive semantics as well; semantic rules in descriptive semantics are also different from the rules held to be true for a particular natural language. To illustrate this point, consider again the example of constructing a descriptive semantics as mentioned in section 3.2.1, in which we undertook radical interpretation of language B. To interpret language B, we would first collect pragmatic facts about this language and then construct a semantic system in accordance with the collected facts. As Carnap himself acknowledges, however, pragmatic facts alone do not uniquely determine the semantic system to be constructed. Suppose, for example, that the word 'mond' in language B is used to talk about the moon 98 percent of the time and about a particular lantern 2 percent of the time. A semantic system that lets 'mond' designate both the moon and a lantern is compatible with these facts about the expression, while at the same time a semantic system letting 'mond' designate only the moon is also compatible with the facts. (For Carnap, "it is a matter of our decision" [Carnap 1939, 6] whether we construct the former or the latter semantic system.) If the former semantic system is constructed, then the use of 'mond' to describe the lantern would be a correct application of the word, but on the other hand, if the latter semantic system is constructed, the lantern use of 'mond' would be an incorrect application.[44] Here the following remarks by Carnap become instructive:

> A question of right or wrong must always refer to a system of rules. Strictly speaking, the rules which we shall lay down are not rules of the factually given language B; they rather constitute a language system corresponding to B which we will call the *semantical system B-S*. The language B belongs to the world of facts ... The language system B-S, on the other hand, is something constructed by us ... (Carnap 1939, 7, italics in original)

Carnap makes it explicit that the semantic rules comprising a semantic system are not the rules of the natural language B, but of the system 'B-S', an artificial language system. That is, in Carnap's semantic project, either with respect to pure or descriptive semantics, semantic rules are understood as rules of an artificial language that we construct, not as the rules held true for a natural language.

Now, let me reiterate Carnap's idea of semantic rules by describing an example that illustrates how semantic rules relate to analyticity.[45] Consider the question of whether the statement 'everything that is green is extended' is analytic. If this statement is analytic, then at least it would not be permissible to apply the predicate

---

[44] This is a clear instance of the indeterminacy of interpretation.
[45] This paragraph is a reconstruction of Carnap's discussion of analyticity in (Carnap 1952).

'being green' to a point in space. It is, however, impossible to determine whether 'being green' applies to spatial points by observing a particular natural language (English in this case). For, speakers of English seldom refer to a single point in space, and if they refer to a single spatial point, there would be no agreement over whether this expression is applicable to it. Moreover, even if it is discovered that speakers do not use 'being green' for a spatial point, there would be no definite way to determine whether this agreement is a coincidence or a semantic fact. As this example illustrates, it is not feasible to describe the concept of analyticity in a definite way by observing particular linguistic activities. On the other hand, the concept of analyticity can be clarified by constructing an artificial language that has semantic rules. If the artificial language L is explicitly designed to have a meaning postulate that excludes the application of 'being green' to spatial points, then the statement 'everything that is green is extended' would be definitely analytic.

To summarize the discussion so far, semantic rules for Carnap are not rules obtaining in a natural language, but the rules of an artificial language system that we construct in accordance with the pragmatic facts about a particular natural language (in the case of descriptive semantics) or in accordance with the pragmatic standard of efficacy for a particular inquiry, whether the resulting rules conform to a natural language (in the case of pure semantics). Grasping this notion of semantic rules is a key to understanding Carnap's semantic project as well as evaluating Quine's criticism of analyticity.

(3) What is undermined by Quine's criticism of analyticity?: Explicatum and explicandum

The discussion so far has elucidated the treatment of semantic rules in Carnap's semantic project. Now, it is time to discuss how Quine objects to Carnap's definition of analyticity, which is based on the Carnap treatment of semantic rules—'truth by virtue of semantic rules'. Consider, first, the relevant passage from "Two Dogmas of Empiricism":

> ... analyticity can be demarcated thus: a statement is analytic if it is (not merely true) true according to the semantical rule.
>
> Still there is really no progress. Instead of appealing to an unexplained word 'analytic', we are no appealing to an unexplained phrase 'semantical rule'. Not every true statement which says that the statements of some class are true can count as a semantical rule—otherwise *all* truths would be "analytic" in the sense of being true according to semantical rules. Semantical rules are distinguishable, apparently, only by the fact of appearing on a page under the heading 'Semantical Rules'; and this heading is itself then meaningless. (Quine 1953, 34, italics in original)

The gist of this criticism is that no improvement would be made by explaining the unintelligible concept of analyticity in terms of yet another obscure concept, that of semantic rules. In order to understand sufficiently what part of Carnap's discussion of semantic rules this criticism targets, it is necessary to figure out which aspect of

Carnap's semantic project Quine really criticizes.[46]

In Carnap's semantic project, one of the goals of constructing an artificial language that is equipped with semantic rules is to elucidate a particular natural language and clarify its logical properties. In other words, an artificial language equipped with semantic rules is constructed as an 'explicatum' for an obscure natural language (the 'explicandum').[47] In an artificial language (an explicatum) the set of semantic rules is unambiguously recognized, since an artificial language is defined by identifying its semantic rules, and so to present an artificial language it is necessary identify its semantic rules explicitly. The functions of such semantic rules are also clear and unambiguous. Semantic rules are definitions characterizing the artificial language system to which they belong, providing the definition of truth in the language and specifying valid inferences. (For this reason, a truth solely by virtue of semantic rules will never change its truth-value when an inquiry is conducted in the same artificial language, regardless of any new empirical fact.)

Thus, the identities and functions of semantic rules are precisely delineated as long as an explicatum, an artificial language, is concerned. When it comes to the explicandum, a particular natural language (ordinary language), however, the situation is different. It would be impossible to distinguish observationally the semantic rules of a natural language (in the technical sense discussed above) from other statements that are considered true. Also, if a theorist arbitrarily selects a set of true statements and labels these as 'semantic rules', we would fail to recognize the defining functions of the statements in the set. That is, semantic rules—though they are explicitly identifiable in an artificial language—have no obvious, recognizable counterparts in a natural language, the explicandum.[48] Recall that Quine's criticism was that appealing to the obscure concept of semantic rules would result in no progress towards understanding the concept of analyticity. The considerations above suggest that this criticism targets the obscurities in the concepts of semantic rules and analyticity in the explicandum. In other words, the lesson to be learned from Quine's criticism of analyticity is that if the concepts of semantic rules and analyticity are unintelligible in a natural language (the explicandum), then they would remain so even when the concepts are precisely defined using the resources of an artificial language.[49]

(4) The disagreement between Carnap and Quine and its root cause

Then how does Carnap respond to Quine's criticism of analyticity, the details of

---

[46] The following two paragraphs present a reconstruction of the discussions in (Carnap 1952; 1963b) and (Creath 1990, particularly the 1954 correspondence).

[47] Carnap characterizes the idea of 'explication' as follows:
> The task of making more exact a vague or not quite exact concept used in everyday life or in an earlier stage of scientific or logical development, or rather of replacing it by a newly constructed, more exact concept, belongs among the most important tasks of logical analysis and logical construction. We call this task of explicating, or of giving an *explication* for, the earlier concept; this earlier concept, or sometimes the term used for it, is called the *explicandum;* and the new concept, or its term is called an *explicatum* of the old one. (Carnap 1956, 7-8, italics in original).

[48] For more details of this discussion, see (Creath 1990, 296-7, 309, 336-8).

[49] Carnap (1963b, 918-9) presents a similar interpretation of Quine.

which are expounded in the preceding discussion? There are two plausible approaches available to Carnap.

1. To elucidate analytic statements in a natural language, the explicandum, by showing the empirical conditions for a statement to count as being analytic.

2. To counter Quine's criticism by arguing that the obscurities in the explicandum (or the lack of clarity in the concept of analyticity) are not detrimental to the concepts in an artificial language system, an explicatum.

It is not easy to identify which approach Carnap adopted to counter the Quine criticism of analyticity. Choosing the first approach may seem natural if the attempt is to defend the concept of analyticity in a straightforward manner. Carnap indeed took this approach to answer Quine's criticism in the 1955 article "Meaning and Synonymy in Natural Languages" (collected in [Carnap 1956]) and also in a section of (Carnap 1963b), titled "C. Empirical criteria for intentional concepts." In a number of other places, however, Carnap suggests that the concept of analyticity can be appropriately used only when dealing with artificial languages. Moreover, the remarks below clearly indicate that Carnap was primarily relying on the second approach to substantiate the concept of analyticity:

> I would agree with his basic idea, namely, that a pragmatical concept, based upon an empirical criterion, might serve as an explicandum for a purely semantical reconstruction, and that this procedure may sometimes, and perhaps also in the present case, be a useful way of specifying the explicandum. On the other hand, I would not think that it is necessary in general to provide a pragmatical concept in order to justify the introduction of a concept of pure semantics. (Carnap 1963b, 919)

Here, Carnap mainly tried to convey that it is not always necessary to have a pragmatic explicandum, specified using empirical conditions or criteria. The places (mentioned above) where Carnap took the first approach to defend the concept of analyticity can be construed as presenting an auxiliary point that it is possible to provide the empirical conditions or criteria for an analytic statement if one shares Quine's objectives; it is not necessary to formulate such conditions.[50]

---

[50] For further illumination of this point, consider the following passage:
Especially *Quine's* criticism does not concern the formal correctness of the definitions in pure semantics; rather, he doubts whether there are any clear and fruitful corresponding pragmatical concepts which could serve as explicanda. That is the reason why he demands that these pragmatical concepts be shown to be scientifically legitimate by stating empirical, behavioristic criteria for them. If I understand him correctly, he believes that, without this pragmatic substructure, the semantical intension concepts, even if formally correct, are arbitrary and without purpose. *I do not think that a semantical concept, in order to be fruitful, must necessarily possess a prior pragmatical counterpart.* It is theoretically possible to demonstrate its fruitfulness through its application in the further development of language systems. But this is a slow process. If for a given semantical concept there is already a familiar,

On this interpretation of Carnap, the disagreement between Carnap and Quine lies in the question of whether concepts such as those of analyticity and semantic rules must be empirically specified in a natural language, the explicandum. Quine (as well as Carnap, of course) would acknowledge that analytic statements and semantic rules are precisely identifiable in an artificial language. When it comes to the counterparts in natural languages, the disagreement between Carnap and Quine stands out clearly. For Quine, if concepts identified in an artificial language (an explicatum) have no counterparts that are empirically recognizable in a natural language, then it would remain unclear what the talk of 'analyticity' is all about—whether all analytic statements are precisely identified in the explicatum. This is what is at the heart of Quine's criticism of analyticity. For Carnap, however, even if concepts in an artificial language have no counterparts that are empirically recognizable in a natural language, it does not follow that the concepts of analyticity, semantic rules, and the like are unintelligible, since the introduction or formulation of semantic concepts does not necessarily require any pragmatic counterparts.

The discussion so far has described the disagreement between Carnap and Quine. Let us now turn to the root cause of the disagreement. I will argue that these two disagree over the goals of the inquiry: whether the inquiry aims at 'describing existing linguistic activities' or at 'making proposals about future linguistic activities'.[51] Below is a quote from Quine that would appear to support the interpretation that Carnap and Quine do not agree on, do not share the goals of the inquiry:

> The lore of our fathers is a fabric of sentences. In our hands it develops and changes, through more or less arbitrary and deliberate revisions and additions of our own, more or less directly occasioned by the continuing stimulation of our sense organs. It is a pale gray lore, black with fact and white with convention. But I have found no substantial reasons for concluding that there are any quite black threads in it, or any white ones. (Quine 1963, 132)

The point of this passage is that what is conventional (namely, semantic rules) is so closely intertwined with everything else in a natural language (which was inherited as lore) that it cannot be distinguished from the rest of the language. The passage clearly points to Quine's approach to analyticity that focuses on describing natural languages and figuring out analytic statements in them. Henceforth, let us call this approach the 'descriptive stance', which attempts to describe the concept of analyticity with respect to a particular, existing language by observing how the

---

though somewhat vague, corresponding pragmatical concept and if we are able to clarify the latter by describing an operational procedure for its application, then *this may indeed be a simpler way for refuting the objections* and furnish a practical justification at once for both concepts. (Carnap 1956, 234-5, italics added, except for "*Quine's*" at the beginning)

[51] Creath (1987) led me to this strategy of interpreting Carnap as taking a 'prescriptive stance'. Yet, the Creath article does not specify Quine's position, the opposing position that will be contrasted with Carnap's here, and further it exclusively discusses Carnap in his so-called 'syntactic phase' during 1930s. This book, by contrast, focuses on his 'semantic phase' (where his treatment of analyticity became perspicuous).

language is actually used.[52] By contrast, the following passages from Carnap's writings clearly exhibit a contrasting position:

> Suppose we have found that the word 'mond' of [language] B was used in 98 per cent of the cases for the moon and in 2 per cent for a certain lantern. Now it is a matter of our decision whether we construct the rules in such a way that both the moon and the lantern are designata of 'mond' or only the moon. (Carnap 1939, 6)

> The task of making more exact a vague or not quite exact concept used in everyday life or in an earlier stage of scientific or logical development, or rather of replacing it by a newly constructed, more exact concept, belongs among the most important tasks of logical analysis and logical construction. We call this the task of explicating, or of giving an *explication* for, the earlier concept; this earlier concept, or sometimes the term used for it, is called the *explicandum* ... (Carnap 1956, 7-8)

> If we are concerned with a historically given language, the pragmatical description comes first, and then we may go by abstraction to semantics and (either from semantics or immediately from pragmatics) to syntax. The situation is quite different if we wish to construct a language (or rather a language system, because we lay down rules), perhaps with the intention of practical application, as for making communications or formulating a scientific theory. Here we are not bound by a previous use of language, but are free to construct [a language system] in accordance with our wishes and purposes. (Carnap 1939, 24)

According to Carnap, establishing semantic rules is not equivalent to describing the rules actually obtaining in a particular language; it is rather like offering proposals to improve clarity and efficacy in achieving the goals of an inquiry.[53] It follows that we never 'find out' but 'construct' or 'propose' the concept of analyticity. In contrasting it to the descriptive stance attributed to Quine, let us call Canap's attitude toward analyticity, discussed here, the 'normative' or 'prescriptive stance'.

Distinguishing the descriptive and the prescriptive stances enables an understanding of the disagreement between Carnap and Quine over analyticity, in particular, over the question of whether a pragmatic explicandum based on empirical criteria is required. Let me elaborate this point. From the perspective of the descriptive stance, it is reasonable to respect Quine's requirement that the explicandum includes the concept of analyticity corresponding to a formally defined concept of analyticity. For defining concepts of analyticity, semantic rules, and the

---

[52] The point I am making here is that Quine took the descriptive stance in developing the criticism of analyticity, not that Quine consistently pursued descriptive epistemology, which was clearly expressed when he made the transition to naturalism.

[53] This consequence is evident in the domain of pure semantics. Also in the domain of descriptive semantics, it is equally justifiable to assume that the semantic rules to be constructed are rules of a system we construct, not among the rules obtaining in a natural language.

like in an artificial language would make no contribution to the goal of describing the facts about existing natural languages that are actually in use if the formal concepts have no counterparts in actual linguistic activities. Therefore, as long as the descriptive stance is concerned, it is natural to follow Quine's view that there needs to be a pragmatic explicandum that is based on empirical criteria.

On the other hand, the conclusion would be different if semantic rules are established to make proposals about future linguistic activities (so the prescriptive stance may be appropriately called the 'propositional' stance). In this case, it is not crucial whether the established semantic rules correspond to actual linguistic activities (whether they are held true in actual linguistic activities).[54] Instead, it is crucial whether the established semantic rules are sufficiently clear or whether they are effective for achieving the goals of the inquiry at hand. Therefore, as long as the normative or prescriptive stance is concerned, it is reasonable to follow Carnap's view that a pragmatic explicandum based on empirical criteria is unnecessary in the construction of semantic concepts.

(5) Is Quine's criticism of analyticity justifiable?

The preceding discussion has, first, clarified the point of contention in the debates between Carnap and Quine concerning analyticity—their main focus was Carnap's characterization of analyticity 'truth by virtue of semantic rules'; the discussion has, second, showed that Carnap and Quine disagree over the question as to whether a pragmatic explicandum based on empirical criteria is necessary for making the concept of analyticity intelligible; and third, it has pointed out that the root cause of this disagreement lies in the two different stances concerning analyticity Carnap and Quine took: the descriptive and the normative or prescriptive stances.

Now, what would be an appropriate evaluation of Quine's criticism of analyticity that it is unintelligible? In this book, I argue that the criticism is not justifiable. Quine's complaint against analyticity was that semantic rules have no counterparts in natural languages and that it is impossible to distinguish, among all the statements that are considered true, conventionally fixed semantic rules from empirically confirmed statements. Certainly, Quine is correct in thinking that there is no reliable method to determine a unique set of analytic statements from a given set of statements that are considered true. However, for Carnap—who espouses the normative or prescriptive stance—it is nonsensical to ask which among true statements are analytic statements or semantic rules. Semantic rules are proposed, rather, as parts of a working hypothesis for a future inquiry, and whether a working hypothesis is appropriate is dependent exclusively on its clarity and efficacy for achieving the goals of the inquiry. In this way, analyticity must be understood as something that we establish rather than something that we discover, and this understanding of analyticity overcomes Quine's criticism, retaining the intelligibility

---

[54] It is true that a descriptive semantics must be constructed in accordance with pragmatic facts. Nonetheless, it is not required in descriptive semantics that pragmatic facts uniquely determine a system of semantic rules or that there be a unique set of semantic rules identifiable among statements that are considered true in the uses of a given language.

of the concept of analyticity. This sums up my diagnosis of the debates between Carnap and Quine over analyticity.[55]

Before moving to the next subsection, I wish to situate this conclusion within a broader picture. A standard view of the historical implications of "Two Dogmas of Empiricism" is that it critically undermined any theories in epistemology resting on the concept of analyticity, and Quine's epistemological holism replaced them. For example, Yasuhiko Tomida, after quoting remarks advancing epistemological holism from "Two Dogmas," writes as follows:

> These remarks clearly express Quine's denial of the so-called essential distinction between analyticity and syntheticity—the idea that a sentence is either analytic or synthetic by virtue of its essence regardless of how it is considered; the remarks also indicate Quine's views on the holistic character of theory revision. (Tomida 1994, 86-7)

However, if what Quine advanced through "Two Dogmas" primarily lies in denying the essential distinction between analyticity and syntheticity and promoting the holistic character of theory revision, then these claims cannot be employed to object to Carnap. For, as has been observed, Carnap did not accept the essential distinction between syntheticity and analyticity because he considered that analytic statements are what is constructed by theorists, and as is widely recognized, he also denied the existence of any statement that is in principle immune to revision. If analytic statements are essentially distinguished from synthetic statements, then it would follow that the distinction is absolute. According to Carnap, however, whether a sentence is analytic or synthetic is answered relative to a system of semantic rules.

I have earlier pointed out that the concept of analyticity is inseparable from Carnap's semantic project, and so to be able to revive the Carnapian model of pluralism it is necessary to counter Quine's criticism of analyticity. It seems reasonable to conclude that the discussion so far has fulfilled this requirement: Carnap's semantic project, if not the entirety of Carnap's philosophy, has been defended against Quine's criticism of analyticity. To summarize, Carnap characterizes the concept of analyticity as truth by virtue of semantic rules, and semantic rules are

---

[55] As is clear from the preceding discussion, the defense of Carnap's semantic project developed in this section relies on the distinction between the descriptive and the normative or prescriptive stances. Indeed, there is an alternative approach to defending Carnap's project if we only aim at upholding the existence of semantic rules: one may as well argue that if physicalism is not adopted, then the underdetermination of semantic rules by pragmatic facts does not necessarily disprove the existence of facts about semantic rules. (This argument is nearly the same as the argument concerning the relation between the indeterminacy theses and physicalism developed in chapter 2.) In this chapter, however, I do not adopt this approach, partly because I wish to defend Carnap's semantic project as a viable option whether one endorses physicalist monism or pluralism. In my view, if physicalist monism is adopted, then there is a constraint imposed on properties that are approved by a semantic system constituting a factual discourse: such properties must supervene on physical properties; yet Carnap's semantic project is still sustainable—the project is illustrated by the idea of semantic rules as rules we construct. There is another reason to eschew the approach that defends Carnap's semantic project by arguing against physicalism. By appealing to this approach, the scope of the semantic project may end up being restricted to descriptive semantics.

not extracted from pragmatic facts about existing languages; they are rather artificially constructed and proposed as a clearer method of discourse (or as a more efficient method for achieving particular goals of a particular inquiry); therefore, Quine's criticism of analyticity does not apply to the concepts of semantic rules and analyticity when they are understood based on the normative or prescriptive stance Carnap adopted.

3.2.4 The characteristics of the Carnapian model of pluralism

The primary reason for examining the Carnapian model of pluralism in this section is that Putnam's views of pluralism, discussed in the previous section, are proven to pose several difficulties and are unable to produce a clear formulation of pluralism, which is the main objective of this chapter. The current section so far has distilled the Carnapian model of pluralism from Carnap's semantic project, addressed several interpretive issues in Carnap's philosophy, and demonstrated a way to overcome Quine's criticism of analyticity, which is usually considered to be an insurmountable challenge to the Carnapian model. In this subsection, drawing on the previous discussion, I will examine the characteristics of the Carnapian model of pluralism in more detail (especially by comparing it with Putnam's views of pluralism) and point out the advantages of this model.

Putnam has criticized Carnap's philosophy over and again in his writings. Nevertheless, Putnam shares a variety of points with Carnap. Consider, for example, the following remarks:[56]

> My position resembles Carnap's (in "Empiricism, Semantics, Ontology"[57]) inasmuch as I hold that differences in ontology sometimes amount to no more than the choice of a way of using words. But unlike Carnap, I do not rest the distinction between questions which have to do with the choice of a linguistic framework and empirical questions on *the analytic-synthetic distinction*. Whether something is or is not any more than a question of how to talk is itself something to which empirical facts are relevant. There is a continuum stretching from choices which, by our present lights, are just choices of a way of talking to questions of what are plainly empirical fact, but there is nothing here which is *guaranteed* to be true no matter what the facts may turn out to be. What I would criticize Quine for is the suggestion that a distinction between fact and language-choice which is not absolute, not drawn once and for all unrevisably, is of no use. (Putnam 1994, 248-9, italics added)

Referring to this passage, Jennifer Case also exposes Putnam's position as follows:
> Putnam considers such a distinction [between fact and language-choice] useful for our purposes as, say, language users and linguistic reformers, but not for such *philosophical* purposes as those in the service of which the logical positivist invoked the analytic-synthetic distinction. Accordingly, Putnam remarks, "unlike

---
[56] Also, see (Putnam 1990, 99), where Putnam interprets Carnap as supporting conceptual relativity.
[57] This is collected in (Carnap 1956).

Carnap, I do not rest the distinction between questions which have to do with the choice of a linguistic framework and empirical questions on *the analytic-synthetic distinction.*" Putnam's convention-fact distinction should not be equated with the analytic-synthetic distinction if the latter is understood to be serviceable for philosophical purposes that call for an *absolute* distinction between convention and fact. His rejection of *an absolute distinction of that kind* is at the same time a repudiation of the philosophical that such a distinction serves. (Case 2001, 423, italics added)

As has been established earlier, however, for Carnap the analytic-synthetic distinction is by no means an 'absolute' or 'unrevisable' distinction unlike it appears to be for Putnam and Case; the distinction is relative to particular linguistic frameworks (see section 3.2.3). Carnap's characterization of analytic statements hardly resembles what Putnam has in mind, according to which analytic statements are "guaranteed to be true no matter what the facts may turn out to be." According to Carnap, the truth-values of semantic rules are internally determined with respect to a proposed semantic system, and they cease to be semantic rules when they are considered with respect to a different semantic system or the proposed semantic system as a whole is abandoned because of the inefficacy of the system (as they become false or meaningless word sequences). Most importantly, there are two reasons to regard Carnap as a 'linguistic reformer' in the sense suggested by Case: first, Carnap primarily studied pure semantics, which aims at producing a useful scheme not placing stress on whether it fits existing linguistic activities, and second, his principle of tolerance allows leeway for a linguistic proposal (a proposal may deviate from the current usage). Therefore, the concept of analyticity Carnap upheld is not susceptible to the objections raised by Putnam and Case.

It is then justifiable to suppose that Putnam in fact sides with Carnap, at least, with respect to whether the analytic-synthetic and the convention-fact distinctions are absolute or not (despite Putnam's own assessment). Moreover, Carnap and Putnam share the same idea in that the choice of a linguistic framework or conceptual scheme depends on the pragmatic standard of 'efficacy for the goals of an inquiry'. Below are Putnam's remarks on this issue concerning the choice of a linguistic framework (section 3.2.1 has already discussed Carnap's views on this point):

Carnap, on the other hand, rejected the idea that there is "evidence" against the "existence" of numbers (or against the existence of numbers as objects distinct from sets). He would, I am sure, have similarly rejected the idea that there is evidence against the "existence" of mereological sums. I know what he would have said about this question: he would have said that the question is one of a choice of a language. On some days it may be convenient to use what I have been calling "Carnap's language" (although he would not have *objected* to the other language); on the other days it may be convenient to use the Polish logician's language. For some purposes it may be convenient to regard the Polish logician's language of mereological sums as "primitive notation"; in other contexts it may better to take Carnap's language as the primitive notation and to regard the Polish logican's language as "abbreviations," or defined notation. And I agree with him. (Putnam 1990, 102-3)

These remarks suggest that Carnap and Putnam agree with one another on the following three points:

- Ontological questions can be questions about conventional linguistic rules.

- No essential or absolute distinction between analyticity and syntheticity is presupposed in a process of conventionally establishing linguistic rules.

- The choice of adopting a linguistic rule depends on the pragmatic standard of efficacy for achieving the goals of an inquiry.

In particular, the second point must be stressed. Putnam misunderstood Carnap as presupposing an absolute or unrevisable analytic-synthetic distinction, which has been shown not to exist, and so it is reasonable to describe both Carnap and Putnam pointing in the general direction of pragmatic conventionalism.

There are, however, three important differences between Carnap and Putnam—or rather between the Carnapian model of pluralism and Putnam's conventionalism:

(ⅰ) Putnam's conventionalism is proposed as a thesis in descriptive semantics—namely, as conceptual relativity—whereas the Carnapian model of pluralism is proposed primarily as a thesis in pure semantics.

(ⅱ) The plurality of linguistic schemes implied by conceptual relativity is restricted to the level of optional languages, and so natural languages are not among the linguistic schemes that are claimed to be plural. By contrast, the Carnapian model is not restricted in such a way.

(ⅲ) Putnam's conventionalism acknowledges there to be invariant linguistic parts (they are invariant in the sense that no alternative conventions are possible), whereas the Carnapian model assumes no semantic rules that must be included in every semantic system, and hence that no invariant linguistic parts exist in a system.

Considering the implications of these closely related differences, it becomes possible to elucidate the characteristics and advantages of the Carnapian model of pluralism. First, difference (i) implies that one of the difficulties pointed out in Putnam's views on pluralism—that no ontological conclusions can be drawn exclusively from theses in descriptive semantics—can be overcome in the Carnapian model of pluralism.

In recent literature it is quite commonplace to develop an ontological claim from semantic considerations (for example, existential claims concerning abstract objects such as number and classes). (For this point, see sections 2.1.1 and 2.1.2, in which a general perspective for discussing ontology was proposed.) As argued in section 3.1.3, however, the current activities involving the use of natural languages may not be optimal, and so no positive ontological claim can be justifiably deduced solely on the basis of descriptive semantics. This becomes the case as descriptive semantics can only entail conditional claims of the form 'if the language use of a group of people is appropriate, then there exists such-and-such an object', and so the antecedents must be verified to derive an ontologically significant claim. In other words, discovering that an ontological claim fits the pragmatic facts about particular linguistic activities is of little use in justifying that claim.

As the discussion above has illustrated, Putnam's argument that some ontological questions are merely questions about conventions is problematic because he bases this argument on an indeterminacy that is found in descriptive semantics. By contrast, Carnap does not suffer from this problem, since his semantic project encompasses descriptive semantics as well as pure semantics, thereby assuming advantages of the pragmatic standard of 'efficacy for achieving the goals of an inquiry', in addition to encompassing the standard of descriptive semantics ('fitting pragmatic facts'); the inclusion of this pragmatic standard enables evaluating the antecedents of the aforementioned conditional claims of the form 'if the language use of a group of people is appropriate, then there exists such-and-such an object'. Therefore, the criticism that no ontological conclusion can be drawn exclusively from theses in descriptive semantics is not applicable to Carnap's semantic project.

Next, let us consider the second difference between Carnap and Putnam, (ii) above, which implies that another problem for Putnam's views on pluralism also pointed out in section 3.1.3—the virtue of clarity in instances of conceptual relativity does not extend to instances of conceptual pluralism—fails to apply to the Carnapian model of pluralism.

Conceptual relativity maintains that there can be more than one artificial and regimented partial language that can be incorporated into a natural language without causing any particular contradiction—that there are multiple 'optional languages'. This thesis of conceptual relativity is formulated in terms of optional languages; the formulation clarifies exactly to what the use of a concept is relativized (optional languages), but at the same time it excludes natural languages and concepts used in the natural languages from relativization. Here, Carnap's semantic project is essentially independent of the natural- and optional-language distinction, and it poses no difficulty to constructing a semantic system defining the uses of predicates in ordinary discourse (such as 'being a desk' and 'being a chair'). Therefore, the Carnapian model of pluralism can account for the examples through which Putnam illustrates the thesis of conceptual pluralism—ordinary discourse that uses ordinary vocabulary such as 'desk' and 'chair' as well as a discourse in physics that uses the vocabulary of fundamental physics; such examples can be understood as different linguistic schemes available in the Carnapian model.

Last, consider one of the important implications of difference (iii): Putnam's views on pluralism admit of no possibility of conventionally revising a natural language, different from the acceptance of this in the Carnapian model of pluralism. This contrast can be clearly observed in Putnam's and Carnap's discussion of linguistic schemes and how they are conventionally established. Compare the following two passages:

> Speaking of "optional languages," as Case suggests here, has the virtue of drawing an important distinction (on which I do *not* claim was clear in my mind before reading Case's earlier paper—thus my present understanding of "conceptual relativity" is in an important respect due to Case herself). The distinction is between parts of language that masters of a language and possessors of the cultural inheritance that is inseparable from being a master of a natural language have no option but to employ and parts that are genuinely optional. We are not, given the material and social worlds in which we live, *genuinely free not to quantify over tables and chairs, for example*. But we are free to employ the conceptual scheme of mereology or not, even in mathematics, even in empirical description, even, for that matter, in philosophy. (Putnam 2001, 434, italics added)

> From these questions we must distinguish the external question of the reality of the thing world itself. In contrast to the former questions, this question is raised neither by the man in the street nor by scientists, but only by philosophers. Realists give an affirmative answer, subjective idealists a negative one, and the controversy goes on for centuries without ever being solved. And it cannot be solved because it is framed in a wrong way. To be real in the scientific sense means to be an element of the system; hence this concept cannot be meaningfully applied to the system itself. Those who raise the question of the reality of the thing world itself have perhaps in mind not a theoretical question as their formulation seems to suggest, but rather a practical question, a matter of a practical decision concerning the structure of our language. We have to make the choice whether or not to accept and use the forms of expression in the [linguistic] framework in question.
>
> In the case of this particular example, there is usually no deliberate choice because we all have accepted the thing language early in our lives as a matter of course. *Nevertheless, we may regard it as a matter of decision in this sense: we are free to choose to continue using the thing language or not* ... (Carnap 1956, 207, italics added)

As is clear from these quotes, Putnam maintains that the commitment to 'the thing language'—the language that refers to observable physical objects such as tables and chairs—is inevitable, whereas Carnap takes a more relaxed position that allows the possibility of abandoning 'the thing language', though acknowledging that we must begin with an acceptance of it (this contrast is closely related to the fact that Putnam is concerned exclusively with descriptive semantics). Of course, Carnap's claim that 'the thing language' can be abandoned must be qualified, since it would probably be required to refer to ordinary objects in specifying the truth conditions of specific sentences when constructing a system of semantic rules. For this reason, if Carnap maintained that it is possible to abandon entirely all at once 'the thing language' that we currently employ, then he would be going too far. It is, however, at least possible to discard concepts that we currently possess one by one, such as those of 'chair' and 'table', thereby changing 'the thing language', with which we must begin; in this way, conventional factors can influence 'the thing language'.

To summarize, Carnap's claim that the use of the thing language can be discontinued entirely must be seen as incorrect as it stands (Carnap himself acknowledges that we must begin with 'the thing language'), but in contrast to Putnam, who denies the possibility of diversity and deviations in natural languages in discussing our possible conceptual revolutions, Carnap acknowledges diversity and deviations in natural languages (as long as they are supported by pragmatic considerations); and Carnap must be recognized for developing this position.

I have so far discussed the differences between Putnam's views on pluralism and the Carnapian model of pluralism and examined their implications. I have argued that two difficulties pointed out for Putnam's views can be overcome by adopting the Carnapian model, in which natural languages may be revised and reconstructed in addition to merely being described (for Putnam, by contrast, natural languages are inevitable and immune to revision). Given these advantages of the Carnapian model of pluralism over Putnam's views, I will formulate 'naturalistic pluralism'—the main thesis of this book—on the basis of the Carnapian model.

It must then be asked why the Carnapian model of pluralism, which was derived from Carnap's philosophy, can be described as 'naturalistic'. In what follows, I will argue that it is justifiable to situate the Carnapian model of pluralism within the naturalist framework.

3.2.5 The Carnapian model of pluralism and naturalism

As discussed in sections 1.1.1 and 1.1.2, Quine criticizes Carnap's epistemological project for several different reasons in the article "Epistemology Naturalized." Through this criticism of the project Quine rejected the first philosophical enterprise of grounding science on a more secure philosophical foundation, and the naturalist perspective finally emerged here. Given this historical development of naturalism, since the primary aim of this book is to formulate a form of pluralistic naturalism by using the Carnapian model of pluralism—the model that succeeds some aspects of Carnap's philosophy, if not quite equating to it—it may seem reasonable to address the question of the validity and coherence of the whole project of this book. To deal with this concern, in what follows, I will argue that the Carnapian model of pluralism can be developed coherently within the framework of naturalism.

First, let me remind the reader of the result of the discussion in chapter 1. There the grounds that justify naturalism are closely examined, and as a result, naturalism is defined as 'minimal naturalism', the view that refutes the existence of any other justificatory procedure than the hypothetico-deductive method and rejects any first philosophical project in which philosophy precedes science and provides its foundation. It was also proposed that varieties of naturalism may be formulated by adding different theoretical options to the minimal naturalism, options like physicalism and natural scientism. This presents an outline of the theory of naturalism advocated in this book.

Based on this outline, naturalists are offered the option to develop their particular positions by adding various theoretical views to minimal naturalism, resulting in the potential for various forms of naturalistic ontology. It would be a mistake, however, to understand this theoretical flexibility to entail that naturalists may hold any idiosyncratic view they may fancy, since naturalism itself is grounded in particular theses such as belief system immanentism and holism, which impose constraints on the possible and acceptable theoretical options that are available to naturalists. In section 2.1.3, I have discussed such constraints on the possible forms of naturalistic ontology and consequently presented the following two constraints:

(1) Constraint arising from belief system immanentism

Naturalists may not understand truth as correspondence to reality in itself (something independent of our belief system). A set of true statements from which an ontology is derived—whether it is a set of ordinarily accepted statements or the totality of science (or a part of it)—has to be located within our belief system.

(2) Constraint arising from the abandonment of foundationalism

The epistemological status of any ontological claim that is derived from a naturalist position will always remain the same: it is fallible and subject to revision. Naturalists may not accept any ontological view that is considered an *a priori* principle immune to revision.

Now, I will consider whether the Carnapian model of pluralism satisfies these two constraints. First, it is clear that the Carnapian model is compatible with the constraint from belief system immanentism because in the Carnapian model of pluralism, the validity of a semantic system is evaluated using the pragmatic perspective of efficacy for the goal of a particular inquiry, not appealing to any correspondence to reality in itself, existing independently of any belief system.

Let me elaborate on this point. According to Carnap, to accept the existence of a kind of objects is "to accept a certain form of language, in other words, to accept rules for forming statements and for testing, accepting, or rejecting them" (Carnap 1956, 208). For example, whether to accept the existence of mereological sums is equivalent to the question of whether to accept a system of mereology. In turn, the question of whether to accept a system of mereology is to be answered by appealing to the pragmatic criterion of efficacy for the goal of a particular inquiry. It then follows that whether to accept the existence of mereological sums must be answered, not by considering reality in itself, but by appealing to the pragmatic criterion of its efficacy for the goal of a particular inquiry.

As has been repeatedly brought up, Carnap and Quine entirely agree with one another on this particular point. Consider the following remarks by Quine:

> We can improve our conceptual scheme, our philosophy, bit by bit while continuing to depend on it for support; but we cannot detach ourselves from it and compare it objectively with an unconceptualized reality. Hence it is meaningless, I suggest, to inquire into the absolute correctness of a conceptual scheme as a mirror of reality. Our standard for appraising basic changes of

conceptual scheme must be, not a realistic standard of correspondence to reality, but a pragmatic standard. (Quine 1953, 79)

Carnap and Quine, notwithstanding their terminological differences with respect to conceptual systems that produce sentences ('semantic system' versus 'conceptual scheme'), share the idea that conceptual systems must be evaluated from a pragmatic viewpoint, rather than by comparison with reality.

The discussion so far has made it clear that in the Carnapian model of pluralism, the truths of statements and ontological claims derived from them never amount to claiming correspondence to reality, and that makes the Carnapian model compatible with constraint (1) above. Let us next turn to the second constraint, that arising from the abandonment of foundationalism. It may superficially appear that the Carnapian model of pluralism is incompatible with this constraint, since the model permits the existence of analytic propositions, statements that are true by virtue of semantic rules alone. To be sure, if they were incorrigible or immune to revision, then the Carnapian model would become incompatible with naturalism.

However, the concept of analyticity for Carnap (and by extension, the concept of analyticity in the Carnapian model) by no means makes analytic propositions incorrigible or immune to revision, as explained in sections 3.2.3 and 3.2.4. According to the concept of analyticity entertained by Carnap, whether a statement is analytic is determined relative to a semantic system. Also, remember that Carnap writes:

Let us grant to those who work in any special field of investigation the freedom to use any form of expression which seems useful to them; the work in the field will sooner or later lead to the elimination of these forms which have no useful function. (Carnap 1956, 221)

That is, semantic systems or systems of semantic rules for Carnap can never specify *a priori* principles immune to revision; a system is proposed as a working hypothesis that purports to subserve a particular inquiry, and it has to be discarded if it turns out to be unsuitable for that inquiry.

These considerations clarify why the Carnapian model of pluralism is compatible with naturalism. This is because, as stated in part (2) of section 2.1.3, ontological claims are compatible with naturalism as long as they are proposed as working hypotheses that can be discarded in an empirical inquiry. It is true that semantic rules in the Carnapian model may have specific ontological implications (for example, if a certain kind of axiomatic system in mereology is incorporated into semantic rules, then the rules logically lead to deducing the existence of a 'null object'). Given the criterion of efficacy for the goal of a particular inquiry, however, ontological claims implied by a semantic system can be discarded *together with the whole system*. In this sense, ontological claims are compatible with naturalism.

The discussion so far has established that the Carnapian model of pluralism satisfies the two constraints imposed on naturalistic ontology. This leads to the conclusion that it is justifiable to formulate a kind of pluralistic naturalism using the Carnapian model.

The current section has examined the Carnapian model of pluralism, yielding the following conclusions:

- The Carnapian model as discussed here inherits many insights from Carnap's semantic project, even if it does not equate to Carnap's own position. (3.2.1 and 3.2.2)

- The model overcomes Quine's criticism of analyticity and thereby offers no insurmountable difficulty that the model has been thought to have. (3.2.3)

- The model overcomes the two problems that have plagued Putnam's views on pluralism. (3.2.4)

- The model is fully compatible with and can be developed within the framework of naturalism. (3.2.5)

Now, I have completed a basic exposition of the Carnapian model of pluralism, the form of pluralistic naturalism advocated in this book. In the remainder of this chapter, to deepen our understanding of the Carnapian model, I will supplement the preceding results by discussing particular cases of conceptual activities and philosophical debates on which the model may shed new light.

3.2.6 Conceptual activities and the Carnapian model of pluralism

In my view, the Carnapian model of pluralism enables not only describing various concepts but also accounting for a dynamic aspect of our conceptual activities: we sometimes transform existing concepts and introduce new ones. In what follows, by way of example, I will discuss the account of our conceptual activities that the Carnapian model offers, presenting some considerations on the conflict between pluralism and monism.

(1) Death in biology and death in law[58]

Let us examine the concept of 'death' and the predicate 'is dead' or 'die'. In everyday life we hold a wide range of views on this concept and assent to some sentences containing the corresponding predicates, and dissent to others. For example, it would be observed through a pragmatic study of English that some speakers assent to 'every person will die', 'the dead doesn't talk', 'only a living creature dies', 'the dead has no consciousness', etc. (Perhaps some would assent to sentences such as 'the dead goes to heaven'.) Certainly, these pragmatic facts do not determine which among the sentences assented to comprise of the semantic rules of English (as argued in section 3.2.3). The Carnapian model of pluralism examined in this chapter suggests, instead, that there is no such 'analyticity in itself'. Asking

---

[58] For the ensuing discussion, I consulted *Encyclopedia of Life Sciences* (Nature Publishing Group, 2002) and *Sekai Daihyakka Jiten* ('World Encyclopedia'), (Heibonsha, 2003).

whether a sentence is a semantic rule (an axiom) or an analytic proposition (a theorem) would be meaningful only relative to a system of semantic rules, and such a question could be answered only relative to a semantic system. At the same time, while succeeding a good part of these ordinary views, we sometimes articulate a clear definition of the concept 'death' and provide explicit rules for using the corresponding predicates, depending on various interests and purposes. Here, as case studies, I will examine the definitions of 'death' in biology and law, elucidating the dynamic aspect of our conceptual activities.

First, in biology, death is defined as 'the irreversible cessation of life activity'. For example, the death of a human being is determined by the irreversible cessation of the functioning of the heart, lungs, and brain, which are considered necessary for sustaining life activity; the death of an organ is defined as the irreversible cessation of its functions; and the death of a cell as the cessation of metabolism. (It follows that the death of a living organism does not entail the death of the organs and cells that the organism consists of.)

This biological way of accounting for 'death' is characterized as follows. The concept 'death' in biology is understood in terms of the cessation of life phenomena. (That is why a semantic system that embodies a biological discourse contains the following semantic rule: 'x died' is true if and only if the life phenomena of the referent of x have ceased irreversibly.) Accordingly, the scope to which the concept 'death' applies is extended beyond individual living creatures to all objects (including organs and cells) to which a life phenomenon can be attributed. Also, since biology is a part of natural science, the conditions of death are specified only in terms of observable biological facts. For example, the death of a human being is determined depending, not on phenomena that are hard to discern from a biological viewpoint such as the irreversible cessation of consciousness, but on phenomena such as the cessation of heartbeat or respiration and a fixed dilation of the pupils.

By contrast, the definition of 'death' in law (jurisprudence) has several different characteristics that are not seen in the biological concept of 'death'.[59] The primary meaning of 'death' in the Japanese Civil Code is the loss of the capacity to hold rights (that is why death is paired with birth, at which the capacity to hold rights is created).[60] Death is established through the completion of statutory procedures by certified experts (such as doctors). (Therefore, at least in Japanese jurisprudence, it is true that for every x, if x has died, then x possesses no legal rights.) As has been illustrated so far, the concept of 'death' in law (the Civil Code) is different from that in biology, the latter of which refers to life phenomena. The cause of this difference lies in the interests and goals of using the concept 'death' in the Civil Code. The primary goal of defining the concept of 'death' in the Civil Code is to deal adequately and uneventfully with legal problems arising from the loss of life for an individual, the basic unit of the Civil Code.

---

[59] I owe the ensuing discussion of the concept of 'death' in law to Attorney Koichi Ohtomo (Subaru Law Firm). I am grateful to his assistance.
[60] Exceptionally, with respect to cases of inheritance and compensation for damages, an unborn fetus may be deemed to have been 'already born'. See Civil Code Articles 721, 886, and 965. For present purposes, there is no problem with the assumption that the capacity to hold rights emerges at birth.

In this way, there is a difference between the fields of law and biology in the semantic rules for the concept of 'death'. Also, death in law and death in biology are not equivalent in terms of how it is established. For example, a human individual may be declared dead in the legal sense through a properly established statutory process, even if it is not possible to determine whether the individual is dead in the biological sense. An example of this is 'Adjudication of Disappearance' (Civil Code Article 30). According to this article, although it is unknown whether a missing person is dead or alive, the person may be deemed legally dead under specific conditions.[61] The article was introduced because of its usefulness in legal procedures (for example, if it is permanently unclear whether the missing person is dead or alive, then the relatives and other interested parties may have difficulty in initiating any legal process). The legal concept of 'death', represented by this example, serves one of the purposes of the law well, dealing with legal issues in an uneventful manner.

Biology and law are also different with respect to the temporal ordering of death. For example, imagine that two deceased individuals are found in a house burned down by fire and it is then asked which individual died first. According to the definition of death in biology, this question must be answered by examining at which point the vital life signs terminated. This would very likely make it remain unclear which of the deceased died first. Under such circumstances, it would not be feasible to apply a biological method to determine the point of death (how could doctors continue monitoring heartbeats during a fire?). In law, however, Article 32-2 of the Civil Code stipulates that the deceased individuals are presumed to have died at the same time in this case unless evidence shows otherwise. (It follows that there would be no inheritance even if the deceased were married or parent and child.) This stipulation was introduced to avoid legal confusion resulting from any answer to the question of who died first; answering this question in any way—doing so in an objective manner would be extremely difficult—could give rise to a legal disparity between interested parties. (There is no need to introduce this kind of stipulation in biology because leaving the question of who died first unanswered would create no serious problem. In biology it would be permissible to leave the question unanswered.)

As the discussion so far has illustrated, a semantic system for legal issues has several rules that are not contained in a system for biology due to its particular interest to deal with legal problems uneventfullly and avoid confusion. In other words, death in biology and death in law are different from one another to some degree in their logical implications, standards for determination, and extensions. Now, it is important to realize that this example of a conceptual activity is nicely captured by the Carnapian model of pluralism. Both biology and jurisprudence started with ordinary views of 'death' and attempted to clarify the concept of 'death' in their distinctive ways in accordance with their own aims and interests. The definitions of

---

[61] The main outcomes of the adjudication of disappearance are the dissolution of the relevant marriage and the commencement of the procedures determining inheritance. Article 32 also defines how to rescind the adjudication of disappearance. An example of the same kind can be found in a notice by the Ministry of Justice: a person over 100 years old whose location is unknown may be registered as dead by the authority of family registration officials (The Civil Affairs Bureau Notice 1358).

'death' proposed in the respective systems are evaluated not on the criterion of whether they fit the ordinary uses of the term 'death'—let alone appealing to any correspondence with the characteristics of the concept of 'death' existing independently of the systems—but on the criterion of whether they are suitable for the purposes and interests of the respective systems.[62]

(2) Philosophy of Mind

The Carnapian model of pluralism may also shed light on the nature of the conflicts in the philosophy of mind. A number of contemporary philosophers of mind have attempted to account for beliefs and other propositional attitudes as well as qualia within the physicalist worldview, whereas others have defended theses such as interpretivism that keeps its distance from physicalism (the former attempts are often described as an effort to 'naturalize mind', but given the argument presented in this book that naturalism can be separated from physicalism, they must be described as attempts to 'physicalize mind'). There is no shortage of debate among philosophers of mind, who develop and defend their own theses and criticize the theses of others. There seems to be, however, no consensus regarding the goals of these theses in the philosophy of mind or on the criteria from which they are to be evaluated.

Let us consider the conflicts in the philosophy of mind under the Carnapian model of pluralism (though with considerable simplification). As a starting point for investigating the mind, some philosophers may begin with the idea that mental states can cause physical acts, among other ideas that are ordinarily upheld, and then attempt to develop a semantic system for mental predicates in such a way that it maintains this idea by modifying and calibrating other views of the mind. Behind this program to understand the mind in terms of its causal roles, there may be a further intention to account for mental phenomena within the physicalist worldview through the causal closure or the completeness of physics (2.2.2). If there is such an intention, theorists would construct different semantic systems depending on what are considered to be causal relata that play the same roles as mental states. (For example, according to the type-type identity theory, it may be the case that 'x is in the mental state A' if and only if the referent of x is in the physical state type α; according to a functionalist system, it may be the case that 'x is in the mental state A' is true if and only if the referent of x is in a physical state type that realizes the functional state β.) Other theorists may focus on the idea that there is some degree of rational connection between the mental states of an individual or that the content of a mental state is understood through utterance behavior, investigating the nature of the mind on the basis of such ideas. This latter strategy is represented by interpretivism, according to

---

[62] It is also important for pluralists that the predicate 'x died' in one system does not supervene on the predicate 'x died' in the other system. As shown by the examples involving 'declaration of disappearance' and 'presumption of simultaneous death', whether one is legally dead and the temporal order of two deaths are not determined by the facts about biological death, and of course, whether one is legally declared dead does not determine whether one is biologically dead. This is illustrated by cases in which one is 'as a matter of fact' legally deemed to have died while biologically surviving also 'as a matter of fact'. (Legal death is determined not by the fact that one is biologically dead, but by the recognition of biological death.)

which the contents of mental states are identified with what the interpreter attributes to the speaker through the construction of a theory of interpretation based on the principle of charity (for example, it would be claimed that 'x believes that A' is true if and only if a theory of interpretation that attributes the belief that A to the referent of x is constructed and accepted).

The question to be addressed is how these conflicting views of the mind must be evaluated. An important point to be noted first is that these semantic systems are constructed in such a way that they fit our everyday linguistic activities concerning beliefs and other mental states as far as possible. For example, it would be misleading to label 'belief' a concept that is defined by semantic rules having little connection to our conventional understanding of beliefs, and it would also make it difficult to relate the new concept of 'belief' to the traditional roles that the ordinarily accepted mental concepts are assumed to play and obscure the purpose of the concept 'belief'.

It has become clear by now that the criterion of whether a system fits pragmatic facts plays some role in evaluating competing systems. It is also worth pointing out that this criterion does not uniquely determine a semantic system to be adopted. I have repeatedly stated that there is indeterminacy in descriptive semantics. In addition, it is questionable in the first place whether all of the commonly accepted views of the mind are compatible with one another, or whether we have developed a variety of views of the mind in such a way that the views are all coherent with one another. In fact, all the views proposed in the philosophy of mind so far have difficulties in accounting for pragmatic facts (non-reductive physicalism and the causal efficacy of the mental, functionalism and its counterexamples by Ned Block, the type-type identity theory and pain in Martians, interpretivism and first-person authority, and physicalism in general and free will, etc.[63]). Given these considerations, the scope of the criterion of whether a system fits pragmatic facts must be qualified in some way.

The current situation in the philosophy of mind seems very similar to what Carnap presented through his semantic project. To be sure, there are a number of important and useful views of the mind, which we wish to retain as far as possible in clarifying the concept of the 'mind'. It would, however, probably be reasonable to abandon some of such views and revise the conventional way of thinking about the mind if doing so would be able to facilitate the various strands of the discussion of the mind. This attitude was shared by Carnap, as represented by his instrumentalist view of language, the view that language is an instrument that is improved and replaced depending on the purpose intended; this can be seen in the following remarks:

> A natural language is like a crude, primitive pocketknife, very useful for a hundred different purposes. But for certain specific purposes, special tools are more efficient, e.g., chisels, cutting-machines, and finally the microtome. If we find that the pocket knife is too crude for a given purpose and creates defective products, we shall try to discover the cause of the failure, and then either use the knife more skillfully, or replace it for this special purpose by a more suitable tool,

---

[63] See (Kim 1998; Block 1980; Lewis 1980; Davidson 2001).

or even invent a new one. The naturalist's thesis is like saying that by using a special tool we evade the problem of the correct use of the cruder tool. But would anyone criticize the bacteriologist for using a microtome, and assert that he is evading the problem of correctly using a pocketknife? (Carnap 1963c, 938-9)

If this linguistic view is accepted, the question of how to understand the mind becomes, at least partially, a pragmatic question. That is, semantic systems that are designed to define the contents of mental concepts would be evaluated not in terms of whether they accurately depict some facts of the world, but in terms of whether they effectively help achieving the goals for which the systems are designed.[64] Some theorists may aim at constructing a philosophical theory of mind that fits our linguistic practice as far as possible; others may prefer accounting for the mind in ways somewhat diverging from the conventional uses of mental predicates by imposing a basic requirement on mental contents—for example, the requirement of intersubjective determinacy and that of decidability by a procedure that can be executed in a limited amount of time. All such goals are meaningful in their own ways and thereby worth pursuing. Given these different goals we may have, it seems justifiable to conclude that whether a semantic system fits pragmatic facts is no longer a prerequisite for accepting that system. Extant natural languages (more specifically, the semantic systems that are constructed to preserve all the pragmatic facts about them) are not in a domain that is separate from artificial languages, but they are 'of equal standing' that must be evaluated for a variety of goals.[65]

Now, keeping all this in mind, let us consider the conflict between physicalist monism and pluralism. As already discussed in section 3.2.1, in the Carnapian model of pluralism, the difference between monism and pluralism is understood in terms of how to evaluate semantic systems—the former appeals to a foundational system that accounts for all other systems whereas the latter appeals to pragmatism. Pluralists,

---

[64] Some of the remarks Davidson made on this point are instructive. For example, consider the following that is concerned with his interpretivist philosophy of mind:
> What I think is certain is that holism, externalism, and the normative feature of the mental stand or fall together: if these are features of the mental, and they stand in the way of a serious science of psychology, then Ryle, Wittgenstein, and Quine in his more pessimistic mood are right. There can be no serious science or sciences of the mental. I believe the normative, holistic, and externalist elements in psychological concepts cannot be eliminated without radically changing the subject. (Davidson 2004, 122-3)

Here, Davidson seems to be committed to the idea that there is the reality of the mental, or at least, the idea that there are essential characteristics of the mental that the mental has to possess to remain mental. At the very least, either idea is incompatible with the strategy suggested by the Carnapian model of pluralism.

[65] In fact, only a fraction of semantic rules are specified in biology and law. It is commonplace to retain the ordinary uses of natural language expressions in a biological or legal discourse, except for expressions such as 'living organism' and 'death' that are provided with a definition different from how it is considered in ordinary usage, and technical terms such as 'cell' and 'DNA'—the root concepts from which they derived are not part of natural languages. I have stated above that natural and artificial languages have equal standing (and this statement would not be undermined by the qualification in this footnote), but more accurately it may be paraphrased as follows: semantic systems that perfectly fit the pragmatic facts about natural languages and semantic systems that are constructed in such a way that they diverge from such pragmatic facts have equal standing.

on the one hand, evaluate a constructed semantic system by relying only on the criterion of efficacy for the goal for which the system is designed; physicalist monists, on the other hand, appeals to physics, a foundational semantic system, and evaluates a semantic system by examining whether all the properties used in the system supervene on physical properties. Accordingly, a monistic view imposes a constraint on our conceptual activities (the constraint that they must be accounted for by a foundational system). By contrast, the Carnapian model of pluralism rejects such a monistic constraint on our conceptual activities.

(3) Contemporary Theory of Knowledge

Considerations similar to those above may be applied to debates in theory of knowledge. Especially since Gettier's seminal 1963 paper, philosophers working in theory of knowledge have been trying to develop a semantic system that precisely captures our linguistic intuitions about how to use the predicate 'know'; that is to say, they have aimed at creating a system that fits the pragmatic facts of 'know'. (Accordingly, an epistemological thesis is commonly criticized by pointing to a discrepancy between what the thesis deems to be knowledge and what we consider to be knowledge.) In short, contemporary debates in theory of knowledge are often concerned with issues involving descriptive semantics.

As indicated in section 3.1.3, however, all that can be revealed by a descriptive semantic inquiry is how the term 'knowledge' is used in a linguistic community, and descriptive semantics can offer nothing of significant import related to whether such a concept of 'knowledge' must be adopted or whether we should believe in what is considered 'knowledge' according to the concept. Contemporary theory of knowledge has provided nothing more than descriptions of the *normal and prevailing* criterion of rationality that is accepted as a fact by a particular linguistic group at a particular period of time.[66]

It is clear that descriptive semantic studies are meaningful in theory of knowledge because they have provided important insights into our concept of 'knowledge' that would not have been available without descriptive semantics (the development of 'externalism' is one such example). Through an examination of Carnap's semantic project, however, it has been argued in this book that semantic inquiries are not exhausted by descriptive semantics (which aims at capturing existing linguistic activities). That is, it must be clear by now that there are pure semantic inquiries that are also available, and in pure semantics a semantic system for 'know' would be constructed in a manner that makes it subserve the purpose of a particular inquiry regardless of whether the system fits pragmatic facts. For example, in order to

---

[66] The following example illustrates the point of this paragraph. Imagine that we make a descriptive study of the native language of an indigenous tribe, and as a result, discover that the word in the language equivalent to 'know' is correctly used on the basis of religious texts that are enshrined by the tribe; and any statement appearing in the texts is considered accurate, and when a statement is found in the texts, a belief in it is considered knowledge. Should we—or the tribe—adopt this concept of 'knowledge'? Should we believe in what is considered 'knowledge' according to this concept? The point I am making above is that such questions fall outside the scope of descriptive semantics.

construct a system of knowledge that is highly objective and manipulatable, it would be effective to require some form of empirical testability for an appropriate use of the predicate 'know' (indeed, this would be a more rigorous requirement than the one Carnap imposed as a theorist who endorses natural scientism). (Let me hastily add that since pluralists promote a diversity of goals of inquiry, they would not exclusively support this particular approach to constructing a system.) By investigating pure semantics it would become possible to explore new horizons of rationality criteria, developing them in a dynamic and diverse way, not merely constrained to acknowledging the accepted criteria.

It would be a mistake, however, to think that the introduction of pure semantic inquiry would radically change the criterion of rationality that we currently accept. For our linguistic intuitions about 'know' reflect a great deal of insight into the ends-means relation, which would be a key to accomplishing a pure semantic inquiry. Still, discussion based on the pure versus descriptive semantics distinction would elucidate the significance and purposes of philosophical inquiry into the concept of 'knowledge', and consequently, it would become possible to evaluate theses in theory of knowledge based on clearer criteria.

In the examination of the three cases above, I have argued that the Carnapian model of pluralism provides a clear vision enabling us to understand our conceptual activities, in which we describe, change, and create new concepts.[67] Moreover, this model of pluralism enables clarifying the conflict between monism and pluralism by distinguishing the two in terms of constraints on acceptable semantic systems.

---

[67] Davidson's criticism of conceptual schemes and Tanji's (1997) 'principle of compensation' illuminate the constraints on such conceptual activities. In this sense, these two play complementary roles in achieving a Carnapian project.

Conclusions

It is generally agreed that physicalism is the dominant ontological view in contemporary naturalism. The form of naturalism revived by Quine, however, neither implies nor presupposes physicalism. In this book, I have shown this by examining the grounds for naturalism (chapter 1) and argued for the development of a non-physicalist form of naturalism by discussing the problems that arise with physicalism when added to minimal naturalism as an ontological thesis (chapter 2). By precisely formulating a model of pluralism, I have demonstrated the possibility of pluralistic naturalism, an alternative to physicalist naturalism (chapter 3).

I have proposed a formulation of naturalism in this book by investigating the grounds for contemporary naturalism, and the formulation is thereby supported from a logical as well as from a historical point of view (though the historical study here is limited to the recent periods). Therefore, the formulation of naturalism proposed in this book is expected to overcome mutual misunderstandings among theorists due to the extant obscure definitions of naturalism, paving the way towards productive discussions of naturalism. The Carnapian model of pluralism presented in chapter 3 is nothing more than a proposal, and not an unavoidable, inevitable form of naturalism necessitated by the pluralistic perspective. Still, I have specified the subject matter of pluralism—that there are multiple semantic systems in the Carnapian model—and the rationale for pluralism—that there are diverse goals in concept formation; and with this it is possible for the Carnapian model of pluralism to stimulate further critical discussion and provide a foundation for a more refined formulation of pluralistic naturalism. Therefore, it is reasonable to conclude that the preceding discussions have largely fulfilled the two main objectives of this book presented in the 'Introduction': to present a clear formulation of naturalism and to develop and defend a model of pluralistic naturalism that can replace physicalist naturalism.

As discussed throughout the book, naturalism is a broad philosophical perspective from which theorists debate over particular philosophical issues. One such major debate is the conflict between physicalist monism and pluralism, discussed in chapters 2 and 3. Physicalism alone has numerous different formulations; theorists have proposed a very large number of variants of physicalism (these debates over the formulations of physicalism are what Todayama calls 'debates over the naturalization strategy'). The various philosophical views within naturalism must be evaluated by examining their implications for particular philosophical problems, based on the plausibility of the answers they can offer to the problems, instead of examining their implications at an abstract level, like the focus of this book. (In this sense, the discussion in chapters 1 and 3 may be regarded as basic research in the theory of naturalism.)

Pluralistic naturalism, the position advanced in this book, is also ultimately to be evaluated depending on whether it can convincingly solve particular philosophical problems. To determine whether pluralistic naturalism is a productive framework for solving particular problems, it is necessary to inquire into the implications of pluralism in specific cases. Such an investigation, however, has to wait for another occasion.

Bibliography

[Bechtel 1980]: P. W. Bechtel, "Indeterminacy and Underdetermination; Are Quine's Two Thesis Consistent?" in *Philosophical Studies*, 38(3), 309-20.

[Block 1980]: N. Block, "What is Functionalism?" in N. Block (ed.), *Readings in the Philosophy of Psychology*, Vol. 1, Cambridge, MA: Harvard University Press, 171-184.

[Borchert 2006]: D. M. Borchert (ed.), *Encyclopedia of Philosophy*, (Vol. 6) (2nd edition), Detroit, MI: Thomson Gale, 206.

[Burkhardt and Smith, 1991]: H. Burkhardt and B. Smith (eds.), *Handbook of Metaphysics and Ontology*, Munich: Philosophia Verlag.

[Carnap 1928]: R. Carnap, *Der logische Aufbau der Welt*, Berlin: Weltkreis. English Translation : R. Carnap (translated by R. George), *The Logical Structure of the World*, Berkeley: University of California Press, 1969.

[Carnap 1932a]: R. Carnap, "Die Physicalishe Sprache als Universal Sprache," in *Erkenntnis* 2(1), 432-65.

[Carnap 1932b]: R. Carnap, "Über Protokollsätze," in *Erkenntnis* 3(1), 215-28. English Translation : R. Carnap (translated by R. Creath and R. Nollan), "On Protocol Sentences," in *Noûs* 21, 1987, 457-70.

[Carnap 1936]: R. Carnap, "Testability and Meaning," in *Philosophy of Science*, 3(4), 419-71; 4(1), 1-40.

[Carnap 1937]: R. Carnap (translated by A. Smeaton), *The Logical Syntax of Language*, London: Routledge & K. Paul, 1937.

[Carnap 1939]: R. Carnap, *Foundation of Logic and Mathematics: International Encyclopedia of Unified Science* 1(3), Chicago: University of Chicago Press, 1939.

[Carnap 1942]: R. Carnap, *Introduction to Semantics*, Cambridge, MA: Harvard University Press, 1942.

[Carnap 1952]: R. Carnap, "Quine on Analyticity," in [Creath, 1990], 427-432.

[Carnap 1956]: R. Carnap, *Meaning and Necessity* (2nd, enlarged edition), Chicago: University of Chicago Press, 1956.

[Carnap 1963a]: R. Carnap, "Intellectual Autobiography," in P. A. Schilpp (ed.), *Philosophy of Rudolf Carnap*, La Salle: Open Court, 1963, 3-84.

[Carnap 1963b]: R. Carnap, "Quine on Logocal Truth," in P. A. Schilpp (ed.), *Philosophy of Rudolf Carnap*, La Salle: Open Court, 1963, 11-915.

[Carnap 1963c]: R. Carnap, "P. F. Strawson on Linguistic Naturalism," in P. A. Shilpp (ed.), *Philosophy of Rudolf Carnap*, La Salle: Open Court, 1963, 933-940.

[Case 1997]: J. Case, "On the Right Idea of Conceptual Scheme," in *Southern Journal of Philosophy* 35(1), 1-18.

[Case 2001]: J. Case, "The Heart of Putnam's Pluralistic Realism," in *Revue Internationale de Philosophie*, 218(4), 417-430.

[Chomsky 1969]: N. Chomsky, "Quine's Empirical Assumptions," in D. Davidson and J. Hintikka (eds.), *Words and Objections*, Dordrecht: Reidel Publishing Company, 1969.

[Chomsky 1975]: N. Chomsky, *Refrections on Language*, New York : Pantheon, 1975.

[Chomsky 1980]: N. Chomsky, *Rules and Representation*, New York : Columbia University Press, 1980.

[Crane 1991]: T. Crane, "Why Indeed? Papineau on Supervenience and the Completeness of Physics," in *Analysis* 51, 32-7.

[Crane and Mellor 1990]: T. Crane and D. H. Mellor, "There is No Question of Physicalism," in *Mind* 99(394), 185-206.

[Creath 1987]: R. Creath, "The Initial Reception of Carnap's Doctrine of Analyticity," in *Noûs* 21(4), 477-99.

[Creath 1990]: R. Creath (ed. and Intoroduction), *Dear Carnap and Dear Van: The Quine-Carnap Correspondence and Related Works*, Berkeley : University of California Press, 1990.

[Davidson 1984]: D. Davidson, *Inquiries into Truth and Interpretation*, Oxford : Clarendon Press, 1984.

[Davidson 1998]: D. Davidson, "Appendix: Replies to Rorty, Stroud, MacDowell, and Pereda," in his *Truth, Language and History*, Oxford : Clarendon Press, 2005.

[Davidson 2001]: D. Davidson, *Subjective, Intersubjective, Objective*, Oxford : Oxford University Press, 2001.

[Davidson 2004]: D. Davidson, *Problems of Rationality*, Oxford : Oxford University Press, 2004.

[Dennett 1991]: D. Dennett, "Real Patterns," in *The Journal of Philosophy* 88(1), 27-51.

[Dewey 1946]: J. Dewey, "Proposition, Warranted Assertibility, and Truth," in his *Problems of Men*, New York : Philosophical Library, 1946, 331-53.

[Dowell 2006]: J. L. Dowell. "The Physical: Empirical, Not Metaphysical," *Philosophical Studies* 131(1), 25-60.

[Dummett 1981]: M. Dummett, *The Interpretation of Frege's Philosophy*, Cambridge, MA : Harvard University Press, 1981.

[Eklund 2006a]: M. Eklund, "Carnap and Ontological Pluralism," in D. Chalmers, D. Manley, and R. Wasserman (eds.), *Metametaphysics: New Essays on the Foundations of Ontology*. Oxford : University Press 2006, 130-56.

[Eklund 2006b]: M. Eklund, "Neo-Fregean Ontology," in *Philosophical Perspectives* 20(1), 95-121.

[Evnine 1991]: S. Evnine, *Donald Davidson*, Cambridge: Polity Press, 1991.

[Field 1980]: H. Field, *Science Without Numbers: A Defense of Nominalism*, Oxford: Blackwell, 1980.

[Føllesdal 1990]: D. Follesdal, "Indeterminacy and Mental States," in R. B. Barrett and R. F. Gibson (eds.), *Perspectives on Quine*, Oxford : Blackwell, 1990, 98-109.

[Gaudet 2006]: E. Gaudet, *Quine on Meaning: The Indeterminacy of Translation*, London : Continuum, 2006.

[Gettier 1963]: E. Gettier, "Is Justified True Belief Knowledge ?" in *Analysis*, 23(6), 121-123.

[Gibson 1986]: R. F. Gibson, "Translation, Physics, and Facts of the Matter," in L. E. Hahn and P. A. Schilpp (eds.), The *Philosophy of W. V. Quine*, La Salle: Open Court, 1986, 147.

[Gibson 1988]: R. F. Gibson, *Enlightened Empiricism: An Examination of W. V. Quine's Theory of Knowledg*, Tampa: Universty of South Florida Press, 1988.

[Hacker 1996]: P. M. S. Hacker, "On Davidson's Idea of a Conceptual Scheme," in *Philosophical Quarterly* 46(184), 289-307.
[Hempel 1950]: C. G. Hempel, "Problems and Changes in the Empiricist Criterion of Meaning," in A. J. Ayer (ed.), *Logical Positivism*, New York: The Free Press, 1959, 108-129.
[Hookway 1988]: C. Hookway, *Quine: Language, Experience and Reality*, Stanford : Stanford University Press, 1988.
[Jackson 1986]: F. Jackson, "What Mary Didn't Know," in *The Journal of Philosophy* 83, 291-5.
[Janvid 2004]: M. Janvid, "Epistemological Naturalism and Normativity Objection," in *Erkenntnis* 60(1), 35-49.
[Katz 1990]: J. Katz, "The Refutation of Indeterminacy," in R. B. Barrett and R. F. Gibson (eds.), *Perspectives on Quine*, Oxford : Blackwell, 1990, 182-3.
[Kim 1988]: J. Kim, "What Is 'Naturalized Epistemology'?" in [Kornblith, 1994].
[Kim 1998]: J. Kim, *Mind in a Physical World: An Essay on the Mind-Body Problem and Mental Causation*, Cambridge, MA : The MIT Press, 1998.
[Kim 2002]: J. Kim (ed.), *Supervenience*, Aldershot: Ashgate/Dartmouth Publishing, 2002.
[Kornblith 1994]: H. Kornblith (ed.), *Naturalizing Epistemology*, Cambridge, MA: The MIT Press, 1994.
[Kripke 1982]: S. Kripke, *Wittgenstein on Rules and Private Language*, Cambridge, MA : Harvard University Press, 1982.
[Lewis 1980]: D. Lewis, "Mad Pain and Martian Pain," in his *Philosophical Papers Vol. I*, Oxford : Oxford University Press, 122-30.
[Loewer 1995]: B. Loewer, "An Argument for Strong Supervenience," in E. E. Savellos and U. D. Yarcin (eds.), *Supervenience: New Essays*, Cambridge : Cambridge University Press, 1995, 218-225.
[Loewer 2001]: B. Loewer, "From Physics to Physicalism," in C. Gillet and B. Loewer (eds.), *Physicalism and its Discontents*, Cambridge : Cambridge University Press, 2001, 37-56.
[Lynch 1998]: M. Lynch, *Truth in Context*, Cambridge, MA : The MIT Press, 1998.
[McDowell 2004]: J. MacDowll, "Naturalism in the Philosophy of Mind," in M. De Caro and D. Macarthur (eds.), *Naturalism in Question*, Cambridge, MA : Harvard University Press, 2004, 91-105 (originally published in *Neue Rundshau* 110, 1999).
[Maddy 1992]: P. Maddy, "Indispensability and Practice," in *The Journal of Philosophy* 89(6), 275-89.
[Moser and Yandell 2000]: P. K. Moser and D. Yandell, "Farewell to Philosophical Naturalism," in W. L. Craig and J. P. Moreland (eds.), *Naturalism: A Critical Analysis*, London : Routledge, 2000, 3-23.
[Neurath 1932]: O. Neurath, "Protokollsätze," in *Erkenntnis*, 3(1), 204-14.
English Translation : O. Neurath, "Protocol Statements," in his *Philosophical Papers: 1913-1946*, Dordrecht: Reidel, 1983, 91-9.
[Ney 2008]: A. Ney, "Defining Physicalism," *Philosphy Compass* 3(5), 1033-48.
[O'Grady 1999]: P. O'Grady, "Carnap and Two Dogmas of Empiricism," in *Philosophy and Phenomenologocal Research* 59(4), 1015-27.

[Papineau 1993]: D. Papineau, *Philosophical Naturalism*, Oxford : Blackwell, 1993.

[Papineau 1995]: D. Papineau, "Arguments for Supervenience and Physical Realization," in E. E. Savellos and U. D. Yarcin (eds.), *Supervenience: New Essays*, Cambridge : Cambridge University Press, 1995.

[Papineau 1996]: D. Papineau, "Reply to Commentators," in *Philosophy and Phenomenological Research* 56(3), 687-97.

[Papineau 2001]: D. Papineau, "The Rise of Physicalism," in C. Gillet and B. Loewer (eds.), *Physicalism and Its Discontents*, Cambridge : Cambridge University Press, 2001, 3-36.

[Price 1992]: H. Price, "Metaphysical Pluralism," in *The Journal of Philosophy* 89(8), 387-409.

[Putnam 1967]: H. Putnam, "Mathematics without Foundation," in *The Journal of Philosophy* 64(1), 5-22.

[Putnam 1975]: H. Putnam, "The Analytic and the Synthetic" in his *Mind, Language and Reality*, Cambridge : Cambridge University Press, 1975, 33-69.

[Putnam 1979]: H. Putnam, "Philosophy of Logic," in his *Philosophical Papers Vol. 1* (2nd edition), Cambridge : Cambridge University Press, 1979, 32-57.

[Putnam 1981]: H. Putnam, *Reason, Truth and History*, Cambridge : Cambridge University Press, 1981.

[Putnam 1988]: H. Putnam, *Representation and Reality*, Cambridge, MA : The MIT Press, 1988.

[Putnam 1990]: H. Putnam, *Realism with a Human Face*, Cambridge, MA : Harvard University Press, 1990.

[Putnam 1994]: H. Putnam, "Comments and Replies," in P. Clark and B. Hale (eds.), *Reading Putnam*, Oxford: Blackwell, 1994, 242-302.

[Putnam 2001]: H. Putnam, "Reply to Jennifer Case," in *Revue Internationale de Philosophie*, 218(4), 431-438.

[Putnam 2002]: H. Putnam, *The Collapse of the Fact/Value Dichotomy and Other Essays*, Cambridge, MA : Harvard University Press, 2002.

[Putnam 2004a]: H. Putnam, "The Content and Appeal of 'Naturalism'," in M. De Caro and D. Macarthur (eds.), *Naturalism in Question*, Cambridge, MA : Harvard University Press, 2004, 59-70.

[Putnam 2004b]: H. Putnam, *Ethics without Ontology*, Cambridge, MA : Harvard University Press, 2004.

[Quine 1953]: W. V. Quine, *From a Logical Point of View*, Cambridge, MA : Harvard University Press, 1953.

[Quine 1963]: W. V. Quine, "Carnap and Logical Truth" in his *The Ways of Paradox and Other Essays* revised, enlarged edition, Cambridge MA: Harvard University Press, 1976, 107-132.

[Quine 1969a]: W. V. Quine, *Ontological Relativity and Other Essays*, New York : Columbia University Press, 1969.

[Quine 1969b]: W. V. Quine, "Epistemology Naturalized," in [Quine 1969a], 69-90.

[Quine 1969c]: W. V. Quine, "To Chomsky," in D. Davidson and J. Hintikka (eds.), *Words and Objections*, Dordrecht: Reidel Publishing Company, 1969.

[Quine 1970]: W. V. Quine, "On the Reasons of Indeterminacy of Translation," in *The*

Journal of Philosophy 67(6), 178-183.

[Quine 1974]: W. V. Quine, *The Roots of Reference*, La Salle : Open Court, Pubilishing Company, 1974.

[Quine 1975]: W. V. Quine, "On Empirically Equivarent Systems of the World," in *Erkenntnis* 9, 313-28.

[Quine 1976]: W. V. Quine, "The Scope and Language of Science," in *his The Ways of Paradox and other essays*, Cambridge, MA : Harvard University Press, 1976, 228-45.

[Quine 1979]: W. V. O. Quine, "Facts of the Matter," in R. W. Shahan and C. V. Swoyer (eds.), *Essays on the Philosophy of W. V. Quine*, Hassocks: Harvester, 1979, 176-96.

[Quine 1981]: W. V. Quine, *Theories and Things*, Cambridge, MA : Harvard University Press, 1981.

[Quine 1986a]: W. V. Quine, "Reply to Morton White," in L. E. Hahn and P. A. Schilpp (eds.), *The Philosophy of W. V. Quine*, La Salle : Open Court, 1986, 663-5.

[Quine 1986b]: W. V. Quine, "Reply to Roger F. Gibson, Jr," in L. E. Hahn and P. A. Schilpp (eds.), *The philosoophy of W. V. Quine*, La Salle: Open Court, 1986, 155-57.

[Quine 1987]: W. V. Quine, "Indeterminacy of Translation Again," in *The Journal of Philosophy* 84(1), 5-10.

[Quine 1990]: W. V. Quine, "Comment on Katz," in R. B. Barrett and R. F. Gibson (eds.), *Perspectives on Quine*, Oxford : Blackwell, 1990, 198-199.

[Quine 1992]: W. V. Quine, *Persuit of Truth* (revised edition), Cambridge, MA : Harvard, University Press, 1992.

[Quine 1993]: W. V. Quine, "In Praise of Observation Sentence," in *The Journal of Philosophy* 60(3), 107-116.

[Quine 1995]: W. V. O. Quine, "Naturalism; or Living within One's Means," in Dialectica 49(24), 251-61 reprinted in his *QUINTESSENCE*, Cambridge, MA : Harvard University Press, 2004, 275-86.

[Quine 2000]: W. V. O. Quine, "Quine's Responses," in A. Orenstein and P. Kotatko (eds.), *Knowledge, Language and Logic*, Dordrecht : Kluwer Academic Publishers, 2000, 407-430.

[Quine and Ullian 1970]: W. V. Quine and J. S. Ullian, *The Web of Belief*, New York Random House.

[Ricketts 1994]: T. Ricketts, "Carnap's Principle of Tolerance, Empiricism, and Conventionalism," in P. Clarke and B. Hale (eds.), *Reading Putnam*, Oxford: Blackwell, 1994, 176-200.

[Rorty 1972]: R. Rorty, "Indeterminacy of Translation and of Truth," in *Synthese* 23 (4), 443-62.

[Rosenberg 1996]: A. Rosenberg, "A Field Guide to Recent Species of Naturalism," in *British Journal for the Philosophy of Science* 47(1), 1-29.

[Searle 1987]: J. R. Searle, "Indeteminacy, Empiricism, and the First Person," in *The Journal of Philosophy* 81, 123-146.

[Steward 1996]: H. Steward, "Papineau's Physicalism," in *Philosophy and Phenomenological Research* 56 (3), 667-72.

[Stoljar 2008]: D. Stoljar, "Physicalism" in E. N. Zalta (ed.), *The Stanford Encyclopedia of Philosophy* (Spring 2008 Edition), URL=⟨http://plato.stanford.edu/archives/

fall2008/entries/physicalism/⟩.
[Varzi 2003]: A Varzi, "Mereology" in E. N. Zalta (ed), The Stanford Encyclopedia of Philosophy (Summer 2003 Edition), URL=⟨http://plato.stanford.edu/archives/sum2003/entries/mereology/⟩.
[Wagner & Warner 1993]: S. J. Wagner and R. Warner (eds.), *Naturalism : A Critical Appraisal*, Notre Dame, In University of Notre Dame Press, 1993.
[Wilson 2006]: J. Wilson, "On Characterizing the Physical," *Philosophical Studies* 131 (1), 61-99.
[Witmer 1998]: D. Witmer, "What is Wrong with the Manifestability Argument for Supervenience," in *Australasian Journal of Philosophy* 76(1), 84-9.
[Witmer 2001]: D. Witmer, "Sufficiency Claims and Physicalism: A Formulation," in C. Gillet and B. Loewer (eds.), *Physicalism and its Discontents*, Cambridge : Cambridge University Press, 2001, 57-73.
[Wright 1983]: C. Wright, *On Frege's Conception of Numbers as Objects*, Aberdeen : Aberdeen University Press, 1983.

(In Japanese)
[Iida 1987]: Takashi Iida, *Gengo Tetsugaku Taizen* I (Summa Lingua Philosophica), Keisou Shobou, 1987.
[Iida 2007]: Takashi Iida, ed., *Tetsugaku no Rekishi 11* (History of Philosophy 11), Chuokouron Shinsha, 2007.
[Igashira 2005]: Masahiko Igashira, "Quine ni okeru Butsurishugi to Shizenka Sareta Ninshikiron" (Physicalism for Quine and Naturalized Epistemology), in *Kagaku Tetsugaku* (Philosophy of Science) Philosophy of Science Society Japan, 38(2), 2005.
[Igashira 2007]: Masahiko Igashira, "Bunsekisei wa Rikaifukanou na Gainen nano ka?" (Is Analyticity an Unintelligible Concept?) in *Tetsugaku* (Philosophy), Japan Philosophical Association, 58, Housei University Press, 2007.
[Kachi 2004]: Daisuke Kachi, "Bunseki Tetsugaku ni okeru Dentouteki Keijijogaku no Fukkou" (The Revival of Traditional Metaphysics in Analytic Philosophy), in *Gendai Shisou* (Contemporary Thought), 32(8), Seidosha, 2004.
[Kaneko 2006]: Hiroshi Kaneko, *Dummett ni Tadoritsuku Made* (How I Have Arrived At Dummett), Keisou Shobou, 2006.
[Kiyozuka 2007]: Kunihiko Kiyozuka, "Kaisetsu Gaibushugi to Hankangenshugi" (Interpreter's Notes: Externalism and Anti-reductionism), in the Japanese translation of Donald Davidson, *Subjectivism, Intersubjectivism, Objectivism*, Shunjusha 2007.
[Tanji 1996]: Nobuharu Tanji, *Gengo to Ninshiki no Dynamism* (Dynamism of Language and Cognition), Keiso Shobou, 1996.
[Tanji 1997]: Nobuharu Tanji, *Quine* (Quine), Koudansha, 1997.
[Todayama 1998]: Kazuhisa Todayama, "Minori Yutakana Research Program toshite no Butsurishugiteki Suugakuron" (A Physicalist Theory of Mathematics: Mathematics as a Fruitful Research Program), in *Tetsugaku* (Philosophy), Japanese Philosophical Association, 49, 1998.
[Todayama 2003]: Kazuhisa Todayama, "Tetsugakuteki Shizenshugi no Kanousei" (The Possibility of Philosophical Naturalism), in Shisou (Thought), 2003.
[Todayama 2005]: Kazuhisa Todayama, "Shizenshugiteki Ninshikiron to Kagaku no

Mokuteki" (Naturalistic Epistemology and the Goal of Science"), in *Tetsugaku Zasshi* (Philosophy Journal) 120, number 792, Yuuhikaku, 2005.

[Todayama et al. 2003]: Kazuhisa Todayama, Hiroyuki Hattori, Masayoshi Shibata, Tadashi Mino, (eds.), *Kokoro no Kagaku to Tetsugaku* (Science and Philosophy of Mind), Shouwadou, 2003.

[Tomida 1994]: Yasuhiko Tomida, *Quine to Gendai America Tetsugaku* (Quine and Contemporary Philosophy in America), Sekaishisosha, 1994.

[Nagasawa 2001]: Hidetoshi Nagasawa, "Gainenwaku toiu Kangae Saiko" (The Idea of a Conceptual Scheme Revisited), in *Tetsugaku* (Philosophy), Japan Philosophical Association, 58, Housei University Press, 2001.

[Nakamura 2001]: Masatoshi Nakamura, "Carnap to Quine: Nani ga Souten Datta no ka" (Carnap and Quine: What is the point of their debates?), in *Tetsugaku Shisou Ronsyu* (Philosophy and Thought Essays), Tsukuba University, 2001.

[Namisato 1997]: Takehiro Namisato, "Quine no Keikouseiron" (Quine's Theory of Dispositions), in *Shisaku* (Reflection), Tohoku University Philosophy Research Group, 30, 1997.

[Namisato 2000]: Takehiro Namisato, "Gainen Zushiki to Dai San no Dogma" (Conceptual Schemes and the Third Dogma), in *Tohoku Tetsugaku Kai Nenpou*, Tohoku University Philosophy Research Group, number 16, 2000.

[Noe 1993]: Keiichi Noe, *Kagaku no Kaishakugaku* (Hermeneutics of Science), Shinyosha, 1993.

[Nobuhara 2004]: Yukihiro Nobuhara, ed., *Series Kokoro no Tetsugaku I Ningen Hen* (Philosophy of Mind Series I Humans), Keiso Shobou, 2004.

[Hamano 1990]: Kenzo Hamano, "Quine no Koudousyugiteki Butsurishugi to Honyaku no Fukakutei These" (Quine's Behavioristic Physicalism and the Thesis of Indeterminacy of Translation), in *Tetsugaku Tankyu* (Philosophical Investigation), Kyoto Philosophical Association, 556, 1990.

[Hamano 2002]: Kenzo Hamano, "Shikouteki Goi no Dokujisei: Kihan o Fukumiuru Shizenshugi no Kanousei" (Independence of Intentional Vocabulary: The Possibility of Naturalism with Normativity), in *Kagaku Tetsugaku* (Philosophy of Science) Philosophy of Science Society Japan, 35(2), 2002.

[Hiromatsu et. al. 1998]: W. Hiromatsu, et. al. eds., *Iwanami Tetsugaku-Shisou Jiten* (Iwanami Encyclopedia of Philosophy and Thought), Iwanami, 1998.

Index

A
all-purpose ontology   124, 125
analytic statement   167, 168, 172, 173, 175, 176, 178
analytic-synthetic distinction   177-179
analyticity   23, 154, 166-179, 184, 185
   concept of analyticity   23, 167, 170-176, 178, 184
   criticism of analyticity   23, 154, 166, 167, 170-177, 185
artificial language   159, 169-173, 175, 190

B
belief system   16, 27-31, 39, 40, 42-44, 46, 48, 52, 53, 56, 58, 59, 64, 75-78, 80, 90, 92, 99, 126-128, 163, 183
belief system immanentism   27-31, 39, 40, 42-44, 48, 56, 58, 59, 64, 75-78, 80, 92, 126, 127, 183
Berkeley, George   21

C
Carnap, Rudolf   vii, 10-15, 20, 23, 26, 45, 131, 146, 153-158, 162-185, 189-192
   Carnapian model   153, 154, 158-162, 166, 167, 176, 177, 179, 180, 182-185, 187, 188, 190-193
   The Logical Structure of the world (*Der logisch Aufbau der Welt*)   10, 11, 13, 26, 164
Case, Jennifer   133, 145, 148, 150, 177, 178, 181
causation   108
Chisholm, Roderick   36
Chomsky, Noam   47, 97, 99
completeness of physics   58, 59, 64, 86-89, 91, 119, 122, 188
Conant, James   124
concept
   conceptual framework   134, 136, 152, 153
   conceptual pluralism   124, 131, 132, 134-136, 145, 147-149, 151-153, 180
   conceptual relativity   131-136, 144-153, 155, 177, 179-181
   conceptual scheme   27, 39, 40, 75, 77, 134, 136, 137-145, 148, 149, 158, 160-163, 178, 181, 183, 184, 192
   criticism of conceptual schemes   136, 140, 143-145, 192
   theory of concepts   8, 9
conception of nature   45, 59, 64
contextual definition   9, 10, 25, 26, 57
convention   132-134, 136, 146, 150, 173, 178-180
   conventionalism   164, 179
   conventionalist pluralism   158, 166
Crane, Tim   81-83, 87
Creath, Richard   171, 173
criterion of pragmatic efficacy   157, 158, 163-166

D
Davidson, Donald   46, 103-111, 115, 116, 129, 136-145, 153, 160, 189, 190, 192

Dennett, Daniel   111
Descartes, René   19, 21, 35, 50
descriptivism   65
descriptive stance   173-175
Dewey, John   27
discourse   10, 112, 124-129, 131, 134, 136, 148, 149, 151-153, 161, 176, 177, 180, 186, 190
dispositional statement   11, 26
Dummett, Michael   73, 75

E
empirical adequacy   80
empirical equivalency   97, 98
empiricism   8, 12-14, 20-26, 30, 33, 38, 40, 58, 122, 155, 163-167, 170, 176, 177
   empiricist foundationalism   21, 30, 31, 58
epiphenomenalism   85, 90, 91
epistemology   vi, vii, 8-24, 26, 30-44, 47, 48, 55, 56, 58, 62-65, 74, 112-114, 174, 176, 182
   descriptive epistemology   33, 35-37, 55, 62, 174
   naturalizing epistemology   9, 14, 16-18
   normative epistemology   36-40, 112, 114
   traditional epistemology   9, 16-19, 21-24, 34-39
experiment   94, 95, 103, 162
   experimental method   50, 52, 53, 55, 60, 81

F
fact of the matter   46, 47, 61, 62, 99, 101-103, 107, 124, 125, 128
fact
   factual property   85, 122
falsificationism   51
Field, Hartry   73, 75
first philosophy   vii, 23-26, 29-31, 47, 49, 52, 55-58, 63, 99, 100
foundationalism   21, 24, 30, 31, 58, 81, 92, 128, 183, 184

G
Gaudet, Eve   96, 102
Gibson, Roger   21-23, 29, 99
goal   8, 15-18, 24-26, 29, 32, 33, 38, 45, 49, 55, 65, 66, 79, 80, 93, 102, 104, 110, 112-114, 116, 129-131, 138, 140, 152, 158, 159, 161-163, 165, 167-169, 171, 173-175, 177-180, 183, 184, 186, 188, 190-193
   concept of 'goal'   114, 130
   purposive rationality   112-114, 130
Gödel, Kurt   22
Goodman, Nelson   128

H
Hale, Bob   72
Hamano, Kenzou   108, 113
Hattori, Hiroyuki   129
Hegel, G. W. F.   21

Hempel's dilemma 86
Hockney, Donald 99
holism 11-14, 25, 26, 30, 31, 39, 40, 43, 57-59, 74, 176, 183, 190
Hume, David 9, 10, 13
hypothetico-deductive method vii, 25, 29, 30, 42, 50-52, 54, 56, 57, 59, 65, 81, 182

I
Iida, Takashi 10, 60, 61, 71, 73
indeterminacy 23, 44-48, 66, 86, 92-103, 105-112, 114-120, 122, 123, 127, 128, 145, 146, 153, 169, 176, 180, 189
indispensability argument 71-75, 125
instrumentalist view of language 189
internal realism 80
interpretation 8, 23, 29, 30-35, 39, 41-49, 52-54, 56-63, 66, 80, 92, 95, 103-111, 115-120, 127-130, 141-143, 153, 155, 162, 164, 169, 171, 173, 189
　indeterminacy of interpretation 103, 105-109, 111, 118, 119, 127, 169
　interpretivism 108, 114, 129, 188, 189
　radical interpretation 103-105, 107, 108, 115, 141, 169
Ito, Haruki 43

J
Jackson, Frank 92
Janvid, Mikael 129
justification vi, 25-31, 35-42, 44, 47, 48, 52, 53, 56-59, 63, 64, 76, 78, 88, 123, 145, 146, 173
　concept of justification 35, 37, 38
　justificatory procedure 50-52, 56, 57, 59, 65, 81, 182
　justificatory process 28, 52

K
Kachi, Daisuke 74, 75
Kaneko, Hiroshi 73
Kant, Immanuel 79
Kasaki, Masashi 122
Katz, Jerrold 94
Kim, Jaegwon 35-38, 44, 189
Kiyozuka, Kunihiko 104, 155
knowledge 13-22, 24, 28, 35, 36, 56, 63, 65, 92, 96, 97, 110, 114-116, 121, 141, 156, 164, 191, 192
　theory of knowledge 20, 35, 36, 191, 192
Kornblith, Hilary 34
Koyama, Tora 122
Kripke, Saul 92, 118

L
legitimacy 16, 50, 56, 74, 85, 95, 97, 114, 116, 128, 158
Leśniewski, Stanisław 133
Levy, Edwin 95
Lewis, David 118, 189
linguistic turn 20, 21

Locke, John 21
Loewer, Barry 82, 83, 118, 120, 121
Logicism 9
Lynch, Michael 149, 160

M

Maddy, Penelope 73-75
manifestability 88, 89, 91, 117, 119-122
materialism 54, 81-83
meaning vi, 12, 13, 20, 21, 25, 36, 42, 45-47, 51, 64, 77, 92, 94, 96-108, 111, 112, 114-117, 119, 120, 123, 127, 128, 133, 134, 141-143, 147, 153, 155-157, 160, 163, 166, 168, 170, 172, 186
  eliminativism about meaning 111
  meaning postulate 156, 157, 160, 168, 170
Mellor, D. H. 44, 81-83
mereology 132-134, 145-147, 150, 151, 181, 183, 184
metaontology 71
metaphor 79, 80
metaphysics 50, 74, 75, 83, 92
  metaphysical realism 46, 78, 149-152
Moser, Paul K. 43

N

Nagasawa, Hidetoshi 145
Nakamura, Masatoshi 45
Namisato, Takehiro 145
Naruse, Takashi 62
naturalism v, vi, vii, 8, 18, 19, 23-25, 27-66, 73-77, 80-82, 89-93, 102, 112-114, 123, 124, 126-131, 154, 174, 182-185, 188, 193
  anti-naturalism 7
  definition of naturalism 48, 49, 53
  epistemological naturalism 50, 112
  interpretation of naturalism 32, 33, 35, 41, 43-45, 47, 48, 57
  minimal naturalism vii, 53, 56, 57, 59-62, 64-66, 76, 90, 92, 124, 128, 182, 183, 193
  naturalistic epistemology 19, 20, 22-24, 33, 38, 113
  naturalistic ontology vii, 183, 184
  natural scientism naturalism 57, 59, 60, 63, 64
  ontological naturalism 50, 90
  physicalist naturalism 7, 59, 60, 62-64, 91, 102, 112, 127, 128, 193
  pluralistic naturalism 5, 7, 59, 124, 127-131, 182, 184, 185, 193
naturalize 6-11, 16-24, 26, 30, 33-40, 43, 44, 47, 48, 56, 58, 62, 79, 80, 113, 182, 188
  naturalized epistemology 7, 9, 16-18, 35-39, 47, 62
natural language 132-135, 144, 146-148, 152, 153, 155, 157-159, 169-175, 179-182, 189, 190
natural science vi, vii, 9, 16-18, 24, 25, 28-31, 33, 42-44, 47, 49, 50, 52, 55, 56, 58-61, 63, 64, 99, 163, 186
  natural scientism vii, 32, 42-44, 53-65, 124, 163-167, 182, 192
neo-Fregeanism 72
Neurath, Otto 14, 18, 193

Nobuhara, Yukihiro   53
Noe, Keiichi   46, 55
normativity   32, 35-41, 43, 62, 112-114, 129, 130
　epistemological normativity   38-41, 62, 112-114, 129, 130
　instrumental normativity   39-41, 62
　normativity chage   32, 35, 37-39, 43, 62
　the normative or prescriptive stance (the propositional stance)   175-177

O
objectivity   109
　observation sentence   14, 94, 95, 97, 98, 100, 115
Ohtomo, Kouichi   186
ontology   vii, 10, 42, 53, 65-67, 69, 71-76, 81, 89, 99, 103, 124-126, 128, 131, 132, 134-136, 139, 143, 146, 147, 149, 151, 177, 179, 183, 184
　naturalistic ontology   vii, 183, 184
　ontological claim   70, 82, 92, 125, 147, 179, 180, 183, 184
　ontological commitment   70-77, 80, 82, 85, 89-91, 123, 125, 126
　ontological option   vii, 65, 66, 75, 76, 82, 92, 126, 127, 131
　ontological problems   69
　the (basic) perspective for ontological debates   76, 80, 89, 92, 126
optional language   133-136, 144, 145, 147-149, 151-153, 179-181

P
Papineau, David   44, 47, 54, 64, 82-89, 91, 116-122
paraphrase   21, 51, 57, 67-70, 72, 73, 129, 140, 190
Peirce, C. S.   12, 13, 20, 79, 80
phenomenalism   14, 85, 90, 91
physical fact   63, 83-85, 101, 103, 107, 108, 119, 125, 127, 128
physicalism   vi, vii, 14, 32, 44, 45, 47-49, 53-66, 71, 75, 81-93, 101-103, 107-109, 111-120, 122-128, 131, 149, 150, 161, 176, 182, 188, 189, 193
　physicalist monism   vii, 46, 65, 66, 76, 123, 126-129, 131, 149-152, 161, 163, 176, 190, 193
pluralism   vii, 46, 65, 66, 76, 93, 123-129, 131, 132, 134-136, 145, 147-149, 151-154, 158-167, 176, 177, 179, 180, 182-185, 187, 188, 190-193
　conceptual pluralism   124, 131, 132, 134-136, 145, 147-149, 151-153, 180
　horizontal pluralism   149, 151
　pluralistic naturalism   v, vii, 59, 124, 127-131, 182, 184, 185, 193
　vertical pluralism   149, 151
pragmatic criterion   40, 158, 161-163, 183
pragmatics   147, 154, 155, 174
　pragmatic facts   146, 147, 153, 155-159, 169, 170, 175-177, 180, 185, 189-191
pragmatism   154, 158, 161, 165, 166, 190
principle of charity   103-107, 129, 130, 142-144, 189
principle of compensation   192
principle of tolerance   157, 158, 161-166, 178
propositional attitude   36, 92, 93, 96, 103, 106-120, 123, 127-130, 153, 188
　elimination of propostional attitudes   106-108, 111, 113
　eliminativism about propositional attitudes   108, 111, 127
　the indeterminacy of propositional attitudes   107
Putnam, Hilary   7, 46, 66, 71, 72, 75, 78, 80, 83, 92, 96, 99, 123-125, 128, 131-136, 144-155, 159, 162, 164, 166, 177-182, 185

Q

qualia 92, 188
Quine, W.V. vi, vii, 8-63, 65-80, 82, 93-108, 112, 113, 115-117, 123-125, 128, 129, 141, 154, 155, 158, 162, 163, 166-168, 170-177, 182-185, 190, 193
   "Epistemology Naturalized" vii, 8-11, 18-24, 26, 30, 33, 34, 39, 40, 43, 48, 56, 58, 62, 182
   "Five Milestones of Empiricism" 8, 24-26, 30, 33, 38, 58
   "Naturalism; or Living within One's Means" vii, 49, 52, 53, 63
   Theories and Things 8, 24, 31, 49, 59
   "Two Dogmas of Empiricism" 12, 13, 22, 23, 40, 155, 167, 170, 176

R

rational reconstruction 10, 15, 16
realism 21-23, 25-31, 42, 44, 46, 57, 59, 71, 78, 80, 107, 109-111, 114, 115, 117, 118, 123, 149-153
   empiricistic realism 21-23
   internal realism 80
   metaphysical realism 46, 78, 149-152
   realistic standard 27, 40, 184
   reationalistic realism 21-23
reductionism 13, 40, 163
   radical reductionism 13, 40
relational property 84, 106
replacement thesis 32, 34-37, 41, 43, 44, 48, 53-55, 60, 62
Ricketts, Thomas 164, 165
Rorty, Richard M. 47, 97, 103
Russell, Bertrand 10, 12, 27, 68, 69, 70
Rutherford, Ernest 82
Ryle, Gilbert 190

S

Searle, John 46, 96
science v-vii, 9, 11, 14-19, 24-31, 33, 34, 36-44, 47, 49-52, 54-61, 63-65, 72-77, 79-83, 86, 87, 92, 93, 96, 98, 99, 112, 124, 125, 131, 146, 156, 157, 163-165, 182, 183, 185, 186, 190
   grounding science 18, 182
   scientism vi, vii, 27, 29, 32, 42-44, 49, 53-65, 124, 163-167, 182, 192
sectarian approach 101-103, 110, 111, 128, 153
semantics 145-147, 153-159, 162, 164-166, 168-170, 172, 174-181, 189, 191, 192
   descriptive semantics 145-147, 153-155, 158, 159, 168-170, 174-176, 179-181, 189, 191, 192
   pure semantics 146, 147, 154-159, 162, 164, 165, 168-170, 172, 174, 178-180, 191, 192
   semantic rules 45, 146, 154, 158-161, 167-171, 173-179, 181, 184-187, 189, 190
sentence meanings 45, 97, 99-102
sensation 137
   sense impression 9, 10, 13-15, 65
   sensory experience 140
singular term 69-73, 75
skepticism 19, 28, 29
supervenience 44, 83-91, 101, 117-121, 125, 149

T

Tanji, Nobuharu　11, 46, 110, 112, 192
Tarski, Alfred　99, 140
theory　8-18, 20-22, 25, 26, 30, 34-39, 46-48, 51, 55, 59-65, 68, 70, 71, 73, 74, 77-80, 83, 87, 90, 94, 95, 97-103, 105-110, 115, 118, 119, 125-130, 132-134, 137, 140-144, 146, 147, 153-155, 167, 168, 174, 176, 182, 188-193
  ideal theory　79, 80
  the underdetermination of theory　46, 47, 79, 80, 95, 97-100, 102, 103, 140
  theory in physics　47, 48, 100, 101
  theory of doctrine　8, 9
Todayama, Kazuhisa　vi, 44, 50, 63, 73, 85, 89-91, 93, 112, 193
token identity　108, 117
Tomida, Yasuhiko　176
transcendental　46, 61, 78-80, 99, 102
translation　v, 10-13, 15, 18, 23, 26, 30, 31, 39-41, 44-48, 52, 56, 61, 66, 72, 92-105, 107-112, 115-117, 128, 136-138, 140-144, 153
  radical translation　93-95, 101, 103, 104, 107, 115, 141
  the indeterminacy of translation　23, 44-48, 66, 92-103, 107-111, 116, 128
  translatability　136, 138, 139, 141, 143, 144
  translation manual　46, 47, 93, 95, 96, 98-101, 103, 116, 153
  translational reduction　10-13, 15, 26, 30, 31, 39, 40, 41, 52, 56
  translational synonymy　47, 100
truth　12-14, 20-23, 28, 35, 38, 42, 43, 45, 50, 52, 55, 56, 58, 65, 73-81, 85, 89-92, 97-101, 103-105, 109, 124-128, 136, 137, 140, 141, 148, 150, 152, 153, 156, 167, 168, 170, 171, 175, 176, 178, 181, 183, 184
  concept of truth　35, 168
  naturalizing truth　80

U

underdetermination　46, 47, 79, 80, 95, 97-100, 102, 103, 140, 176
unregenerate realism　25-31, 42, 44, 57, 59

V

verification　12, 20, 21, 78
  verificationism　14, 51

W

Wagner, Steven　42
Warner, Rcihard　42
White, Morton　38, 40, 62
Wittgenstein, Ludwig　190
world in-itself　27-31, 58
Wright, Chrispin　72, 73

Y

Yandell, Keith　43
Yatabe, Shunsuke　153

About Author
Masahiko Igashira（井頭昌彦）

He was born in 1975 and obtained Bachelor of Science and Ph.D in philosophy from Tohoku University. After working as a Japan Society for the Promotion of Science research fellow and as an assistant professor at Graduate School of Frontier of Biosciences and also at Graduate School of Human Sciences, Osaka University, he is currently an associate professor at Hitotsubashi University (tenured).

The Possibility of Pluralistic Naturalism
Understanding the Continuity Between Philosophy and Science

©2016 Masahiko Igashira
All rights reserved.
Published by YOUKOODOO Co., Ltd.
1103 City Square Tukiji 6-4-5 Tukiji Chuo-ku Tokyo 104-0045
Tel：(81)3 6264 0523 ; Fax：(81)3 6264 0524

ISBN978-4-906873-67-8　C3010
Printed in Japan